SUNDOWN AT SUNRISE

A Story of Love and Murder, Based on One of the
Most Notorious Ax Murders in American History

SUNDOWN AT SUNRISE

*A Story of Love and Murder, Based on One of the
Most Notorious Ax Murders in American History*

MARTY SEIFERT

BEAVER'S POND
PRESS

Edited by Wendy Weckwerth

ISBN 13: 978-1-59298-794-8
Library of Congress Catalog Number: 2016918980
Printed in the United States of America
First Printing: 2016
20 19 18 17 16   5 4 3 2 1

Book design by Athena Currier

Beaver's Pond Press, Inc.
7108 Ohms Lane
Edina, MN 55439–2129

(952) 829-8818
www.BeaversPondPress.com

CONTENTS

Contents. v

Preface ix

Acknowledgments xiii

1. The Petries 1

2. Going to Redwood 7

3. The Dance that Changed Lives. 13

4. Plans at the Restaurant. 21

5. Getting Serious at the Dance 25

6. Heading Home. 35

7. Killer in the Coop. 41

8. Getting to Church 47

9. Looking at Options 57

10. The Boys Go To Town. 69

11. The Suitor Finally Calls 91

12. Painting the Buggy and the Shed. 99

13. Off to Clements 107

14. A Surprising Fall 117

15. The Carriage Ride. 121

16. Henry Runs for Sheriff. 127

17. William's Big Decisions 131

18. Getting the First Car 135

19. Poppin' The Question 141

20. Convincing the Folks 145

21. Changing Frank's Location 155

22. Getting the Minister 159

23. Gettin' Hitched 163

24. Leaving for the Honeymoon 169

25. The Newlyweds Return 175

26. New Kids and a New Car 181

27. Checking out the New Place 187

28. Home Forever 207

29. Seeking a New Member of the Flock 211

30. The School Board Asks a Question 217

31. The New Teacher Takes a Look Around 225

32. The Boarder Takes Up Residence 233

33. School Starts 241

34. Breaking the Moral Turpitude Clause 247

35. Sunday Beckons 255

36. Mary Takes Ill 259

37. Till Death Do Us Part 267

38. The Discovery 283

39. The Inquest 297

40. Claiming the Bodies 303

41. Moving the Bodies to Town 321

42. The Boys Come Home 331

43. Preparing for the Funeral 339

44. Negotiating Burials 347

45. Funerals 355

46. The Aftermath 361

Now I lay me down to sleep.
I pray the Lord, my soul to keep.
If I die before I wake,
I pray the Lord, my soul to take.

—Children's Nighttime Prayer

PREFACE

The following is a fictional tale based on a true story that took place only several miles from where I grew up near Clements, Minnesota. It was one of the worst ax murders in the history of the United States—a crime many readers might be surprised to learn occurred in rural southwestern Minnesota.

This tale has been in my mind for decades. The original idea came from my father, Norbert Seifert, who would periodically point to a mysterious abandoned farm site north of our hometown and say, "Something terrible happened on that farm."

That intriguing statement was followed by a few additional pieces of information that grew more detailed as I matured. The quick synopsis is that a farmer killed his wife and kids with an ax and then hung himself.

A large metal hand pump stood alone across the road from the farm, and Dad often mentioned that a teacher had boarded at the farm and taught at the school, of which only the pump now remained. The murderer, I learned later, was born only three years before my paternal grandfather.

The historical fiction you're about to read comes out of my imagination, but it's the direct result of this event that happened so close to my home and was told to me repeatedly during my childhood. Many details and characters—and certainly all dialogue—are entirely fictional. It is based on the true story of the gruesome murder that took place in 1917.

If not for my late father, I wouldn't have had the idea to write this book, so I owe him a debt of gratitude for planting the seed of the story. Growing up, I never knew if the ax-murder tale was a fictional yarn or an actual crime, which led me to investigate the question as an adult. After conducting research and interviews, I discovered that on March 24, 1917, a farmer named William Kleeman murdered his wife and four young children with an ax and then committed suicide. In looking at comparable cases, it appears to be one of the worst ax murders in history, along with the 1912 Villisca ax murders in Iowa and a few others. As far as I can tell, no one has closely examined the Kleeman story since the initial newspaper articles reported the story of the murder-suicide at the time.

I anticipated that looking into the event would likely unveil some interesting facts, but I was astounded at some of the discoveries I made—and surprised about some I couldn't make. It turns out my great-uncle, Dr. Frank Brey, was the Redwood County coroner who examined the bodies, helped preside over the inquest, and signed the death certificates for the Kleeman family. Minnie Kleeman refused to attend her own son's funeral. Mary Snelling, the young schoolteacher who lived with the Kleemans, essentially disappeared after the murders. Also, I haven't been able to locate the graves of Maud Kleeman and Gordon and Rosadell, the two youngest Kleeman children, despite the efforts of experts, historians, and cemetery officials.

Odd coincidences surround the research related to this book. When trying to locate the original site of the Church of the Holy Communion in Redwood Falls, I discovered that once the church was removed, the parcel was eventually purchased by a Seifert, although not a relative of mine. When reviewing an old plat map of Three Lakes Township from the era around the time of the murders, directly across the road from the murder site read the name *M. Seifert* on the section of land in the plat book.

One memorable day of research for this project held three particularly noteworthy twists. My wife, children, and mother-in-law accompanied me on a clear Sunday in early December to take pictures of the abandoned farm site where the murders occurred and to retrieve my father's weathered copy of the 1919 *Plat Book of Redwood County* from my mom's house nearby. We drove from our home in Marshall, Minnesota, forty miles east to the murder site. Twenty miles into our drive, just as we entered Redwood County, a wall of fog converged upon us, making it difficult to drive and impossible to take any pictures from the road.

As the five of us discussed the book earlier that day, we had debated what type of dog William Kleeman would've owned. While we came to no consensus on the breed, we agreed that it should be a black dog. Despite the dense fog, we decided to drive near the farm where the murders were committed, hoping that perhaps we'd still be able to catch a glimpse. With the fog thicker than ever, we gave up when we pulled to the side of the road next to the farm and couldn't see anything to photograph. However, we did notice a freshly killed black lab lying on the road's shoulder immediately west of the former Kleeman farm.

I took the opportunity to remind my family that when I was nineteen years old, I had a horrific accident that totaled my car and sent me to the hospital in Redwood Falls. Where did this accident happen? It occurred a few hundred feet north of the murder site.

After the eerie sights of the dog and my own accident site, we drove the four miles to my home farm and entered the house I grew up in to retrieve the plat book. The book had been sitting in a writing desk in the same spot for forty years of my memory, but for some reason, it was now missing. I took every book and scrap of paper out of the desk and looked all around my mom's house—no sign of the book. My mother and brothers didn't recall it ever being moved either. My uncle Lawrence, who lives in the house next to ours on the same farm, said he knew the book had always been in the writing desk, for decades, just as I had remembered, but he also had no idea where it was now. My father had obtained the book from Lincoln Clements, son of the man who founded Clements.

The sudden appearance of the thick fog—which, according to weather reports, was isolated only to a small area in and around Redwood County—the dead, black dog next to the murder site, along with the missing plat book, all on the same day, combined into something of a sinister shadow over the eventual completion of this book, as if someone or something didn't want this dark story told.

ACKNOWLEDGMENTS

I WANT TO THANK THE MANY PEOPLE WHO HELPED ME gather some background on the Kleeman farm, the characters, and the time period, including Jan Louwagie from the Southwest Minnesota History Center, located on the campus of Southwest Minnesota State University; the Redwood Falls Public Library and its staff; the Blue Earth County Historical Society and its staff; the Minnesota Historical Society and its staff; Troy Krause, editor of the *Redwood Falls Gazette*; and Don Reding, grandson of the second person to arrive at the murder scene. Don still lives on the same farm just down the road from the murder site, where his grandfather lived in 1917.

Immense thanks to the editor and publisher for helping put the final product together.

Finally, special thanks to my wife, Traci, and my children, Brittany and Braxton, for their patience and support in assembling this book.

CHAPTER 1

THE PETRIES

HENRY PETRIE WAS A PROPER EPISCOPALIAN who was prominent and well known in western Redwood County, a large rural county in southwestern Minnesota. Henry and his wife, Clara, owned one hundred sixty acres of prime farmland in the south-central portion of Three Lakes Township. By chance, the Chicago Railroad was looking for an ideal rail line that could jut to the west and travel to Marshall from the east. Small hamlets started to pop up along this minor rail route, and they became settled: Wayburn, Clements, Rowena, Wabasso, Seaforth, Lucan, and Milroy, among other towns, suddenly became platted and introduced rail depots, grain elevators, and new Main Streets across Redwood County in an east-west line.

At the turn of the twentieth century, a deal was struck in which Petrie sold his land so the railroad could establish a station. Peter O. Clements, a Swedish immigrant, named the new town for himself,

1

and the community soon swelled to more than one hundred people, mainly of German and Scandinavian descent. A saloon, two churches, a grain elevator, a railroad depot, and the various other trappings of a small, rural village dotted the landscape of Clements.

Henry gained a bit of money from the sale and moved to different locations in the area, but he generally lived between Redwood Falls and Clements his entire life.

He and Clara had only one daughter, Maud. She exuded the same class and poise that her mother modeled as an example. The Petries also had three sons—two died before they reached the age of eight, but Johnson Claude Petrie, who was several years younger than Maud, survived. Claude, who was always known by his middle name rather than his first, was a handsome and lanky boy. As the Petries' only surviving son, he was lavished with almost the same intensity of attention as his sister. Claude was blessed with an enviable social ease, and he treated his peers with respect and kindness. He was popular and well spoken, and he was often invited to stay with his chums from country school.

Like many area farmers, Henry employed a hired man. Unlike most, though, this hired man had stayed on for more than five years, longer than the average. Frank Schottenbauer was a strong and stocky fellow, with a light tan complexion and a respectful demeanor. He had attended the local country school until sixth grade, when he dropped out to start helping area farmers with chores and fieldwork. Most neighbor boys ended their formal education after eighth grade, and like them, Frank enjoyed hard work, not books.

At age twenty-eight, he was already viewed as an aging bachelor, rather than an available suitor for the young women of the area, including the alluring Maud Petrie, who was almost ten years his junior. Frank rarely went to town or socialized, other than with the Petrie family. Wishing to avoid his authoritative father, Frank rarely returned to his family's farmstead to see his folks or younger siblings, even though they lived a short four miles away.

Early on in his time with the Petries, Frank lived with the family, but within a few years he moved into an aging farmhouse less than half a mile from his employer. The house was larger than what he needed, but Henry never charged him rent, and it provided a convenient location for him to commute to the main farm to do chores and assist Henry. When the weather was acceptable, Frank would simply walk to the Petrie farm with a lantern, whistling a tune as he shuffled.

The Petrie livestock was divided between the two farm sites. The beef cattle, a small number of pigs, and one team of workhorses were kept with Schottenbauer, and the six dairy cows, additional beef cattle, chickens, and another set of workhorses were kept at Henry and Clara's farm.

Mrs. Petrie was especially kind to Frank, feeding him three meals a day and sending delicious treats home with him, especially if she knew they'd be away visiting elsewhere.

The hired man would usually arrive by six in the morning to start milking cows by hand, gathering any eggs that were laid overnight and seeing to other menial tasks that needed doing. Some nights, he would leave right after supper and others he would linger a bit later, but never too late out of respect for the Petries' privacy.

Frank always admired Maud from afar. He was hired on at the Petrie place when Maud was just a teenager, but she was attractive and only grew more so as she got older. Her picky ways and occasionally petulant attitude toward her parents frustrated him. He'd been taught to respect his elders without question. However, he was old-fashioned and from a much larger family. He figured he was probably too judgmental, and she should be excused for her behavior.

Maud, in turn, viewed Frank as an older uncle, someone who did the dirty work and was just an employee of her father's. She privately lusted after boys her own age when she spied them at church in Redwood Falls or on the occasional trip to Clements for supplies.

While Henry Petrie enjoyed the challenges and rewards of farming, he shied away from any manual labor that was too smelly or made him work up a sweat. Daily farm chores and related drudgery included picking up the chicken eggs in a basket and washing them, usually a task reserved for Clara Petrie. Henry, and especially Frank, did more of the "menfolk" chores like milking the cows, cleaning the manure from the stalls, feeding oats to the horses and alfalfa to the cattle, making sure the troughs were full of water, and taking care of any needed repairs around the place.

Because the farm lacked electricity, cream was separated from the milk by hand-cranking a machine. The sewing machine, feed grinder, butter churn, clothes washer, and corn sheller all had to be powered by hand. The backbreaking chores, whether in the farmyard or in the home, were usually conducted chiefly by Frank and Henry, with some assistance from Clara and the children. Maud would help periodically, but she was rarely recruited to help with any outdoor farm chores.

In the fall of 1909, on a gentle Minnesota Saturday, Henry, Clara, and Maud were feverishly making preparations for a grand trip to Redwood Falls. And young Claude was staying with a friend that weekend. They all needed a break from bereavement. Earlier in the summer, William Henry Petrie died of typhoid just shy of his seventh birthday. It added extra anguish for the elder Petries that another son, Frances, had died of the same disease at the age of six back in 1900.

CHAPTER 2

GOING TO REDWOOD

HENRY PETRIE HAD AGREED TO BRING MAUD AND A FRIEND to the Saturday evening dance in Redwood Falls in his brand-new car. After the family took their usual Saturday baths in the afternoon, it was determined that Henry and Clara would entertain themselves at the best restaurant in Redwood Falls for a long supper while Maud and her friend enjoyed the dance.

Henry had just traded his grand high-wheel surrey in for a Buick automobile after the cash came in from the 1909 crops. He enjoyed that the car was reliable, large, and didn't need the attention his ill-tempered horses required when they went to town. The Buick was deep blue and had an ornate amount of brass affixed in various places that gleamed in the Minnesota sun. The wheels had large wooden spokes stained a deep brown. Automobiles were a sign of prominence in 1909, and Henry Petrie wouldn't fall behind the times.

"Maud, I want you and Julia to refrain from any drink," Henry warned as they made arrangements for their trip. "It makes people do things they otherwise wouldn't." Henry frequently gave stern advice to his daughter. Maud was a bit naïve, he felt, and her looks were well above average compared to the drab farm girls she'd befriended as a youth. He knew his daughter would catch the eyes of more than one man.

"Daddy!" his daughter answered indignantly. "You know better. I just want to have some fun with Julia tonight, not to partake in liquor."

Julia Christensen had been a good friend of Maud's since their time in country school. She was a bit plumper and more pompous than the thin and attractive, yet often reserved, Maud Petrie.

"Your mother and I will be at the restaurant until eight o'clock. Then we'll come to pick you up. Be ready," Henry warned his young daughter. "I'm not fond of driving in the dark. Those carbide headlights are tricky."

While Henry Petrie had learned to operate his new automobile with adequate satisfaction, the massive brass headlamps were vexing and complicated devices, requiring special chemicals and mixtures to ignite them. It provided an additional reason to hasten his girl out of the dance and back to the safety of his farmhouse.

"But, Daddy, this dance is scheduled to go until ten o'clock. It will barely be started by that time," Maud protested. "It'll be equally dark either way. I need to stay until at least nine."

Henry Petrie knew everything was a negotiation with his petulant daughter. He had purposely set the exit time early, knowing she would argue with any deadline he set as too early. If he had suggested picking her up at nine, no doubt Maud would've argued for ten. Just as he was finishing that thought, Clara entered from the kitchen and whispered in her husband's ear. Maud could tell her father was being chastised by her mother, the more permissive of the two, for his overly protective nature. The brief scolding led to success.

"Fine, Maud," Henry conceded to his daughter with a sigh. "Your mother and I can pick up you and Julia at nine o'clock sharp. I can get the headlights lit, and we'll take our time coming home. Remember that we plan to attend morning services, so we'll need to come all the way back to town tomorrow."

The Petries were members of the Church of the Holy Communion in Redwood Falls. Despite its misleading, Catholic-sounding name, it was an Episcopal church. While it was one of the oldest congregations in Redwood County, it was also one of the smallest, with only a few dozen believers filling the rolls of the membership roster. Henry, Clara, Maud, and Claude rarely missed Sunday services at ten thirty, especially when the weather allowed easy travel.

After dressing in his town clothes, Henry cranked his massive Buick to life and drove it around the yard to pick up the women from the front of the house. Henry sighed as he sized up his alluring daughter.

Maud had purposely prepared herself to be especially striking for the event, applying slightly more rouge and extra-bright lipstick. Her blue dress, newly made by her mother, was trimmed with a gleaming white lace and matched her bright eyes. She'd spent an inordinate amount of time on her hair, using long strings of warm cloth intertwined in it for an hour that afternoon to give her light-brown locks extra curl. She puffed on the fragrant perfume she'd received from her parents just the month before as a birthday gift. A stately broach was snapped at the top of her collar, allowing Henry some relief that she didn't choose a dress with a low neckline that might expose cleavage.

Frank's shadow appeared at the door of the shed. He peered across the yard, spying on Maud, who looked especially beautiful this evening. The distance to the house was too far to eavesdrop, so he just stood there, staring at the ravishing girl from afar.

"Are we taking you to a simple dance hall or dropping you at your own wedding ceremony?" Henry asked his daughter sarcastically. "You are too graceful, my dear."

Clara had dressed more modestly, putting on a simple smock, with her hair pulled back in a bun. She didn't need to impress anyone this evening.

Henry left his car running. He usually did, in order to avoid having to start the engine by hand-cranking it each time the automobile was shut off. Many in the area had broken a wrist cranking cars that backfired, and he didn't want to join the rolls of the injured. Henry slid the brake handle back to keep his machine from making an escape and moved the transmission lever loosely to ensure the car was out of gear. He dismounted the Buick and assisted his wife up to the front passenger side, then helped Maud climb the black running board to enter the spacious back seat. The car's black leather seats had deep-set buttons, with thick padding that made the ride immensely more comfortable than the thin buggy seats they'd grown used to in previous years.

He pulled the car into gear and jerked the clutch, killing the automobile in its tracks.

"Damn it!" Henry shouted at the dead car. "I'm still learnin' this machine."

Witnessing the car's quick death, Frank dashed across the yard.

"Let me crank 'er up, Mr. Petrie," he said helpfully, holding up his grubby right hand. "Put it in neutral, and I'll get ya goin'."

Henry pushed in the clutch and snapped the car out of gear. He nodded at Frank. The car bellowed to life in just one crank, and Frank stepped aside. Henry stepped on the gas pedal several times to get the engine warmed up.

"Thank you, Frank!" Maud called from the back seat in a sweet, singsong voice.

Frank tipped his straw hat to Maud and admired her as the car roared out of the driveway, turning left to head straight north into Redwood Falls. He would watch the dust clouds settle and spend one more weekend evening alone, brooding at the Petries' barn and then in his solitary farmhouse. The Petrie family navigated the Buick from their farm in New Avon Township to the Christensen place three miles away to pick up Maud's friend. Henry swung his gangly car into the Christensen driveway and pulled near the front door, stopping suddenly. The jerk nearly knocked Clara into the dashboard.

"Henry!" Clara scolded. "Watch how short you're stoppin'!"

"Sorry, ladies," Henry said apologetically. "I'm still learning the brakes on this car."

A portly Julia Christensen stepped off the porch and walked near the awaiting vehicle. Julia's gown was plain and too tight for her heavy body, and her makeup had been applied too generously, the Petries noticed.

Henry spotted Lars Christensen, Julia's father, standing on the wraparound porch and waving to the visitors. "Lars!" Henry called in a friendly greeting. "We'll have her back here before ten tonight!"

Lars Christensen was an old homesteader in Redwood County. He sported a thick mustache and wore heavy, wire-rimmed glasses. Julia was an only child and, as a result, was both protected and somewhat spoiled. The Christensens considered themselves blessed that

Julia was born healthy, since her mother, Olga, was past forty years of age when Julia was conceived.

"Dat's fine," Christensen barked in his broken Dutch accent. "Olga and I vill have da lantern burning until you return."

"You got a car to drive," Olga called out. "Dat's a high-class ting."

Henry jumped out of the Buick and opened the car's rear door, assisting Julia onto the running board and into the cavernous back seat, where an eager Maud Petrie greeted her. He whisked around and climbed back into the car with a glint in his eye. While the girls exuded eagerness to drive to town for their evening fun, Henry also showed some elation to flee the farm and enjoy the civilization of the city for one night. He also enjoyed showing off his shiny new vehicle to the primitive neighbors who were still relegated to using horses for their transportation needs.

"I'm so excited to go to town tonight," Julia giggled as she greeted her old friend. "Thank you for taking me along."

"You behave yourself, young lady," Olga warned as she stood near the car. "We vill see you ven you get home."

They pulled out of the Christensens' driveway, waving at Lars and Olga on the way out. Henry and Clara visited about their possible menu selections at the restaurant as the girls carried on with laughter and whispering in the back seat.

Since finishing secondary school, Maud fretted about never landing a husband. The rare times she made it to town, other than for church services, had left her without a beau each time.

The car successfully traveled the requisite three miles and wheezed to halt at the Redwood Falls Ballroom, the largest gathering spot in the whole county that wasn't a place of worship or formal education.

CHAPTER 3

THE DANCE THAT CHANGED LIVES

"You girls have a good time tonight, but not *too* good of a time," Henry warned sternly as he helped his daughter and her friend to the ground.

"Daddy, we shall see you at nine thirty?" Maud joked.

Clara shot a scowl in Maud's direction.

"I'll meet you nine o'clock sharp, Miss Petrie," Henry said resolutely. "The livery stable will be busy down the street, so I want to meet you at this corner."

"Thank you, Mr. Petrie," Julia said politely, quickly ending the conversation so they could traverse to the awaiting dance.

"Happy to have you," Henry replied with a tip of his black dress hat. "You two behave yourselves now, you hear?"

Henry returned to the car, which he had left running. He retrieved his bejeweled pocket watch out of his vest and clicked open the case.

"Clara, it's almost six thirty, and I'm hungry," Henry stated. "The girls will be fine."

He shifted the Buick into gear and let open the clutch. As the car pulled away, he saw two young men eyeing his daughter while ignoring the homely Julia Christensen.

Maud and Julia nattered for a few minutes about trivial matters as they stepped toward the ballroom, but suddenly, Maud became more serious. "I've just turned twenty-one years old," she said, turning to Julia with a forceful stare. "I cannot fathom being a spinster and forced to be alone my whole life. I think of the old ladies in church and can't bear the thought of being relegated to a life of isolation."

"Maud Petrie," Julia chastised. "You are so slender and beautiful. Being alone isn't going to be a worry for *you*."

As they entered the dance hall, they could hear music, talking, and laughter. Wafts of cigarette and cigar smoke plumed toward the ceiling and hung in the air like a smelly cloud. The place was dimly lit, and fresh sawdust was scattered on the hardwood floor to ease the dancers' swaggers.

William Kleeman, a stunningly handsome bachelor farmhand, sat near the bar. He was sipping a Schell's beer and laughing with his friends. He was a devout follower of the Schell's brand, a fine local beer that was brewed in New Ulm, the county seat of Brown County, the neighboring county to the east. The German owners must have known his exact taste, William thought.

The crowd was abuzz about a brutal murder that had happened several weeks earlier in Delhi Township.

"Did you hear about that widower by Delhi who beat his daughter to death?" William's buddy Forest Van Sant asked. "He killed the housekeeper's daughter too."

Willis Tibbetts was a widower who had gone berserk and resorted to murder and suicide in September of 1909. The sensational story roared across southwestern Minnesota as family and neighbors tried to piece together a motive and provocation.

The crime was never solved.

"They found him hangin' by a strap in the barn, I heard." William replied without emotion. "Guess that's the best way to end it after you done somethin' like that."

The famous Kramer Band from Seaforth was the featured entertainment at the dance for the evening. Made up of a whopping nine brothers and three sisters, they filled out the entire stage.

"There's Anton, John, Arnold, Michael, Mathia, Romulad, Henry, Nick, and Peter," William announced to his friends breathlessly as he pointed out each band member by name. "The girls are Mary, Magdalen, and Anna."

This wasn't the first time the Kramer Band would play for William Kleeman. He attended dances across the county to sweep young prairie girls off their feet.

"It's the reason they're chargin' a dime instead of a nickel tonight," Forest said in a hushed voice. "There's so many of them, it takes more money to pay. I heard they each get two free beers for the night too."

"I wanted to date that youngest girl," William said, pointing to the fair Anna Kramer. "But they're all devout Romans, and that wouldn't sit well with my folks."

While William didn't really belong to an organized religion, his Protestant parents would likely object strenuously if he started courting a Catholic girl. Any potential for a "mixed marriage" would be avoided if he could help it.

As the band struck up another tune, William spied the stunning Maud Petrie enter the smoke-filled and sweltering ballroom.

Maud was a bit spoiled by her parents, but she'd also been shy and somewhat reclusive in her youth. Some thought it might have been partly the impact she felt from losing two of her younger brothers at an adolescent age. As the Kramers entertained the attendees, Maud awkwardly clung to Julia's arm while they moved toward an empty corner of the dance hall. She looked up to the room's balcony to see aged widows with large-plumed hats and looking glasses, searching for any sign of immorality or sights worthy of gossip.

As Maud's curvy figure strode across the dance floor, it was love at first sight for William Kleeman. Boastful and popular, he sized up his prey from a distance, poking his slender friend Arthur Davis in the ribs.

"What do you think of *that* one?" he asked his startled chum, pointing to Maud. "Looks like she's single."

Arthur looked Maud up and down carefully. She did look stunning through the smoky haze.

"You should ask her to dance," Davis teased, jabbing his friend back. "She'd be worth the risk."

Davis had been William's friend for over three years. They were hired-out farmhands together by day and beer-slurping chums by night. William would persuade his employer, Omer Streeter, to hire on Arthur temporarily as they worked through the heavy threshing season.

"Tell you what, Art," William quickly bargained. "I'll buy you a beer if you ask her friend to dance too."

Arthur squinted to see Julia Christensen's stocky frame standing next to Maud.

"Better be a damn good beer," Davis retorted. "You're gettin' the better end of the deal."

"C'mon, Art," William begged. "This type of beauty ain't available in these parts that often."

"All right," Arthur relented. "I'll do one dance. Who knows? She might have a great personality."

"Glad I took my bath this afternoon," William said confidently to his buddy. "She's gonna have high standards. I can tell."

William and Arthur bid farewell to Forest and their other buddies, who continued to talk smart and gulp down glasses of cold beer.

By this time, the band had stopped playing music to take a well-earned break. The gaggle of musicians moved to the bar to swill beer for a few minutes, filling the open spot in the lounge just created by the absence of William Kleeman and Arthur Davis.

William intently shuffled his way across the room, pushing his way past young suitors, middle-aged philanderers, and giggling teens. Davis was in tow right behind him.

All this time, Maud and Julia were looking over the crowd, surveying the massive assembly to make snap judgments about people's hair, clothing, and looks. Twenty minutes had passed since Maud and Julia paid their dimes to enter, and so far there were no men of interest to Maud Petrie, either familiar or unfamiliar.

Suddenly, a striking young man with light-brown hair, a chiseled chin, and bright blue eyes appeared directly in front of her. It was William Kleeman, focused on his goal of sweeping the inexperienced girl off her feet with his audacious charm.

"Hello, ma'am," William said seductively, focusing his steely eyes directly into hers. "Are you here on your own tonight?"

Maud was taken aback by his bold manner and handsome appearance. She turned to look at Julia and blushed.

"Well, actually, I'm here with my friend tonight," Maud replied, tossing her head in Julia's direction. "But not with a man."

"Name's William Kleeman, miss," he said politely. "When the band starts, I'd be honored to take up a dance with you."

Maud and Julia, amateurs at romance, were stunned and temporarily incapable of a response. The momentary silence was broken by William's quick-witted second offer, semi-rehearsed with Arthur as they traveled across the dance floor.

"This here is my buddy, Arthur. Maybe the four of us could dance," William said, losing a bit of his cool demeanor and slipping into a more awkward stammer. "I mean not all dancin' at once. You with me. Your friend with my friend," he mumbled, losing a bit of confidence.

Ending the uncomfortable scene, William grabbed the gangly Arthur and shoved him in front of Julia, who immediately brightened with delight. At this point, she was willing to take *any* man, but considered herself blessed to share a dance with someone almost as handsome as William.

Arthur, thin and clumsy, wore a rumpled suit and crooked bow tie. He stuck out his right hand toward Julia.

"Hi, ma'am," he blabbed, looking toward the floor. "My name's Arthur Davis, and I'd be obliged to dance with you."

Julia drew a deep breath and shoved her hand back to Arthur. "I'd be honored, Mr. Davis," she said quickly, clutching his hand with a sweaty grip.

The band had ended its intermission and began to play a familiar, upbeat German polka. Maud, wearing the beautiful blue dress sewn by her mother, felt that fate might be calling.

"Could I get your name?" William asked. "Might be good if I knew your name."

"I . . . I'm Maud. Maud Petrie," she said sheepishly. "Pleased to meet you."

William quickly thought about her last name. It was vaguely familiar. He wondered if she might be related to that Petrie family who had sold the land that was platted out for the new village of Clements, which was located south of his folks' place. There would be plenty of time to investigate details like that later. For now, William just needed to get his hands on the beautiful maiden. Regaining his confidence, William put his arm around Maud's waist tightly and held her hand with the other.

"Your eyes are blue, just like your dress," William teased, struggling to bring out some initial conversation from the young virgin.

He pondered what lay underneath the blue gown as he gave her an impish grin. Maud hesitated to look William in the eyes, but his piercing baby blues were dazzling to behold. She admired his smooth, clean-shaven skin, freshly tanned after a long season of shocking grain and threshing in the hot August sun.

"Yours eyes are blue too, Mr. Kleeman," she responded. "Bluer than mine."

"Call me William," he responded, bringing about informality. "My ma calls me Willie, but I don't care for it much at my age."

William and Maud danced tightly and comfortably, but that wasn't true for the accompanying couple. Arthur struggled to get his lanky arm across Julia's paunchy frame and ended up stepping on her feet frequently. Julia sweated profusely in the crowd of sticky dancers. Her putrid underarm odor was only slightly concealed by the smoky stench of spent cigarettes and spilled beer that had been slopped to the floor from clumsy drinkers.

William Kleeman would owe Arthur Davis more than just a beer for this travesty, he thought. Their conversation was hesitant and inelegant.

"My family is Dutch," Julia said, struggling to bring interest of some sort from Arthur. "Daddy farms south of town."

"Well, we're English," Arthur said, seeking an excuse as to not continue the brief relationship. "We farm *way* east of town."

In reality, the Davises were less than seven miles from Redwood Falls, but for Arthur, it could just as well be at the end of the earth by Winona for the purposes of this discussion.

"We just got a few acres," Arthur continued, insinuating poverty. "Daddy just gets by."

Factually, the Davis family owned a large amount of land. William and Arthur worked part-time for Arthur's dad on his vast tracts of rich farmland near Gilfillan Station. But Arthur didn't want to inspire a gold-digging attitude from his stout dance partner.

As the seemingly endless song continued, Arthur tried everything to make himself as unattractive as possible to the admiring lass, including audibly passing gas, dancing out of time, and complaining of stomach cramps. As the polka finally concluded, Arthur released Julia and excused himself to flee the dance floor.

"Sorry, Miss Christensen," he lied. "My ma made a big supper of beans, and I need to use the indoor water closet."

"I'll wait right by this stool for you," Julia said firmly. "I won't move from the spot."

Arthur rolled his eyes and sighed with a slump. He retreated to the dance hall's water closet, pretending that he urgently needed to relieve himself.

CHAPTER 4

PLANS AT THE RESTAURANT

AT A RESTAURANT IN DOWNTOWN REDWOOD FALLS, Henry and Clara Petrie were indulging in good food and fretting about their daughter. Cigar smoke lingered throughout the room, and murmuring conversation filled the place.

"I wonder how Maud is doing," Henry wondered as he looked at his gold pocket watch. "Maybe we should leave early and go up in the balcony."

A waiter poured drinking water into their crystal glasses with an icy plop and moved quickly to the next table.

"Henry Petrie!" Clara admonished. "Spying on your own child! Give her a little privacy."

She carefully sliced the well-done steak that filled her plate, with bits of charred fat falling off the edges.

"I'm just wanting her to be safe, Clara," he said protectively. "I

21

know what these young men want, and Maud looked ripe for the pickin' tonight, just as beautiful as her mother."

His old-fashioned chivalry and charm reignited their old romance.

"Henry, we need to let Maud venture out more," Clara stated plainly. "This is one of the few places we've allowed her to even find someone to court her, other than perhaps church."

Henry thought for a few moments. He realized that Maud was isolated on their farm, and he sort of liked it that way. He took his fork and poked at the charred pieces of fat that Clara had carefully cut off her steak, and he ate them.

"We'll see," Henry said, chewing the burned gristle. "She's got time."

Henry sopped up bloody juice off his plate with soft white bread and finished his main course. He always enjoyed a rare steak.

Changing the subject, Henry wanted to get his wife's thoughts on their future as landowners.

"I saw a half section of land for sale south of us in Willow Lake Township," Henry said in a businesslike manner. "They want seventy dollars an acre."

Clara hated discussing money over dinner, but realizing the girls needed more time at the dance, she accommodated her husband's wish to discuss the topic. She was adept at math and calculated out the three hundred twenty acres multiplied by the asking price. "Henry, that's over twenty-two thousand dollars for a farm," she said in a hushed voice, not wanted to get the attention of those at neighboring tables. "We have some money, but that's just too much."

The Petries were renting their current farm and had good relations with the owners. As a package deal, they were also leasing the site where Frank Schottenbauer lived. In addition, they had use of a small pasture and one hundred eighty acres of rich and tillable land.

"At some point, we'll have to move, Clara," Henry warned. "The car shed will go with us. I'm not leaving anything that we paid for on the place."

"Are you saying that we need to move soon, Henry?" Clara questioned. "Why did we buy that car if that's the case?"

"No, Clara. We're set for the next year," Henry clarified. "I'm just thinking about the future."

Clara breathed a sigh of relief as the waiter returned to take their dessert order, and they both requested a slice of fresh apple pie.

Henry deliberated a few moments and blurted out something that had been nagging him the past few weeks.

"Clara, I'm thinking of running for sheriff," he said flatly. "I've been considering it for some time. It's one of the reasons I bought the car. I thought it would be easier to campaign in next year."

"You *what*?" Clara said, dropping her fork on her plate with a clang. "Why haven't you said anything about this before?"

"I wasn't sure what your reaction would be," Henry replied. "It's not a done deal."

"Well, I hope not, since you've never uttered a word about it to me," Clara protested with a reddened face. "What if Schueller runs again?"

B. C. Schueller was the incumbent Redwood County sheriff from Morgan. His given name was the unusual Baltazzar, but for simplicity, he always went by his initials. He had gained some recent notoriety investigating the Tibbetts murder case by Delhi in the last several weeks. Henry thought they handled it clumsily. They hadn't discovered a motive behind the murder, and information wasn't being provided to the public in a thorough manner. Many citizens were hungry for details, and Henry was puzzled about why the sheriff didn't provide more to the public.

"Schueller needs to tell the *Sun* and the *Gazette* more details on the Tibbetts case," Henry said, referring to the two large rival newspapers based out of Redwood Falls.

Henry knew that the thought of running for any political office wouldn't be agreeable to his privacy-seeking wife.

The waiter placed a piping-hot slice of flaky apple pie in front of each patron.

"Incumbents can be beat, Clara," Henry said defensively, grabbing his silver fork and picking over his dessert. "We're both Republicans, so I'd have to take him out in the primary."

"More wine, ma'am?" the waiter interrupted. "We have another shot left in this bottle." The waiter held up a tall, mostly empty bottle. Clara's lips tugged back.

"One last pouring of wine, please," she said as she held out her glass.

"I'll take a cup of coffee with my pie," Henry interjected to the waiter. "Bring some cream and sugar too, please."

"There's just a number of questions about this sheriff's position, Henry," Clara warned. "I think Schueller is liked by a lot of folks. You might think that the public should know more in the Tibbetts case, but keep in mind that the families probably don't want lots of information out there on their dead children."

"Clara, we can discuss this another day," Henry begged. "Let's enjoy our evening."

As Henry finished speaking, the large decorative fireplace in the front of the dining room roared higher, and the large mahogany clock in the corner chimed eight times.

CHAPTER 5

GETTING SERIOUS AT THE DANCE

UNLIKE THEIR MISFIT COMPANIONS, ARTHUR AND JULIA, William and Maud were laughing, teasing, and flirting after they finished their dance. Maud was falling head over heels for the dashing young farmhand.

"My folks farm east of town," William informed Maud. "We just rent. Daddy tends to frown on borrowin' any money to buy land like most folks."

"My parents farm south of town," Maud replied. "We live in New Avon Township, west of Clements and south of here."

"I bet your daddy is the feller that owned the land Clements is at!" William said eagerly, connecting the dots in his mind from her last name. "You must be right proud."

Maud nodded and turned a shade of pink. She didn't want her father's prominence or wealth to hook her a man. Maud Petrie would attract her own suitor.

"We like to do some trading in Clements. My father is rightfully proud of his history," Maud explained. "But it was just an ordinary land transaction, not unlike any others you might see. The railroad was looking for land, and he happened to own the right piece. In many ways, Peter Clements got the legacy, not my father."

Maud downplayed her family's status and changed the subject quickly.

"What happened to your friend?" she asked William, observing Julia Christensen standing alone by a barstool. "Did he have to leave early?"

William scowled. He was certain Arthur had bolted as soon as their first dance concluded. The new couple darted toward Julia, who had stood an eternity of ten minutes solo near the lounge.

"Your friend has apparently taken ill," Julia huffed to William. "He left for the water closet at least ten minutes ago, and I haven't seen him since."

"Let me check on him," William said hopefully. "We had a pork chop and some bread at the restaurant downtown before this shin-dig started, and maybe that food ain't agreeing with him," he offered, inadvertently exposing his friend's lie to Julia.

"He told me his ma made a pot of beans for supper tonight!" Julia yelled. "I see that he's not a very good fibber."

William grimaced and withdrew to the water closet to find Arthur Davis hiding in the corner.

"Art!" William scolded. "What are you doin' hidin' in here? Get your skinny rear back out there!"

William grabbed Arthur by the back of the collar.

"Hold on, Willie," Arthur begged. "That girl smells and ain't got nothin' in common with me. I ain't wastin' the whole night when I got other womenfolk to choose from."

"But I told you I'd buy you a beer—"

"You said *one dance*, Willie!"

"All right, I'll buy you a beer every weekend for the next month if you can humor that girl for the rest of the night, Art," William negotiated. "Free beer—how can you turn that down?"

Arthur thought about briefly and decided he didn't have much of a choice. His conscience gnawed at him, but only slightly.

As William pushed Arthur back to the lounge area, he informed the fabricator that he was caught in a lie regarding his supper story to Julia and that an apology to her was in order.

"I should've told her I needed to use my folks' outhouse seven miles away," Arthur asserted. "That would've gotten me outta here."

William smirked and shoved his resistant friend to where Maud and Julia were standing.

"Ahhh, here we are," William announced to the awaiting women, prodding Arthur to stand by Julia. "Art, don't you have something to say to Julia?"

William immediately grabbed Maud to rejoin the dance floor and abandoned Julia and Arthur a second time.

"Well, I'm sorry I told you eatin' Ma's beans was the cause of my diarrhea, Miss Christensen," Arthur stammered, looking at the floor. "I thought you might think lesser of me if you thunk William was my dinner companion and not my ma."

It was a pathetic apology, lacking any extended thought or contrition.

"Apology accepted!" Julia said in a delighted outburst. "I'm ready to dance again, Mr. Davis."

She pulled him back to the sawdust-strewn floor for another round of uncoordinated dancing.

William and Maud finished their dance and eventually moved to the lounge area.

"May I buy you a drink, Maud?" William asked. "Anything you want."

Maud recalled getting chastised by her father hours earlier to avoid alcohol. She would obey his wishes and be a teetotaler for the evening. It might not look good to drink alcohol anyway, being a young, refined woman.

"Some kind of soda would be fine," Maud said, sticking with her alcohol-free promise to her father. "The flavor doesn't matter."

William stepped to the sticky bar. The majority of it was covered with dirty beer glasses, heaping ashtrays, and empty peanut shells.

"Hey, Ted!" William called to the familiar barkeep over the ruckus of music and laughing. "Over here!"

The age-old trick of using friendship with the bartender to garner favor over other waiting customers was a familiar ploy for William Kleeman. The waiter, wearing a dirty black apron and stained white shirt, moved toward William. Maud could easily tell they were familiar with each other.

"Willie, you lucky dog!" the barkeep said, staring over at Maud. "What can I get you for drinks tonight?"

"The usual for me and a pop for the lady," William told Ted confidently. "Your choice on the fizzy drink."

Ted pulled on a large wooden tap, pouring out Schell's beer into an awaiting empty mug and plopping it on the counter. He searched underneath his bar and stood up to reveal a cool, glass bottle of Coca-Cola. Pulling out a steel bottle opener, he tore the metal cap off of the chilled bottle and shoved it toward William.

"Fifteen cents," the barkeep said in a routine manner. "Dime for the beer and a nickel for the soda."

William fumbled in his pocket, pulling out his pocket watch to make room for his hand to search for the requisite coins. He produced a dime and nickel, placing an extra Indian Head penny on the bar to tip his friend for his services.

"Ted, I know you charge more than normal at these dances," William said with a wink. "But she's worth it."

William handed the bottle to Maud and found an empty table where they could take a rest. They caught a glimpse of Arthur and Julia on the dance floor, stepping awkwardly as the band played a German tune that contained no words.

"Looks like Art and your friend are having fun," William lied. "What time do you have to go?"

Maud suddenly panicked. She could hear her daddy's voice booming in her head: "Meet us at this corner at nine o'clock sharp!"

"Could I bother you for the time, please?" Maud begged. "I need to leave by nine."

William produced his pocket watch, an open-faced timepiece that was a bit cheaper than her father's encased version. He studied his watch and frowned.

"You got less than five minutes, Miss Petrie," her new companion stated in a disappointed voice. "That ain't much time."

Maud looked at her bottle of pop, which she'd only sipped from a few times. It would be rude to have William purchase a whole nickel's worth of product, only to abandon him minutes later.

"Excuse me, William," she said quickly, sliding her oak chair backward. "I need to tell my father to wait a few more minutes."

Maud jumped up from the chair and shoved her way through the smelly crowd. Upon exiting the dance, Maud was relieved to have a cool breeze freshen her smoke-permeated clothes. She looked to the east corner of the street, where a massive blue Buick was parked with its engine running. Two passengers were waiting impatiently in the front seat.

Maud lifted up the bottom of her long dress and raced to the corner to find an irritated Henry Petrie waiting in the driver's seat.

"Daddy, just another ten minutes," Maud pleaded, catching her breath. "Julia has met someone, and it could be true love!"

Henry audibly groaned. "*Julia* needs to stay later?" he asked in a genuinely shocked voice. "How long does your mother have to put up with this, Maud?"

"Only ten minutes, Daddy," Maud continued. "I will peel that suitor off her by then!"

The dishonest excuse to reenter the dance was clever. Maud thought it was the best thing she could come up with in the short time she had to mislead her father. She would arrange a second rendezvous with William in the next ten minutes and then relieve the gangly Arthur Davis from the clutches of her friend Julia. She burst back into the dance hall and saw William sitting exactly where she left him, drinking his beer and looking at his watch.

"William Kleeman," she said forthrightly to her startled new beau, "I wish to see you again."

Maud plopped back in her chair and lifted the pop bottle to her lips. The excitement and oppressive heat in the building had parched her mouth. She consumed the remainder of her cola with a series of gulps and gurgles.

"Well, that was direct for a shy, little farm girl," William teased. "Do your folks have a telephone on the party line?"

"Why, yes, they do," Maud said immediately. "You can ring the switchboard out of Wabasso. We live too far south to be hooked to the Redwood line. Tell the operator it's Henry Petrie's place. Our ring is three shorts and a long."

Maud thought about the time and her impatient parents. She would have another two minutes to retrieve Julia before risking the wrath of her father for her tardy behavior. It was a hasty exit. Maud knew she could neither kiss nor hug her handsome new acquaintance.

She patted his muscular shoulder, running her hand to his right biceps and giving them a seductive squeeze. "You take care now, and please ring me," Maud said as she scanned the room for Julia. It was the boldest Maud Petrie had ever been with a man in her entire life.

"I'll ring you this week," William promised. "If you're looking for Art and your friend, they're over there." William pointed to an isolated corner of the room, where Julia had Arthur Davis trapped.

Maud raced to the corner and pulled Julia toward her.

"Julia, it's after nine, and my folks have been waiting forever!" Maud begged. "We have to leave *right now*."

Julia Christensen finally had a man in her grasp and the beautiful Maud Petrie was going to ruin the opportunity.

"Maud, do we *have* to leave?" Julia cried. "I feel like we just got here!"

"Julia, my daddy is going to kill us if we don't get our hind ends out in that car!" Julia pleaded. "I'm not dying young."

Julia knew that Henry Petrie had only so much patience. She had witnessed his temper flair periodically when she had visited Maud as a child, and she didn't want to provoke any unnecessary anger from the elder Petrie. With a disappointed sigh, Julia grabbed Arthur's right hand.

"Will I see you again?" Julia asked in a provocative voice.

"Umm . . . maybe. Let's see," he stumbled. "I'd ring you at the Hans Christensen place north of town?"

"No!" Julia snapped. "The *Lars* Christensen place *south* of town."

"Perhaps William can get the four of us together again in the near future," Maud stated politely, concluding the unpleasant discussion.

"I enjoyed this fine evening with you," Julia called out to Arthur as Maud pulled her away.

Arthur gave a nod to the women and looked anxiously for his so-called friend. He spotted William at the table where Maud had left him, finishing his beer and surveying the remaining pretty women, three of whom circled the north side of the lounge area.

"Willie Kleeman!" Arthur called out as he stomped toward William. "You got some nerve stickin' me like that."

"Calm down, Art," William admonished his friend. "Let me buy you your first free beer of the month."

He handed Arthur a dime and told him to order whatever brew he wished.

Arthur made his way to the lounge, and after a quick minute of the usual banter with Ted, he rejoined William with a cold Schell's in his hand.

"Those women look mighty fine," Arthur stated, pointing in the direction of the three ladies who were staring William up and down.

"They sure do," William agreed. "But I'm thinkin' that Petrie girl is worth a pursuit."

"Well, she may be worth pursuin'," Arthur answered, "but I ain't doin' any more courtin' with her friend."

"I ain't ever hit it off with a gal like that before," William said with a devilish grin. "She made me stiff with love from the minute I first saw her."

The crude humor between the two men was nothing new.

"She is mighty perty," Arthur responded. "Funny, she ain't hitched with someone by now?"

"She just turned twenty-one, only a couple years younger than me," William said thoughtfully. "She ain't experienced much with menfolk. I can tell that."

"An untouched virgin of the prairie," Arthur declared in a vulgar, but honest, assessment. "I think you might land her."

As the hall emptied out, William and Arthur stayed until the place closed down, but for the first time in his life, William Kleeman only danced with one woman.

CHAPTER 6

HEADING HOME

JULIA CHRISTENSEN AND THE PETRIE FAMILY coasted south in the Buick, moving only in second gear, due to Henry's uncertainty about driving the bulky car in the dark.

"We're in no hurry, Henry Petrie," Clara scolded. "I want to get home in one piece tonight."

Henry referenced Maud's earlier exaggeration about Julia and Arthur Davis. "Sounds like you met someone special tonight, Julia," Henry teased. "Maud said you hooked yourself a man at that dance."

"Well, ain't as close to courtin' with my man as Maud is with hers," Julia stated plainly.

"Daddy, what Julia meant to say is that we were both able to find someone to share a dance with this evening," Maud interrupted as she nudged Julia to silence.

"What is this?" Clara asked, pretending to be startled. "You found men to dance with?"

"You're lucky we aren't Baptist!" Henry chuckled. "No dancin'. No nothin'."

"Henry, be respectful," Clara admonished. "We all believe in one Lord."

"Who were these lucky chaps?" Henry asked. "Are they local folks?"

"Well, their names are William Kleeman and Arthur Davis," Maud answered in a matter-of-fact manner. "They are both gentlemen and very handsome."

Henry knew how "gentlemanly" boys were in their early twenties and winced when he remembered how attractive his daughter was this evening.

"I'm sure they were fine men," Clara stated. "We can't expect these girls to become spinsters, Henry."

Maud explained that William Kleeman might ring the telephone this week to set up a time to come calling on her.

"Daddy, William will be calling in the next few days, and I wish to speak with him," Maud said politely. "Please let me know if I'm not in the house."

"You know that I'm not staying by the telephone much, Maud," Henry goaded. "Might miss that ringin' this week. Lots of work to do."

"Henry, stop it!" Clara exhorted Henry.

"Make sure you ask him about Arthur, Maud," Julia interrupted.

"We'll take the call and let you know, dear," Clara said in a kind voice. "And I'm sure that he'll be askin' about your man too, Julia."

The car made its way first to the Christensen farm, where both parents impatiently waited by lamplight for their only daughter to return. Henry pulled up to the front steps, parked the car, and escorted Julia from the back seat. Olga Christensen's shadow appeared on the ornate porch.

"Thank you for taking Julia to town tonight, Henry," she said, appreciative of the extra trouble. "Would you like some coffee or bars?"

"Sorry, Olga," Henry called. "We got church in the morning, and I'm sure Julia will want to tell you about the nice fellas she met tonight."

Julia looked to the ground, flushed with embarrassment. While she was bold in the presence of her friends and even strangers, her aging and old-fashioned parents expected her to be unassuming and reserved.

"Well, I know you must be going," Julia said hurriedly. "Thank you so much for taking me along tonight."

"Bye-bye, dear," Clara said sweetly. "Thank you for joining us this evening."

"We'll talk," Maud stated in a hushed voice to her friend. "I'll find out more about that Davis fellow."

There was much more to discuss with Julia, but it would be in secrecy, away from both sets of parents. The giddiness they felt couldn't be fully released in the car ride home with the elder Petries.

Henry mounted his vehicle and shifted it into gear. The Petries took their time returning home. The Buick rolled into the car shed, a new building Henry had built for his grand car. He wouldn't risk damage to the new vehicle from a passing hailstorm.

As they started toward the house, the Petries heard coyotes howling in the distance, and a cool breeze brought a chill to their skin. They were puzzled to see light flickering in their kitchen window. Frank had always gone home after finishing chores, and there were no other members of the family home to await them since Claude was staying with friends for the weekend.

"Maud, Clara, you stay right here," Henry warned as he crept toward the front door. "I want to see why that light is on."

Various scenarios raced through Maud's mind. Was it a robber? Was the kitchen on fire? Did their relatives from out east come calling and not inform them?

Clara and Maud could see through the windows as the flicker moved from the kitchen to the front foyer. Henry stepped carefully toward the house.

The door suddenly swung open to reveal Frank Schottenbauer filling the entrance.

"Frank!" Henry chastised. "What on earth are you doing here at this time of night?"

"Sorry, Mr. Petrie," Frank said sadly. "I wanted to wait up for you folks to make sure everything was all right."

Clara and Maud had made their way close enough to the house to hear the conversation.

"You sweet man," Clara declared. "Always lookin' out for us."

Maud thought it would be awkward to discuss her handsome new dance partner with Frank and her folks.

"I'm very tired," she announced to the three as they entered the kitchen and lit more lamps. "May I go to bed so church doesn't come too early?"

It was a perfect excuse that had a lot of truth weaved into it.

"Of course, dear," Clara said, holding Maud's chin up to inspect her glowing face. "I'll wake you by nine tomorrow morning so we can get to church on time."

"I lit this for you, Miss Petrie," Frank said in his plainspoken tone, shoving a red lantern shining brightly at her. "Don't want you stumblin' to the outhouse. Just pumped some new cistern water in your pitcher upstairs too."

Frank had memorized Maud Petrie's evening rituals.

"Why, thank you, Frank," she answered politely, grabbing the lantern from his strong hands. "Please excuse me."

Maud held up the lantern and first marched upstairs to a small closet next to her room, retrieving something unbeknownst to Frank. She bounced down the stairs moments later, exited the front door, and went straight to the small, white outhouse that sat a few yards from the home. The toilet was a needed respite for the girl. The cola had she gulped down earlier was ready to be released, and her monthly had started—dual reasons to spend some time in the stench-filled building.

"Frank, I must say, you spoil us," Clara said. "Shall I put on some coffee?"

"Not for me, ma'am," Frank responded. "I best be gettin' back to my house. Have a good night," he said, looking at the scripted walnut clock that adorned their wall. "It's late, and you folks need to get to bed."

The hired hand moved to the porch and lit a dusty, aged barn lantern. He blew out his large wooden match and waved good night to his employers.

Instead of taking the driveway out to the road on his half-mile walk home, he decided to quietly tiptoe past the outhouse as an unnecessary shortcut.

CHAPTER 7

KILLER IN THE COOP

THE OLD ROOSTER CROWED LOUDER THAN EVER on Sunday morning at the Petrie farm.

Daybreak arrived too soon for the groggy family. Clara had consumed three glasses of wine, thrice the amount she normally drank on such occasions, and Maud had been up past her usual bedtime. Henry hoped Frank would be doing the chores this morning, which was the usual routine on Sundays.

The main-floor clock rang eight times and helped awaken the clan from their slumber.

Henry slid out of bed and pulled away the curtain that faced the barn. He spotted Frank in his Sunday overalls, crossing the yard to fetch a pail of water for the horses.

"Good ol' Frank," Henry announced to his unsurprised wife. "What a noble hired hand."

Clara Petrie audibly yawned and stretched her short arms across the bed.

"Henry, he's more than a hired hand," Clara admonished. "He's almost like family. Been with us for so many years, he's like an adopted son."

Her husband hadn't contemplated Frank in such a way. His relationship with Frank had been more formal than Clara's. He paid Frank barely adequate wages twice per month, worked alongside him doing chores, and treated him professionally.

"Yes, Clara," he responded upon deeper thought. "Frank indeed is more than just a hired hand."

As Henry dressed in his Sunday clothes and Clara picked at her hair, Maud burst into the bedroom.

"Can you learn to knock, young lady?" her father chastised. "What is your urgency?"

"Daddy, I cannot stop thinking about that William Kleeman," she gushed. "I do so hope that he calls."

Henry exhaled loudly, blowing air audibly in Clara's direction.

"If he doesn't come callin' on you, *he's* got a big problem," Henry answered as he fixed his complicated dress tie.

"You get upstairs and pretty yourself up, Maud," her mother instructed. "I'll get started on breakfast, and then we'll have to get to church."

"Tell Frank to come in for breakfast," Clara told Henry. "He's doing all the work this morning."

It was customary that Frank would arrive to do chores, but on every day except Sunday, Henry Petrie also helped with chores. He didn't want the smell of livestock or sweat clinging to him before attending church services.

Frank rarely attended his home church near Wabasso, so Sunday-morning chores weren't a burden. He was somewhat estranged from his large family and only attended the Lutheran church services at Easter and Christmas, which he did out of respect for his ma, he would occasionally reveal. It was an ideal situation to have Frank working for the family, even though Henry and Maud often took his work ethic and polite demeanor for granted.

Henry put on his black dress shoes and stood erect. Other than his black beaver-skin cap, he was fully dressed to attend services at the Church of the Holy Communion. He walked out to the barn to search for Frank and saw that an inordinate number of chicken feathers were lying around the toolshed.

"Frank!" Henry yelled out in the direction of the barn. "Time for breakfast!"

Frank ambled around the corner of the toolshed, startling Henry.

"Mr. Petrie," the exasperated hired hand called out. "The chickens, they're almost all dead!"

Frank led Henry behind the shed, which hid the carnage. Blood was spattered against their small chicken coop, and white feathers were scattered everywhere.

"We've only got two hens and the rooster left," Frank said. "The rest of 'em are dead or gone."

The loud cry of the morning rooster was one of survival, not of routine that day.

"It must have been a fox or some weasels!" Henry stammered in anger. "Get the gun!"

Frank trotted off to the house to grab the rifle that they used to kill various vermin on the farm.

Henry didn't want to get blood on his Sunday best, so he instructed Frank to walk the perimeter of the property and shoot anything that moved if it wasn't his livestock or chickens. Ten laying hens that were providing fresh eggs for eating and cooking were prematurely dead. As a general rule, the Petries would butcher most of them in the fall to provide chicken meat for the winter. All that remained now were two wounded fowl that hobbled toward the coop, seeking safety from their predator.

"Circle the farm and shoot any bastard critter you see, Frank!" Henry bellowed. "Come on in for breakfast after your first round."

Frank nodded and headed behind the barn, inspecting bushes, hollowed-out trees, and any other place where a fox or similar varmint might hide.

Henry was crushed. Anytime a farmer loses animals to accidental or predator deaths is a disappointment. Much-needed meat goes wasted, and hard-earned money is squandered.

Clara called for the men to come in for breakfast. Henry heard her, but Frank was too far away to hear.

"Lost almost all our chickens, Clara," Henry snorted as he threw open the door. "Feathers and blood everywhere. All we got left is the rooster and a couple of crippled-up hens."

"Oh, Henry, no!"

Clara Petrie was the true steward of the farm chickens. She sometimes treated the long-lasting ones as pets. The older chickens and the rooster usually ended up in the soup kettle, because the tough meat was harder to chew if it was fried or baked. More often than not, Clara helped keep their metal pans full of water and ground corn and picked the eggs in the late morning before she started dinner (their midday meal).

Clara sat down by her large kitchen table and wiped a tear with her apron. Just then, in the midst of her brief moment to mourn the lost fowl, she realized her bacon was starting to burn, and she ran to the cookstove to slide the cast-iron pan to a dead burner.

"Mother, what is the commotion about down here?" Maud asked as she descended the steps. "I thought I heard Daddy yelling."

"Something got into the chickens, dear," Clara said calmly. "It killed almost all of them."

Maud had sometimes adopted a chicken in the spring. She knew what they meant to her mother.

"Mother, I am so sorry," Maud said, embracing her as if a relative had passed. "How many are left?"

"Maybe two or three," Clara answered as she threw a slab of butter over some cut-up potatoes.

Crack! A gunshot was heard in the distance.

Maud and Clara peered out the front window to see Frank carrying a bloody fox by its disheveled red tail. They heard Henry let out a cheer and a whistle as the men stood and admired the executed villain.

Frank dropped the carcass in the middle of the yard, and Henry aggressively pushed and pulled the handle on the well pump, releasing a fresh stream of water into Frank's filthy hands. They trotted to the front door, chattering about the method Frank used to kill him.

"Did you see it, Clara?" Henry exclaimed as they entered the house. "Did you see that dead fox Frank got?"

"My knight in shining armor!" Clara called out as Frank arrived to a hero's welcome. "You sit down and have some breakfast."

Frank grinned as Maud, Clara, and Henry waited on him with biscuits, fried chopped potatoes, and fresh bacon. It was the best he'd ever been treated in his life. All for killing something.

"Henry," Clara warned, "we must get going; I need to be at church early to play organ."

CHAPTER 8

―――――――――

GETTING TO CHURCH

WHILE THE MASSACRE OF THE CHICKENS and subsequent execution of the fox delayed them slightly, the Petries still had time to get to church early enough for Clara to play the organ, her usual weekly task at the small parish. She had been teaching Maud to play the piano and organ since Maud was young, and she was improving, but she wasn't as musically skilled as the experienced Clara.

Clara played for the vast majority of services at the Church of the Holy Communion. She was even called in for special events like weddings and funerals from time to time. Maud was gaining enough confidence to play organ one Sunday per month, and the aging Sadie Brewster played out of tune in emergencies when the Petries couldn't attend.

As Clara piled the dirty dishes in the sink and pumped a few splashes of water from her small cistern pump over the soiled plates, she heard the Buick's engine crank to life outside. Maud and Henry had already beaten her to the car shed. The car roared in reverse to cross the yard quickly.

"No time for chivalry!" she called above the engine noise to her husband as she came outside, cautioning him not to get out and assist her into the car.

Henry nodded and kept the car stopped, with his dress shoes pressing the clutch tightly to the floor. Clara opened the door, climbed up onto the running board unassisted, and slammed the door shut. Frank was slurping a drink of cool water from the tin cup that usually hung on a nail near the well pump. It was a well-deserved treat for his efforts that morning. The Buick pulled forward, and the three passengers waved to Frank as he beamed a broad, toothy smile in return.

A mixture of buggies, wagons, and cars awaited the Petries at the Church of the Holy Communion in Redwood Falls when they arrived for services, the only one of the day. The church boasted a roster of forty-one souls. Its small white frame gave it a humble appearance, and the inside matched the exterior for its modesty.

Henry killed the engine and assisted his wife and daughter off the tired vehicle.

Pastor Joss, rector of the local chapel, greeted the Petries as they entered. He was wearing bright white robes and a red stole. "As usual, thank you for playing organ, Mrs. Petrie," the pastor said gratefully. "I don't know what we'd do without you."

"My pleasure, Reverend," Clara said kindly as she abandoned Henry and Maud for the creaky organist's bench.

Joss was known to be devout and stern. He was a proud Protestant who worked to bring more members into his shrinking flock of believers. But his demanding demeanor may have led more believers to stay away than to come.

Henry sat with Maud in the second pew, a place of prominence they were proud to occupy that was also conveniently located near Clara's seat at the organ keyboard, which was in the front left of the sanctuary. Henry was a generous donor to the tiny church, one of its few patrons.

The service took the usual routine of an opening hymn, Old and New Testament readings, a long sermon, communion for the believers, and several more hymns, including one at the conclusion.

Across the aisle in the second row sat twenty-year-old Andrew Churchill, a lifetime member of the church and an attractive young man. He had suffered from acne earlier in life, leaving a few pocks and scars, but still displayed a handsome appearance. He was tall and thin as a rail. His demeanor was always polite—and when he was out of the presence of his elders, he was a risible young lad, quick to humor and slow to judgment.

Since childhood, Andrew had felt a passion for Maud Petrie. She had a soft glow to her skin, gentle flowing curls, and bright blue eyes that Andrew couldn't find in other girls their age.

Only one year her junior, Andrew stared across the aisle, admiring Maud's well-developed figure. His bright eyes blinked, and his pupils trained below her neckline.

Henry noticed the gawking and cleared his throat, gazing over to Andrew to give fair warning that the protective father was paying attention to anyone pursuing his daughter.

Maud thought Andrew was a nice young man, but he was nothing like William Kleeman. For some strange reason, the edgy persona that William demonstrated the previous evening was indescribably attractive to her. A customary churchgoing regular like Andrew would be all too ordinary.

As the service droned on, Maud noticed Andrew taking periodic peeks at her face and figure. Since she'd worn her better dress at the dance and it was infused with smoke from the dance hall, she now wore her red dress, which lacked the decorative lace but still complemented her curvaceous figure to anyone paying the least bit of attention.

Maud had dozed off in a drowse as she sat for the homily, but after a few minutes, was jolted awake.

"Your body is to remain chaste until the bounds of matrimony!" the bespectacled minister thundered, looking down at the voluptuous Maud Petrie. "It is a *sin* to partake in the forbidden fruit of lust."

The minister turned to Andrew Churchill and glared momentarily, as if he saw the inner workings of the boy's hormones activating at the sight of Maud's well-endowed figure.

Pastor Joss's fire-and-brimstone sermon had Maud Petrie thinking the reverend might have witnessed her antics the previous evening, although she'd done nothing physical enough to warrant such chastising.

"The devil is real!" the parson bellowed. "He is cunning, and he is devious!"

A chill went down the spine of every congregant. Maud swallowed hard and briefly deliberated about Churchill's ogling. As the sermon ended, the minister's voice and tone changed immensely from a booming voice to a hushed warning.

"Lucifer lurks where we least expect him," Joss concluded in a quiet and eerily predictive way.

Andrew Churchill gulped audibly.

As the service concluded with "Bringing in the Sheaves," accompanied by Clara Petrie, Maud exited into the middle aisle at the same point Andrew Churchill spilled out of his pew.

"Hello, Maud," Andrew whispered while shifting his eyes to hers. "You look right nice today."

The routine pleasantries didn't impress Maud. Only the night before, she was with a gorgeous and muscular gent who might strike the prudes in the congregation as a cad. But that's what Maud Petrie liked about him. There would indeed be a bit of a risk in running off with the likes of William Kleeman. A suitor like Andrew Churchill might meet minimal expectations, but choosing him would relegate her to a life that would simply be too routine.

Following the unwritten rule of silence upon entrance and exit in their church aisle, Maud waited to say anything until they left. She gave Andrew a slight nod of acknowledgment. As they left the church, their barely audible church voices could now return to a normal tone outside. Henry was visiting with Pastor Joss, soon to be joined by Clara, who clutched several song sheets as she greeted the pastor and her husband.

Maud moved toward the awaiting Buick, while Andrew Churchill lingered close behind. The bright Sunday sun was making the temperature particularly balmy for Minnesota in September.

"I'm thinkin' of going swimmin' down by the river today, Maud," Andrew said innocently, with a naïve smile. "Would you be interested in coolin' off this afternoon?"

The swimming hole on the east side of the Redwood River hugged the western border of the Redwood Falls city limits. The lagoon jutted off the main bank and provided cool respite from the scorching Minnesota summers for area residents. It was an infamous location for young couples to have trysts in the privacy of its weeds that grew thick along the shore. Maud guessed this wasn't a simple invitation for swimming, but for a more intimate liaison.

She quickly turned down Churchill's flirtatious attempt. "My presence is no longer available to you or any other men, I'm afraid, Andrew," she said, half lying. "If you had asked last week, I likely would've taken you up on the offer, but I simply cannot out of loyalty to my suitor."

The fancy language Maud was in the habit of using was difficult for most of the country boys to decipher, but Andrew calculated that he was being rejected after his gutsy invitation. The inexperienced and gullible lad had no intention of molesting Maud Petrie at the local swimming hole, but thought it might be one way of setting up a date. Maud, older and worldlier, viewed his attempt with suspicion.

"Well, if you ever change your mind, I'd be right appreciative to keep company with you sometime," he said in a disappointed tone, kicking the sand on the street. "I've been meanin' to ask ya for a couple of years now."

Andrew shuffled away to a small buggy, with his mother and father atop, patiently waiting for their son to return. Maud could see Andrew shaking his head at his folks, signaling that the parents had likely been in on practicing for the romantic solicitation. After Andrew had mounted the back seat of his parents' surrey, Henry and Clara arrived to confront Maud about the conversation.

"I'm excited to see that Churchill boy might have taken a likin' to you, Maud," Henry said glowingly as he helped her into the back seat of the Buick. "He's been such an upright young man all these years."

"Daddy, I'm *not* interested," Maud said in a forcefully hushed voice. "I rebuffed his advances just now."

Clara Petrie climbed into her seat and took her husband's hand.

"But, Maud," Clara responded, "I always thought you liked Andrew."

"Mother, he's nice, but I don't like him *that way*," Maud countered. "Besides, I told him I'm unavailable."

Henry cranked the Buick to life and mounted the driver's seat to rejoin the fray, continuing a long conversation for their trip back home.

"How can you say you're unavailable when you just met that Kleeman fellow last night?" Henry wondered. "You've known Andrew Churchill since you were knee high to a grasshopper."

"Daddy, that's the issue," Maud pleaded. "There's something about William Kleeman that I don't feel about Andrew Churchill—or any other boy, for that matter."

Henry stopped the car abruptly, yielding to a large black Chalmers car that whisked past while letting out a loud toot on its horn.

"I just think you need to take your time and look around, dear," her father begged. "Tellin' folks you're unavailable after one evening seems a little quick."

"Sounds like you fell hard for that man," Clara said with a smile. "That's how I felt about you at first, Henry Petrie." She grabbed her husband's arm and gave it a flirtatious squeeze.

As usual, Clara Petrie would support her daughter's wishes. This time it was about courting, and it was backed up by her own first-hand experience. Henry would have difficulty refuting her perspective. Nonetheless, having never met the young beau from the previous night, Maud was putting her mother in the position of defending the unknown.

The Buick growled down the dusty road with a frustrated Henry Petrie at the helm, outnumbered two to one. The usual odds.

The Petrie family returned to their farm where their hired man stood waiting near the front door of their home. After exiting the vehicle, they saw that Frank Schottenbauer was beaming as he held up the skinned carcass of the freshly killed red fox that had vexed them earlier in the morning.

Frank had carefully butchered the animal, cutting off its head and removing its innards and legs. He carefully opened the body from top to bottom and scraped the flesh and fat off the insides, making a furry pelt.

"I done made this up for you, Miss Petrie," he said proudly to Maud. "You could use it as a rug or blanket. I'll tan up the skin for you later."

With an expression of horror, Maud cringed and backed away slowly in silence.

Clara, sensing Maud's disgust, interjected. "Frank, you did a marvelous job with that fox," she complimented. "I'm sure Maud would love to have it after you're done tanning it."

Henry pulled the fuzzy carcass away from Frank and held it high, admiring the crafty taxidermy job his hired hand performed while they were in church.

"I am amazed you could make such a fine pelt so quickly, Frank," Henry said cheerfully. "Where are the guts?"

"Buried 'em out behind the barn, Mr. Petrie," Frank answered, a little disappointed at Maud's reaction. "Didn't want 'em stinkin' up the place, and we don't need no more varmints comin' in and eatin' at 'em."

"I'll have dinner ready in a bit," Clara said quickly as she grabbed Maud's arm gently. "Maud will need to help in the kitchen.

Henry, I want you to pick up Claude from the neighbor's place pretty soon too."

It was a clever exit strategy for what was becoming an increasingly uncomfortable scene. Frank and Henry stood to admire the fox fur. Over time, it would become apparent that Frank would like to execute more than just this cunning rascal.

CHAPTER 9

LOOKING AT OPTIONS

WILLIAM KLEEMAN PACED BACK AND FORTH in his shabby old farmhouse. Though also a farmhand, he didn't enjoy the benefit of free housing that Frank Schottenbauer enjoyed with the Petries. He was required to pay eighteen dollars per month for the use of a ramshackle abandoned house. The small farm site consisted of an aging barn that would barely hold a team of horses, a well pump that periodically ran dry, an ancient empty granary, and a drafty, run-down, one-bedroom house. A small outhouse with a rotting roof and loose-hanging door rounded out the place.

While his conservative parents modeled how to manage money quite well, William squandered some of his meager pay on beer, dances, and the occasional woman he was able to lure on the weekends. But his dilapidated surroundings or lack of money did not cause of William's restless pacing. The cause was the ravishing Maud Petrie, who had haunted his dreams the night before. Her shy beauty, voluptuous figure, and naïve innocence intrigued him greatly. It was Monday morning, and he was still thinking about the young lass.

William had rounded out his Saturday evening by bragging up Maud with his buddy Arthur Davis, who was trying to forget the pawing of Maud's friend Julia Christensen.

Now William brooded over his next move. Maud had plainly invited him to ring the Petrie household and set up another rendezvous, but he faced a monumental problem: His primitive residence lacked a telephone—and worse yet, he lacked any transportation to begin courting her.

William rented the shanty from his main employer, a farmer named Omer Streeter. The place had once belonged to Streeter's bachelor uncle, who had passed away years before. The Streeters owned more land than the average Redwood County farmer. William was hired on when he decided to move off his folks' place over in Paxton Township and enjoy more freedom near the city of Redwood Falls. It was the end of his third season helping the Streeter family with their endless chores and farmwork.

Unlike Henry Petrie, Streeter was a demanding and impolite boss. His grueling tasks never seemed to end, but William knew he couldn't stay living with his parents forever. He hoped to own a farm of his own someday.

Streeter's lack of dental hygiene had caused a majority of his teeth to fall out, causing a slight lisp when he spoke. He wore a medium-length beard that was black in his youth and was now streaked with gray.

His wife, Grace Streeter, was as stern and irritable as her husband. Short and slight, she was a good cook who was frequently adorned with a dirty apron. Other than Sundays, she always had her hair fixed with a bun on top of her head. It was expected that William and her boys help with some of the house chores and not just stay in the sheds and fields doing "menfolk work" that hired hands on other farms were doing. With no other girls in the house, it was a logical proposition.

Mr. Streeter cut corners wherever he could to save money, so the ultraconservative landlord refused to have a telephone installed for William, even though the tenant had offered to share the cost.

Like most farm homes in Redwood County, William's house had no running waterworks, no electricity, and poor insulation. The shack was only one story and was heated by an undersized potbellied stove in the living room. A modest and rarely used cookstove, heated mainly by wood, stood in the kitchen and helped supplement the heat supply.

Despite his exceptional good looks, William spent many nights alone in the drab shack, playing solitaire and roughhousing with his dog, Duke, a dark and larger-than-average canine that was a frequent guest inside the home. The hound had suddenly appeared the year before as a stray, and he'd grown very protective of William.

Some of his evenings were spent reading through the Sears, Roebuck and Co. catalog, which contained every imaginable article of clothing, kitchen tools, farm machinery, guns, and other types of ware. It had brief, vivid descriptions of the items and included periodic illustrations.

The Sears catalog was patronized heavily in Redwood County. Richard Sears, the founder of the company, got his start by selling surplus watches up the road in North Redwood. Sears shipped the timepieces out from the railroad depot there. After making some money, he left Redwood County and ended up in Chicago, pairing up with a business partner, Alvah Roebuck, to form a giant mail-order company. The frugal farmers of the area remembered that Sears got his start nearby, and it instilled a sense of pride that one of the locals made good.

William spied an ad in the mechanical section of the book: "Coming new for 1910, the Sears Automobile."

William knew that Sears had a car in its previous catalog, but now they were available in different types. He scanned through the various options and prices. A cheap Model G, without a top or fenders, but with lamps, a horn, carpet, oil, hard tires, and a tool kit, could be purchased for three hundred seventy dollars. As he looked at the additional models that included tops, pneumatic tires, side curtains, and more, the prices continued to rise, topping out at five hundred twenty-five dollars.

How impressed would Maud Petrie be if he owned an automobile? Sure, it wouldn't be an expensive car like her father's, but it would be a status symbol above the average farmhand in these parts. William thought over his options.

Through his farm toils and scrimping and saving from childhood, he'd saved a few hundred dollars at Farmers & Merchants Bank of Redwood Falls. Other than his frequent beers and attending dances with his friends, he didn't have many expenses, since the Streeters deducted rent from his pay but provided him with meals. With the brutal Minnesota winter coming, an automobile wouldn't be practical. Most car owners jacked up their vehicles in a shed and hooked up sleighs to horses to navigate the deep snow that would pile up on the roads. Since it was only September, it might be best to buy a team of horses and save up diligently to buy a car in the spring.

Under the Sears car listing, the catalog said, "cash up front" and indicated that the car would be shipped by rail from Chicago with "some assembly required" to operate it. Sunup to sundown, most of William's time was spent doing chores for Mr. Streeter, who lived less than a mile away. This kept him from squandering the money he earned, and it was a blessing in disguise. Now, with the dawning of Miss Maud Petrie in his life, he decided that it was time to purchase transportation. It would be practical to purchase his own team of horses in the fall and stable them in the ramshackle barn located at his leased property. After all, what type of girl would want to date a man who didn't even have his own team of horses?

William decided he'd saved up enough money to purchase an average team. He wouldn't have to rely on his folks, friends, or the boss to cart him around any longer. Then the winter months would provide time to save up money to buy the Sears Motorbuggy in the late spring, when the soft roads would harden as the weather improved.

The first challenge was to convince his employer that he could keep his new team in the frumpy shed that had been built more than fifty years earlier and was now in disrepair. He only had a couple of specifications for the animals: They had to be black, and they had to be cheap.

Monday dawned, and William dressed to make his usual walk to the main Streeter farm. As he walked, he rehearsed how he'd ask about the horses. Duke, his loyal companion, followed behind, chasing a bird along the way and sniffing deeply into the ditch grass. The dog was shared between the two farms, but everyone understood it was William's mongrel to master.

"Mr. Streeter, sir," William said with uncommon politeness as he arrived at the Streeters' large red barn. "I got a favor to ask you."

William wasn't intimidated by the scowling Omer Streeter like others in the neighborhood were. His boss was lifting straw into a pen that contained dozens of small pigs and looked like he didn't want to be bothered.

"What do you want, Kleeman?" Streeter retorted with a huff. "I'm busy."

William cleared this throat as pigs squealed with delight to receive fresh bedding.

"I was thinkin' of gettin' a team of horses to help out around here. I was wonderin' if I might stable 'em over at my place," William asked with a gulp.

"We got plenty of horses around here, Kleeman," Streeter snapped back. "No need for more."

A large sow ambled over to where the men were standing and snorted. She was protecting her small piglets from the conversing trespassers.

"Back up!" Streeter screamed, shaking his pitchfork. The hog originally ignored the irritable farmer, then turned its head to see William standing there.

The enormous pig immediately grunted in fright, turned around, and hurried away, a dozen piglets following close behind. William's inquiry went unanswered by his boss.

"We have to clean manure out of the barns this week," Streeter instructed, changing the subject. "But the woman is doing laundry today, and she'll have a fit if we stink up her linens."

Monday was the traditional day for the womenfolk to do laundry in southwestern Minnesota. It was no different on the Streeter property.

"I'll get right on it first thing tomorrow," William answered as he grabbed a second fork and helped his boss dump in more straw. "This barn will be spick-and-span by suppertime tomorrow."

"We've got firewood to saw too," Streeter added. "We can use the gas engine that Ma is using today."

The Streeters owned two gasoline engines that were single cylinder, with large-spoke flywheels. The power units were attached to steel-wheeled carts and hauled around the farm to help with various chores. The belt pulleys attached to the large flywheels had thick belts running from the motor to the unit doing the work. The smaller engine, a Fuller & Johnson rated at three horsepower, was always reserved for Grace Streeter's use on Monday morning to run the washing machine. It powered the agitator and wringer, so she avoided having to crank her machine by hand. While the engine was a little larger than needed for a simple washer, Omer Streeter was too cheap to buy a smaller engine for the once-a-week chore.

Since the three-horse engine was also used to power a pump that sucked water out of the main well into the cattle and hog troughs, it was a Monday routine for William to start the engine with a crank and fill all the water troughs. He would then shut it down and drag the contraption near house's open porch. At nine sharp, Mrs. Streeter would pour a large kettle of water heated on her cookstove into the washing-machine tub. With the water cooling by the minute, there would be hell to pay if William didn't have the engine pulled to the porch, belted up to the washing machine, and running by the time his boss's wife was dumping dirty laundry into the rinse tub.

The Streeters' larger engine, a six-horsepower International Harvester, was used for grinding corn into feed, shelling corn off the cobs, and powering a hay press that compressed loose straw into bales. William and the Streeter sons, Lester and John, would pull the heavy engine where it needed to go for its various chores.

"That saw could use the six-horsepower instead of the three," William corrected. "The last time we used the little one, we kept jamming the saw blade."

"Fine," Streeter conceded. "You and the boys use that thing more than I do."

Streeter had surprisingly modern equipment for being an old-school farmer. However, when it came time to operate the tractors or engines, it was William, Lester, and John who did the handling, not Omer. When horses had to be handled, it was usually Old Man Streeter and his boys who handled them, not William. The Streeters generally worked more with the livestock and William with the equipment.

Lester and John were younger but not necessarily less mature than William. Like many farm boys, they dropped out of formal schooling after eighth grade. The Streeters were training both boys to be farmers, and they saw little need for "too much extra schoolin'," as Omer would say.

Lester, the older boy, was eighteen, almost four years younger than William. He was tall compared to most men, well over six feet in height and weighing more than two hundred pounds. His swarthy skin was permanently tanned, and his dark brown eyes looked black from afar. His many years of farmwork had turned him muscular and strong. William often teased Lester that if his father had let him attend high school in Redwood Falls, the girls might be callin' on him. The isolated location of the farm coupled with infrequent visits to town kept Lester secluded from any pretty girls who might be interested.

John, the younger boy, had just turned fifteen. He hadn't completely matured into a man yet, and his body would never be as brawny as Lester's. His face was innocent, and he had a slight hint of freckles along his nose. John spoke with a stutter, which would alternately soothe or frustrate his stern father, depending on the day. Nonetheless, his scrawny frame was still able to handle the usual chores, and his face showed a boyish charm. His complexion wasn't as dark as his olive-skinned older brother.

The Streeters had hoped for more children after John, but an untamed horse had kicked Omer in the testicles back in 1895, less than a year after John was born, rendering the patriarch sterile.

From Omer's initial reaction, William knew that his employer didn't want to address the issue of getting more horses, so he decided to try a new tactic—bargaining, something the elder Streeter enjoyed.

"Mr. Streeter," William coaxed again, "I'd be willin' to pay ya some extra rent if you were to let me have a team of horses." William knew the way to his boss's heart.

"What you thinkin', boy?" he retorted, leaning his fork against the filthy wall. "Another dollar a month?"

Knowing the scraggly pasture at his rented place wasn't sufficient to feed a team of horses, William pondered a deal that might make him come out ahead.

"How about two bucks a month and I get to use a scoop of oats once in a while to keep their stomachs goin'?" William rebutted. "They can eat at the pasture over at my place for the most part."

"Well, that ain't *your* place; it's *mine*," the farmer retorted. "That grass belongs to me. I just ain't usin' it right now."

The old man's hard bargain frustrated William. "I won't be borrowin' your horses anymore," William teased, even though he rarely, if ever, used them. "That'll save wear and tear on 'em."

Streeter stroked his scraggly beard, thinking the negotiated terms over again. "You win, Kleeman," he conceded. "Go git your horses sometime, but not during daily chores or when we have other work to be doin'."

William thought over how much time he spent working during daylight hours. There really *wasn't* any time outside of chores or extra work, unless it was pitch black outside. He made a mental list of work items that needed to be completed this week, which would, when done, allow him time to sneak into Redwood Falls and purchase a team. The woodpile had to be sawed and split; the cattle fence needed mending; they had to grind corn into feed for the pigs; the barn manure had to be scooped into the steel-wheeled manure spreader and taken out to be dumped in the fields; and the small shed needed painting.

Then there were all the regular, ongoing chores—milking the cows, feeding and watering the animals, cream separating, butter churning, and egg picking. All of those had to fit in around the extra work that needed to get done. In addition, it was expected that Grace Streeter would have help bringing up wood for her cookstove, dumping and rinsing the filthy chamber pots, and doing any necessary repairs to the house.

William decided the barn could be cleaned the next morning, and the manure could be dumped in the afternoon. They'd start cutting wood immediately after that, and considering they'd need to fit in the daily chores, they'd likely finish with the wood on Wednesday. The cattle fence could be fixed Wednesday morning, and they could grind up corn in the afternoon that day. Thursday made sense as the day to buy his horses and rig, since the unnecessary painting could get squeezed in on Friday. Of course, with Lester and John out of school and available, he would enlist their help for each job, as he always did.

He didn't want to call Maud until he had his own team and buggy, not a borrowed one. So he'd wait, and so would she.

As the week continued, William grew more excited at the idea of owning his own team. He knew he'd take more oats from the Streeter farm than Omer was expecting. William was growing tired of walking as his main mode of transportation, and the introduction to Maud the previous weekend was the perfect excuse to make the leap to being a horse owner like other men his age. He'd gotten by for several years without horses, but he was a full-fledged adult now and ready to be a suitor.

As Thursday approached, William finalized his plan. Lester, who was fully capable of driving the family's red Maxwell sedan, would drive William to the Redwood Falls livery stable and tack shop. William would find an acceptable team and make a good deal, and that would be that. He knew that the team would have to be black, just like the Streeters' horses, regardless of the breed.

CHAPTER 10

THE BOYS GO TO TOWN

THE MORNING CHORES WERE FINISHED EXTRA EARLY on that cool day in September. Lester Streeter was pulled aside by William as they finished putting away the water buckets.

"You ready to take me into town?" William asked, his hand on Lester's shoulder. "Time for me to get a team and a buggy."

"That's a mighty big step for you," Lester replied. "You got the money for this?"

"We have to stop at Farmers & Merchants on the way," William said proudly while holding up a barely used savings booklet. "Got my plan right here."

The men bounded to a small shed that used to hold the family's buggy but now held a moderately sized Maxwell touring car. It had a brass radiator and deep red paint. The top could go up or down, making it a convertible in the summer. It was a common car for the time, and its cost was below average for a vehicle. That was attractive to the frugal Omer Streeter.

"I gotta turn on the gas and spark, Willie," Lester announced. "I'm not sure Daddy put any fuel in this thing."

The Maxwell required that a small metal petcock be turned left to shut off the fuel to the engine when it wasn't in use so the carburetor didn't flood. A coil box was attached to the battery, and it required that a lever be pushed up to retard the spark, which prevented the car from kicking back and breaking the wrist of whoever was cranking the machine to start it.

Lester grabbed a clean, smooth stick about three feet long and opened the gas tank, which was a round container that sat above the engine. He screwed open the lid and dipped the stick into the tank, slowly lifting it up to reveal a wet, gas-soaked stick.

"About half-full," he told William confidently. "That'll get us to town and back easy."

"Glad to see that, Lester," William replied with a grin. "Your daddy is so tight, he'd charge me to put a drop of fuel in this thing."

John Streeter wasn't always included in the older men's activities. He peered around the corner, watching them fiddle with the car from the front of the shed. William, who was by far the kindest person on the place to the stutter-prone younger brother, spotted him from afar.

"Johnny, you want to ride along?" he asked with a wide smile. "Could sure use your help, buddy. Did you pick up all the eggs like we told you to?"

John immediately lit up and bounded over to jump in the back seat.

"Th–th–th–thank you!" John exclaimed to William from the rear seat. "I g–g–got the eggs picked." It was the only thing he uttered until they reached Redwood Falls.

"Daddy knows we're goin' to town, 'cause I heard him talkin' at breakfast about it," Lester said as he dropped the side panels down on the car's engine. "We'd better skedaddle before he changes his mind and finds extra chores for us to do before he leaves for Rowena."

Lester checked to ensure the car was in neutral, so he didn't run himself over as he cranked over the car in the front.

"Let's go, Lester!" William called impatiently from the front seat. "We ain't got all day."

Lester pulled the iron handle up quickly, and the engine roared to life, smoke billowing out and engulfing the small shed. It was the first time the car had been started since the family had gone to church five days earlier. John and William waved smoke away from their faces and squinted from the blue cloud. Lester mounted the vehicle and moved the spark lever to advance, making the engine run more smoothly. He pulled down the throttle, engaged the transmission, and slowly lifted the clutch to drive the car out into the warm sun. The impatient Omer Streeter liked to back the car into the shed, so when it was time to leave for a destination, they could simply drive forward and speed out through the yard.

William and Lester visited about what expectations for the new team of horses would be when they reached the livery stable. Cheap and black—that really was all. Now that they'd left the overbearing presence of Omer Streeter, William turned their conversation to Maud Petrie.

"Met myself a gal Saturday night at the dance hall," William said proudly to Lester, with an eavesdropping John Streeter listening intently from the rear seat.

Since Lester didn't have the opportunity to interact with women in general—even though William had promised multiple times that

he'd bring him along to one of the Saturday dances at some point—
he was excited to hear details.

"What'd she look like?" Lester inquired impatiently. "Is she local?"

"Lives south of town about seven or eight miles," William
answered. "She looks like one of the gals out of the Sears catalog. Her
daddy was the fella that sold the land where Clements is platted to
the railroad."

Lester and John knew that Maud must be well above average if
she looked like a model in the mail-order book they were all familiar
with.

"How far did you get with her?" Lester asked with a curious
smirk. "Did you sneak a kiss?"

John's right leg started to twitch up and down nervously. This
was the most interesting conversation the teenager was allowed to
witness in his entire life. Periodically, William would boast of his
weekend adventures with his friends when Lester and John were
working on the farm, providing some excitement to their otherwise
mundane chores.

"Didn't get a kiss," William said, staring at the floor of the car.
"But got my hands tight around her waist and got to rub up against
her some when we got to dancin'."

Lester and John, while virgins, were not impressed.

"You seem pretty excited about her," Lester continued. "I bet
you're wantin' to get these horses to impress her."

"Well, unless your pa is going to borrow me this car, I need
somethin' to get me over to her place. She said for me to call on her
again."

The car creaked to a halt in front of the bank. A mixture of
cars and horses stunk up the main street in Redwood Falls, with

alternating whiffs of manure and engine smoke polluting the air. A police officer keeping watch down the block tipped his hat to the three as they entered the bank. Steel bars protected the front window, and a massive iron double lock held on to the door. The front entrance was surrounded entirely by brick. The bank had two teller windows, both staffed by middle-aged women.

"You two wait here, and I'm gonna get my money," William said in a hushed voice.

Lester and John plopped into ornate walnut chairs that were neatly arranged by an unlit fireplace. A matching wooden clock with a quick-swinging brass pendulum was mounted above the fireplace mantel and showed ten forty-five on its ivory face.

William stepped to the left teller window and slapped his savings passbook on the heavy wooden counter.

"I'd like to withdraw two hundred fifty dollars, please, miss," he said, giving a handsome smile to the blushing clerk. "All in ten-dollar bills."

"Must be something special," the woman commented as she opened her cash drawer. "That's a bit of money."

"Goin' down to buy me a team of horses and a buggy," William answered proudly. "If the livery ain't cheap enough, there's other places to go."

The woman slowly counted out William's cash, slapping down the bills neatly in front of him as she announced the running total.

"The men at that livery are a little different, but they're cheap," the woman stated, scribbling on his rarely used savings register. "You have a little over four hundred dollars left. Thank you, and come again."

William winked at her with his usual flirtatious signal.

He rejoined John and Lester at the reception area and gaped at the large, crystal chandelier that hung above them. "Makes you wonder how they pay for all this," William commented. "Lots of fancy stuff in here."

John shrugged as Lester grabbed the ornate brass door handle to exit. Financial literacy wasn't their strong suit. William shoved the cash in his front shirt pocket and started parting ways with his two workmates, moving south toward the livery.

"I'll meet you boys at the stable!" he hollered, abandoning John and Lester. "We're only a couple of blocks away. I can walk!"

William was too anxious to go through the complicated and time-consuming sequences of starting the Maxwell. He was excited to start viewing his choices of horses and begin the negotiation. It'd be better to negotiate a deal without Lester's second-guessing anyway.

After a short walk along the dusty, windswept streets, William stood before the Vastetsov Livery and Tack Shop, located just off the main street in Redwood Falls. It was conveniently located between the railroad and hotels, so travelers could rent livery rigs to transport them to their local destinations. The business was owned by four brothers who had emigrated from Moldavia in eastern Europe. The siblings were known around Redwood County for being reasonable negotiators, for their difficult-to-understand accents, and for their strange, triangular goatees. The Scandinavians and Germans who dominated the local landscape viewed the four brothers with some suspicion.

Just the horsemen I need, William thought. *Cheap and willing to bargain.*

William threw open the door and saw the oldest brother, Josef Vastetsov, standing at the long counter. He had dark eyes, swarthy skin, and a black goatee that came to a sharp tip at the bottom of his chin.

"Goot mornin', sir. How I help you?" Josef asked his new customer.

"My name's William Kleeman, and I'm interested in buying a team of black horses and maybe a buggy," he stated forthrightly. "I'm payin' cash, but I need 'em cheap."

"Ahh, Mr. Kleeman," Josef responded. "I make you good deal. Come thees way."

The elder Vastetsov led William through a creaky side door to a large livery stable that held dozens of horses. The front pen held various colors and breeds. Most were along the feed bunks eating fresh hay and oats.

The men shuffled along the long wooden fence, looking first at a pure white mustang, followed by one with a red tinge, then an untamed black steed, and finally a pale colt with a greenish hue. The four horses stood next to the fence, staring at William without moving. All the other horses in the place turned around and pushed quickly to the far back of the wall.

"My brothers and I, we enjoy these horses and feel like you are destined to buy some from us," the man said confidently. "We find what you want."

A younger gray filly that was somewhat apart from the others spotted William at a distance and reared up high, letting out a loud whinny.

"Strange," Vastetsov said. "Dhat horse has been broke in for some time. She should not act like dhat."

"I'm only interested in getting black horses," William said forcefully. "It's a requirement."

"Thees way," the owner replied in his broken dialect, leading William to an isolated back stall that contained two average-sized steeds that were the darkest shade of black possible. "I have ideal team for you."

William closed the barn door behind him and looked at the team's dark eyes as they switched their tails to whip annoying flies off their buttocks.

"Their names are Abaddon and Damion," Vastetsov said proudly. "They are very good team and, of course, you can change names if you choose."

"Nice horses," William said as patted their stringy, ebony manes. "How much you need?"

"Thees team of horses. They older in age. But they too good for glue factory," he responded, predicting the eventual doom of many horses when they reached the end of their lives. "You say you need buggy? I make you deal."

William nodded. He looked over the horses, who were calm and clopping their hooves from time to time. They seemed well broken in and as if they could be used for different purposes.

"If the price is right, I can buy this team and a surrey off ya," William stated. "What's available for buyin'?"

Josef led him down a narrow, straw-strewn path to a separate shed, where a dozen wagons and buggies were parked.

"I make you deal on thees one," Josef offered, pushing his way to the rear of the shed.

A midsized, high-wheeled buggy with no canopy sat isolated in the corner with a layer of dust on it. Josef added, "Buggy no longer used, and my brothers say to get rid of."

William looked it over carefully. The black lacquer was chipping off, and the once bright red wheels were faded. The leather seat was missing several of its buttons and showed a small rip on one side. William guessed it was likely from the 1800s.

"I sell horses and buggy to you for three hundred dollars," the owner stated abruptly. "I throw in harnesses and tack you need so you drive away today."

William was taken aback by the sudden price offer but also glad since time was of the essence. Lester and John would be arriving any second, and he didn't want them to know what he was paying for his rig.

"I ain't got three hundred dollars, mister," William replied confidently. "I'm interested in the team and the rig, but two hundred dollars is what I'm thinkin'."

"We no bullshit around," Josef shot back. "We split at two fifty, and that is what I do."

William looked over the buggy again. The Streeter boys could help him paint the vehicle to make it look newer, and his folks could probably help him repair the seat. The horses looked acceptable. They'd easily be able to pull the aging buggy.

"I still want the tack and gear I need for harnessin' them up, and the bottom line is two forty-seven, total," William replied. "I can pay you now if you want. If you ain't wantin' that deal, I got a neighbor back home who might sell his rig for that."

William wanted to get the better end of the bargain and thought that landing on his side of two hundred fifty dollars would make him the winner. He blatantly lied about a fictional neighbor having a team and buggy for sale.

"Deal," the merchant responded after a brief moment of thought. "You pay up front."

They shook hands on the deal, and William became the proud owner of two aging black horses with a beat-up buggy to match.

The men returned to the front office, where Josef scratched out a bill of sale with a thick pencil on a yellowing receipt.

As William pulled the twenty-five ten-dollar bills from his shirt pocket, Lester and John thrust open the door, hoping to catch the tour and witness the negotiation.

"Bought myself a team and buggy, boys." William beamed. "Just finishin' up."

"Dang it!" Lester exclaimed, cursing his delayed status. "We had trouble gettin' the car started. Done left the gas on and flooded it."

William pushed twenty-five bills to Josef Vastetsov, who to William's relief didn't count it audibly. He knew his younger counter-parts were anxious to know what he paid. The horse trader put three silver dollars down in front of William, providing him his change.

"Thank you, Mr. Vastetsov," William said quickly, putting the large coins in his pants pocket. "Can you have your men hitch up the team and bring the rig up front?"

"Yes, sir," he answered. "My youngest brotha, Victor, do dhat. You meet out front in one hour."

John's stomach audibly rumbled, causing William to crane his head toward him.

William pulled his pocket watch out and looked at the time. It was getting to be time for dinner. The boys ate breakfast very early that morning since the elder Streeters planned to visit Omer's brother, who lived near Rowena and had taken ill that week. Grace Streeter always prepared breakfast for the men after morning chores, but she cooked it extra early this day because of their haste to exit and visit Omer's ailing sibling. Omer had chosen to take his wagon and team on their visit so he could deliver some fence posts to his brother. William was relieved he'd left the Maxwell behind since it simplified his trip to town.

"I've got three dollars to spend on some grub," William announced to the famished brothers. "I can treat you to dinner downtown."

"Can we take a peek at the horses?" Lester asked. "Gotta see what you bought, Willie."

"Real quick," William replied. "Johnny here is starvin'."

"We'll crank up the car and go over to Randgaard's to eat," Lester said. "But after we look at the horses."

William led them down the front side of the building and over to the separate stalls where the newly purchased steeds were waiting.

Lester was unimpressed. "They look a little old, Willie. Did you look at their teeth to check their age?"

William swallowed hard. In his haste to purchase the animals, he did precious little investigation as to their age or health.

"Well, I got such a good deal, don't matter," William replied defensively. "They ain't really workhorses; they're for pullin' my new buggy."

"All right, Willie, where's the new buggy?" Lester teased. "I can tell these horses are ready for the funeral parlor pretty quick."

John let out a sudden guffaw.

"It's over here in this shed," William said as he trotted over to where all the wagons and surreys were parked.

He led them to the back corner where his drab buggy looked rougher than it had a few minutes earlier.

"Ha, ha, ha," Lester laughed. "*That's* your *new* buggy?"

"Yeah, I know it needs a little work, but we ain't all rich like your pa," the irritated William snapped back. He was growing tired of the mockery of his new purchases.

79

"Hold on, Willie," Lester responded. "I'm just teasin' ya a little. No need to bring Daddy into this."

"Time t–t–to eat," John interrupted, breaking the tension and speaking his first words since arriving in town.

"You are correct, Johnny," William said as he put his arm around his favorite farmhand. "I'm still treatin' you boys for food, even if you be insultin' my fine steeds."

The men exited the buggy shed and cranked the Maxwell to life. William was waiting in the front passenger side for Lester. Since they planned to eat at Randgaard's, they'd move the car to the opposite end of the main street from the bank.

William knew Saint Catherine's Catholic Church was along the route, with its ornate statues and crucifix showing grandly along the front steps, but he had another place in mind as a destination along their path to dinner. "Let's go past Sebo Implement to see if they got any new tractors outside," William requested. "We don't have to stop; just slow down and look. You'll have to turn the car around and go this other way."

Lester didn't protest. He liked to look at farm machinery as much as any other farm kid. He shifted the Maxwell into gear and turned the car around to detour through the bustling downtown. John, who rarely was in the city, peered up at the stenciled windows and colorful signs that spelled out the wares each merchant was peddling.

Hillig Brothers Jewelry, the first place they whisked past, was in a tidy brick building. The younger Streeter remembered that his tightwad father had bought a piece of jewelry for their ma as a gift one time. Because it was such a rare occasion, the name of the jeweler was seared into the youth's mind.

"Slow down, Lester!" William called as they roared toward a large corner lot. "Sebo's is over there on the right."

Soon the car was crawling past tractors, gas engines, and the various other pieces of farm machinery on display. Sebo Implement sold McCormick-Deering farm machinery and International Harvester equipment. The larger gas engine used on the Streeter farm was bought at Sebo's, as well as their threshing machine and the large tractor that powered it.

"I like that smaller tractor with the narrow front wheels," Lester said as he pointed out a gray tractor with bright red steel wheels. It was about half the size of their current tractor.

"It'd be easy to handle," William replied. "That big ol' tractor you got now is tough to steer."

William spent an inordinate amount of time on the Streeter tractor. It was used to thresh, plow, and run the silo filler. While it was an extraordinarily helpful machine, it was very large. Omer had chosen one of the biggest tractors available, knowing it could handle any job that would be required.

"Looks like a fine tractor for small jobs, Willie. I'm turnin' left here to get to the café," Lester stated. "Shouldn't be more than a couple of blocks."

The *Redwood Falls Gazette* building was on their way, John noticed. The newspaper provided all the news for his folks. The other town paper, the *Redwood County Sun*, was farther away. The rival media outlets had polar opposite political bents, with the *Gazette* leaning heavily Republican in its editorials and the *Sun* opining more for the Farmer-Laborites. With three major political parties in Minnesota, the Democrats sometimes finished in third place in major races, especially in Redwood County.

John felt as if he'd barely blinked before they were parking. RANDGAARD'S CAFÉ AND CONFECTIONERY was stenciled in neat, gold lettering across a large plate-glass window. The restaurant had similar locations in Montevideo and Benson, a little food chain for southwestern Minnesota in 1909.

"I could eat a horse!" Lester exaggerated. "But not the tough meat on the nags you bought, Willie!"

"Shut yer mouth," William said with a sigh. "Ain't in the mood for your lip."

"I'm just joshin' ya', Willie," Lester replied. "Can't take a joke?"

The car was parked at an angle right beside a black Stanley steam car that had a coffin-shaped front end. Water was dripping from its front, and Lester, an inquisitive and mechanically minded man, looked it over.

"Boy, am I glad Daddy didn't buy a steam car," Lester said as he shut off the gas line to the Maxwell's engine. "Takes a half hour to get the boiler started on those things."

William nodded and circled the car. The car had a reputation for being reliable, but it was time consuming to start. Other steam engines, both tractors and cars, had exploded after running dry of water. That frightened some potential customers from buying such contraptions.

"It looks solid, but if I'm gettin' a car sometime, it'll have a gas engine," William stated. "I think steam is headin' out and gettin' replaced."

The group finished their inspection and entered the café, looking around for an empty table. The aroma of fresh-brewed coffee permeated the air. Men were playing cards in the back, and several businessmen ruffled newspapers as they took a quick break from their stores. The friendly policeman they'd seen earlier was sitting alone at a table, puffing on a cigar and scanning the room with a curious eye.

They scratched their high-backed chairs back on the hardwood floor, seating themselves at a small table for four.

"Where are you gonna get money for your own car, Willie Kleeman?" Lester asked as he looked around for a waitress. "You just blew your money on that fine team that should be headed to the glue factory."

"No more jokin' about my team, Lester. I got some money left, and I been checkin' on some cars for next year."

John cocked his head to the side, wondering how William could save enough extra money from his father's miserly salary.

"You can't say a word to your pa," William warned sternly. "Neither of you."

Lester and John knew William was serious. His glad-handing demeanor had melted away and had been replaced by deep-voiced intensity that showed he was serious.

"Y–y–you have my word," John said innocently as he peered at William with true sincerity.

"Me too," Lester reluctantly agreed.

"All right, I've been lookin' over that Sears Catalog at my place, and they're comin' out with a Sears-brand car in different types," William said. "It'd be brand new and pretty cheap."

"But you don't even have your new team home, Willie. Now you're buyin' a car?" Lester asked in astonishment.

"I'm goin' to save up over winter and spring, and by that time, the team might be takin' a back seat to the car. Besides, you're makin' it sound like they'll be dead of old age by that time."

They all laughed now that William was poking fun at his own team, taking Lester's place in mocking the aging horses.

A pretty waitress appeared and poured water into the empty glasses. She handed out three heavy-paper menus.

"Special today is a bowl of vegetable-beef soup with either a ham or turkey sandwich for sixty-five cents," she stated routinely.

John looked at her curvaceous figure and swallowed hard. He didn't want to embarrass himself with his stutter in front of a beautiful woman. She didn't look over twenty and would be more suited to Lester's age than his.

"I'll have the s–special. Ham sandwich," he said confidently. "Just water."

Lester and William looked at each other. John had never spoken that well before.

"Me too," Lester added. He didn't want to take advantage of William's generosity by ordering expensive food. "Soup and a ham sandwich for me."

"You look like *you're* special," William boldly flirted. "But I'll just have your food special for eatin'. Make mine turkey."

Although impressed with his chiseled good looks, the waitress wasn't seduced by William's overt teasing.

"*Turkey* for you," she answered in a slightly mocking manner as she turned and walked away. "Fine, I'll be back in a while."

"I need your guts with women, Willie," Lester said, admitting his weakness and viewing the waitress from afar. "I don't know how you got the gumption to talk to them like that. Momma would slap my face if I ever talked that way."

"You just gotta belt it out," William replied. "The womenfolk like it that way more than lookin' at your shoes and stumblin' around."

John smirked. He knew he'd never be able to be bold with women like William Kleeman, but he admired his spunk and loved to tag along with William when the chance arose.

William changed the subject back to cars. "I can get a car for three hundred seventy dollars, and I can afford that, boys," he said in a hushed voice. "Like I said, it's in the Sears book."

"Maybe my daddy would be willin' to sell you the Maxwell next year," Lester said plainly. "It'll be three years old by then, and I think he might take an offer of that much."

"It's more impressin' to the womenfolk if I got a *new* car, Lester. I want to have something sparklin'."

The waitress returned with three bowls of soup and set them down around the table. She dropped large spoons in front of the men.

"I'll be back with your sandwiches," she added. "One turkey and two hams."

The famished men picked up their silverware and started gulping the warm soup.

"You got lots of time, Willie," Lester said as he slurped the broth. "Six months or more to think about what kind of car you want."

The waitress returned with three sandwiches and placed two modest-sized ones in front of the two older men. A noticeably larger one was placed in front of John. The curvy woman squeezed his arm softly.

"You deserve a good sandwich, honey," she said with a grin. "I made that one just for you."

She blinked slowly several times and walked away with a provocative wiggle. The three customers sat for a minute in stunned silence.

"Holy shoot, Johnny!" William blurted out after she left, spitting pieces of his soup across the table. "That woman was just puttin' moves on you!"

For the first time, John Streeter turned beet red in embarrassment from the seductive advances of a woman. And it felt good.

The men finished their meals, kidding with John about women and talking cars. When the meal ended, William paid up accordingly, and they returned to the Maxwell. He left a dime for the waitress on the table as a tip, hoping she'd be impressed with their generosity.

"Let's drive by Sebo's one more time," William requested. "Just want to look at that tractor again."

Lester obliged, and another detour took them past the farm implement dealer again to ogle over tractors, plows, and manure spreaders.

The car squeaked to a halt in front of the livery. William's black team was waiting alongside the building, hitched up to his buggy and ready to go. Lester kept the car running as John and William exited the vehicle.

Victor Vastetsov, the youngest brother of the four horsemen, was wiping the buggy off with a soiled rag.

"You must be Mr. Kleeman," Victor said. "My older brother is eating, but he said you paid in full. Your team is ready to take."

William looked over his steeds and the newly purchased buggy. The tack used to harness the horses was obviously used, with stretch marks and scuffs visible throughout. However, the buggy looked marginally better, and the horses seemed ready to work.

"I ain't really in the mood to follow you when I can go a lot faster," Lester said, sitting atop the driver's seat. "Will you be all right, Willie?"

"You go ahead, Lester," William replied. "Me and Johnny will get back soon enough."

Lester waved and steered the car forward to make a return to the farm. William and John looked the buggy over. The removal of the multiple layers of dust made it look somewhat more presentable.

"We're gonna repaint this thing to look brand new, Johnny," William said. "Think you can help me?"

John nodded eagerly. William was like a fun and carefree older brother, and swiping a paintbrush would mean more time to enjoy with him.

"This team is very broke in and gentle, Mr. Kleeman," Victor said. "Do not overwork them, and they will last you long time. We hope to do business again."

William thanked Victor for preparing the rig and bid him farewell. John hopped up on the buggy and held the reins firmly for William, who climbed up the step and swung his body onto the awaiting seat. He pushed the surrey's small brake handle forward, releasing pressure off the wheel.

"Hy-ahh!" he called out to the horses as he took the reins from John. "Johnny, we might go travelin' a bit more now that I don't have to pester your pa to use the car."

John lit up. "I—I'd like that," he replied. "P—P—Pa don't take me out much."

William knew that well enough. The two Streeter boys were rarely allowed to leave the farm. Farm chores were the masters of their time. William worked for them almost full-time but sometimes hired out with his friend Arthur Davis to work on shocking and threshing crews from late July through early September. Since Omer Streeter owned the tractor and threshing machine, William generally was one of the lead workers, engineering the rig from farm to farm. Streeter made good money from the per-bushel fee he received for use of his tractor and thresher. At times, Lester was allowed to help with thresh-ing at the farms of the more distant customers, but John was relegated to staying behind and helping his folks with their daily chores.

"I'm gonna see if I can convince your folks to have you and Les-ter go with me to a dance sometime," William said gleefully, nudging John in the ribs. "I bet you'd like that."

John spent many lonely weekend nights listening to his ma read the Bible and his pa tell stories of moving to the area from Chisago County, north of the Twin Cities. It was a repetitive and dull life for a maturing fifteen-year-old boy.

"W–w–would you, Willie?" he asked, delighted. "I–I would behave."

"I know you'd behave, Johnny. You're about the best-behaved man I know. Could use you to rein me in—and Art Davis too."

The horses were clopping past the city limits at a steady pace.

"I'm thinkin' that I'm going to call that gal Maud Petrie tonight, Johnny," William said with a blush. "She's the one we were talkin' about on the way into town this morning."

John Streeter was a frequent and appreciated confidant for William. While he rarely talked, he listened intently and found Wil-liam's antics interesting. Since he had difficulty communicating, John Streeter was the perfect person to share intimate secrets with.

"I know your folks don't like me usin' their telephone," William said cautiously. "I don't want to get you in trouble, but I gotta call this gal and get set up with her again."

"W–w–what about Art? H–h–h–he has a telephone."

John knew Arthur Davis from his periodic visits to the farm. His father sometimes hired Art to help with big jobs that the four of them couldn't handle, especially threshing.

"Holy shoot, Johnny!" William yelped. "I forgot all about Art!"

"Art is a g–g–good guy."

William plotted his next moves to borrow Art's telephone and shared secrets of what he was hoping to someday do with Maud. The naïve fifteen-year-old was awestruck by the consultation, but he grew up a lot that day under William's wing.

"I'm thinkin' we oughta go fishin' together one of these next Sunday afternoons over at Daubs Lake," William said with a grin. "Maybe on a Saturday, if your folks let us."

The young boy smiled broadly. Today, life was good for Johnny Streeter.

CHAPTER 11

THE SUITOR FINALLY CALLS

Clara Petrie decided that Frank's shooting of the chicken-killing fox deserved accolades from her spoiled daughter, not rudeness. As she finished preparing supper, she scolded her daughter.

"Maud Petrie," she whispered in the kitchen, "Frank skinned that fox and wants to give it as a gift. It'd be ladylike of you to show some appreciation."

"But, Mother. What am I to do with a dead animal?"

"You can allow him to tan the skin and use it as a soft rug after you bathe," Clara suggested. "Or put it at the foot of your bed."

"Mother, I will pretend to like that fox, but it will *not* be in my bedroom. We can talk to Daddy and figure out something."

"Fair enough. Now call your father and Frank in for dinner."

Maud retreated to the porch and hollered for the men to come in to eat. Henry and Frank had been working with the livestock, with Claude still sleeping away because of a sudden flu bug.

As she came back to the kitchen, she heard the jingling of the walnut telephone that hung off to the side of the room. Her heart skipped a beat.

Clara picked up the earpiece. "Yes, we can take the call, Operator," she said politely. "Petrie residence. . . I can get her," Clara said in a singsong voice. "Maud, this call is for you."

Maud frowned at her mother and swung her head to one side quickly, instructing her to leave the room.

"This is Maud Petrie," she answered.

"Miss Petrie, it's William Kleeman. I met you at the dance last Saturday," William called into Arthur Davis's telephone as Maud's blood pressure skyrocketed. "You said I could ring you."

"Yes, I remember you, William," she said, pretending to be vaguer in her recollection than reality. "Thank you for calling."

"I was wonderin' if I might be able to call on you Saturday afternoon, Miss Petrie. Maybe just to talk a little. I could pick you up with my rig if you give me directions to your folks' place. Hope the notice ain't too late."

Maud was exhilarated beyond anything she'd felt before. Here was the first man to ask her to spend time with him in a meaningful and romantic way. Andrew Churchill from church didn't count.

"I would be honored, William," Maud replied with a heavy breath. "What time do you suggest?"

William knew Omer Streeter would demand that he squeeze as much labor as possible out of William, but he tended to be a bit more generous on Saturdays if he had advance notice. Outside of the shocking and threshing season, which had just ended, Saturday evening and a good portion of Sunday were the times he'd be granted respite from work on the Streeter farm.

There was a brief moment of silence on the telephone.

"Let's say three o'clock on Saturday, since it's still light out," William offered. "I have chores to get done before that."

Maud explained the location of her parents' farm in New Avon Township and that she'd need to get permission from her father, which would likely not be a problem.

"Shall I ring you back to confirm my father's permission?" she asked, tapping her foot nervously against the floor.

William swallowed hard. He didn't want Maud to know he lacked a telephone, so he had to think of a quick excuse about why she couldn't ring him.

"I'm really busy doin' chores, and there ain't anyone in my house to answer the telephone," he cleverly explained. "How about if your pa ain't OK with me comin', you just turn me away that day on your yard. I'd understand."

Maud knew she would be able to persuade her father, so she agreed to the deal.

"I will be waiting for you," Maud said, a little breathlessly.

"Take care until I'll see your pretty little face on Saturday," William said, knowing the sweet line would enthrall Maud to the bone.

Maud set down the earpiece and threw her back straight against the wall, gazing into the air. Clara reappeared from the porch and started stirring the stew she'd made for supper. She slopped some onto the burner, which created some smoke.

"Land sakes, let's open the window!" Clara cried as smoke billowed up from the burner. "Get some fresh air in here."

Maud opened up the kitchen window as far as she could push it up. The front door creaked open, and in strolled Henry, with Frank close behind. The men slid onto their seats, with a hint of animal smell from the milk cows and horses on their clothing. Maud took out dishes and set them around the table with accompanying silverware, paying special attention that the utensils were placed perfectly in front of her father. Clara took the heavy kettle off the stove with a rag to protect her hand from the heat and scooped the steaming stew into the awaiting bowls.

"Looks wonderful, my dear," Henry said as Frank nodded. "Smells good too."

"Claude is up in his room, Henry. He's not feeling well," Clara said as she put the kettle back on the stove. "I'll save him some stew for later. Maud, would you please say the blessing?"

Maud started the prayer, flattering her father in an over-the-top manner. "Dear Lord, we thank you for your gifts. We thank you for a wonderful father who provides for his family. Who is loved and respected by all."

Henry rolled his eyes as Clara scowled. Frank stared straight ahead.

"We thank you for this man who has blessed us with his presence and is generous to those who ask for appropriate things," she continued awkwardly. "Ummm, we also thank you for Mother, our wonderful cook, and for Frank, who shot the fox dead. Amen."

The prayer was clumsy and self-serving, but Maud was pleased she remembered to include her mother in the prayer—and Frank as well, after her mother's earlier admonishment to show appreciation to him for executing the fox.

"Amen," everyone said in unison with a relieved sigh. The dishes and silverware clinked as they were passed around and used.

Henry knew his daughter wanted something, but he wasn't about to pander to her wishes by inquiring, especially in front of Frank.

"We've got some cattle to sell at the end of the week, Frank," Henry blurted, breaking the momentary silence and immediately changing the mood from the cumbersome prayer to business on the farm.

"Yes, sir. I'd say the two biggest Hereford steers are ready," Frank answered. "I can get the cattle wagon hooked up to the team Friday, first thing after milkin'."

The Petries had owned cattle for years and often made contracts with townspeople to purchase their fresh beef. Henry and Frank would prod the animals into their cattle wagon, lock the back door of the trailer, and pull the enormous cart to the butcher shop in Clements. The meat was processed, packaged, and sold from the butcher shop. It was a profitable venture, and the Petrie meat was considered delicious among the town dwellers who had no livestock.

Maud fidgeted with her soup spoon. She impatiently waited for her father and Frank to conclude their discussions of farming, so she could interject and ask permission to date William. However, she looked at the clock and realized there was plenty of time to corner her father without embarrassing herself in front of Frank. The request could be made later.

"Daddy, I think the cattle look especially wonderful this year," Maud said, barging her way into the agricultural conversation.

Henry looked at Maud in disbelief. She had rarely engaged in conversation about farming, the livestock, crops, machinery, or work in general.

"Why, yes, dear," he answered, beaming. "They are bigger and healthier than ever, thanks to Frank."

Frank stirred his soup and refrained from looking at Maud. He was suspicious about her motives for indulging her father during the prayer, and he surmised her trip to Redwood Falls on Saturday night likely resulted in a beau of some sort. Henry and Clara didn't discuss Maud's liaison with William Kleeman, so he kept quiet, knowing he'd be kept out of the affair entirely.

"I should be goin' home, Mr. Petrie," Frank said as he finished his stew. "The meal was delicious, Mrs. Petrie, as usual."

"Why, thank you, Frank," Clara said as she took his bowl to the sink. "Make sure you come hungry for breakfast tomorrow morning."

Frank slid out his chair slowly and stood up. "Thank you, Mrs. Petrie," he said as he put on his straw hat. "Much obliged."

Frank left, carefully closing the door behind him. As soon as the door clicked shut, Maud started on a tirade.

"Daddy!" she shouted as Henry jolted in his chair. "I need your permission to see William Kleeman again this Saturday! He just called before you came in!"

"What are the arrangements?" Henry asked, determined not to allow an unbridled, all-day excursion with a stranger. "I would like to meet this young man."

She swallowed hard as Clara pumped water over the dirty supper dishes. Maud knew if William was coming to the farm, meeting her parents would be unavoidable.

"He's set to arrive around three o'clock in the afternoon. He said we may just take a carriage ride in the country for a while."

"Clara, what do you think?" Henry asked his wife, trying to deflect any responsibility.

"I'm perfectly fine with a carriage ride. I'm excited to meet him," Clara responded. "After all, our Maud isn't a spring chicken anymore."

"Then it's settled," Maud proclaimed. "Mother, I'll need help with my hair that day."

"Frank and I are planning to scoop manure that day, Maud," Henry teased. "The yard may smell a fright when he arrives."

"Daddy!" Maud scowled. "You can clean barns another day, *not* on one of the most important days of my life."

Henry enjoyed baiting his daughter. He decided to up the ante by requiring some manual labor in the barn from his daughter in exchange for the reunion with William Kleeman.

"Well, my dear," he said in a gloomy voice, "we can't work on the Lord's day, and Frank and I are taking cattle in for butchering Friday. Monday is washday, and we can't have cow manure smelling up our clean clothing. That leaves Saturday."

Maud slumped down in her chair. She wanted everything to be perfect for William's arrival. It didn't even occur to her that William was a farmhand who smelled manure every day. A manure spreader full of dung parked in the yard on Saturday would simply ruin her date. Her father had her cornered.

"I'd be willing to wait until Monday afternoon when laundry is finished, Maud, but it's simply too big a job for Frank and me to handle in a short period of time," Henry explained. "Perhaps if you helped in the barn, we could refrain from doing the manure on Saturday."

Maud crossed her arms as Clara wiped off the dishes, and Henry barely contained an immense smile.

"All right," she steamed. "I'll do it for William. You and Frank will have to show me what to do, Daddy."

Clara's mouth dropped open in disbelief. Maud must really have fallen for this young man to volunteer to help with one of the farm's dirtiest jobs.

"Thank you, my dear. We'll wait with the manure until Monday afternoon," Henry said with enthusiasm. "Clara, you may have to start the wash early that day."

Outside the open kitchen window, the bright September moon outlined the shadow of Frank Schottenbauer.

CHAPTER 12

PAINTING THE BUGGY AND THE SHED

WILLIAM SHOWED AN EXTRA AMOUNT OF ENERGY when Friday morning arrived. What a week. He'd bought a new pair of horses and a surrey, found a telephone through his chum Arthur Davis, and arranged a date with Maud Petrie.

He brought his new rig to the main Streeter farm. He pulled into the yard and stopped the team by the far shed to keep it out of Omer Streeter's sight. Pulling back tightly on the reins, he stopped his team and flung back the brake lever to hold the surrey in place.

Jumping off the buggy, he started to admire the cart, rubbing his hands over the chipped frame.

The buggy! William remembered. *My ride with Maud is tomorrow, and the buggy ain't painted!*

A plan had to be hatched quickly. William couldn't pull up to the Petrie place with such a drab-looking buggy. He had an idea.

The Streeters planned to paint their small shed a deep red. He could push his buggy behind the building and alternate painting the shed and the wheels while Omer Streeter was busy doing other chores. Painting was a task Mr. Streeter despised, so it was unlikely he'd be nearby when the work was being done. William knew there was some leftover black paint from recent projects, and the pail was still sitting on a shelf in the barn entry. He'd borrow the paint and get started right after breakfast. He'd need to enlist Lester and John to help with his scheme to pull it off.

"Good morning, everyone!" William beamed as he entered the Streeter kitchen. "How is your brother doin', Mr. Streeter?"

"He'll be fine, Kleeman. We had a good visit," Streeter said with unusual calmness. "Appreciate you askin' about him."

"I'm plannin' to paint the shed today, Mr. Streeter," William said with his eyebrows raised. "Could sure use the boys to help me out."

"Did you get all the corn ground and the fence fixed? We have higher priorities than painting."

"Got that all done, sir," William replied, knowing his boss's preferences. "I know you don't much care to paint."

"Absolutely hate it. Might be good to do it before it gets too cold and the rain comes. You boys help out with that paintin' so it gets done."

"We'll get right on it this mornin', Mr. Streeter," William said as he lifted his fork. "Lots of paintin' to do."

"I hate to be gone two days in a row, but Grace and I need to take the car to town and get some supplies," Omer said with a bit of frustration. "Won't be able to help with the paintin'."

William smiled to himself. He couldn't have planned this any better. Both elder Streeters would be gone, which would make painting his buggy even easier. Instead of alternating between the paint jobs, he'd have the boys help him get it done right away.

"I'm makin' the list for town right after breakfast," Grace interjected. "If you boys have somethin' you think we gotta have, let me know when you're done eatin'."

"Will do," Lester added. "Do we have enough paintbrushes?"

"I counted three out in the shed the other day, and it looks like we got enough leftover red paint from doin' the barn last summer that it'll cover the shed and then some," William answered. "That should be enough."

As they finished breakfast, William and Lester gave the elder Streeters ideas on items that were needed around the place: a ball of twine, a quart of oil for the gas engines, a mousetrap or two, and a rubber-tire kit to help repair the tires on the car. The more items they had to fetch, the longer they'd be gone. William whispered into John Streeter's ear as Grace wrote down the supply list, and Omer got money out of a tobacco tin hidden on a high cupboard shelf.

John reappeared in a minute with a pair of his work gloves and held them up. They were missing six of the ten fingers and one had a huge rip across its side.

"M–M–Momma, I could sure use new g–g–gloves," he said.

Everyone paused. If this hardworking boy with a stutter couldn't move the hard, frugal heart of Omer Streeter with the display of shredded work gloves, nothing could.

Omer was the first to speak. "We'll get you some gloves, son." It was the kindest tone of voice William had heard Omer Streeter use in his years of working for him.

"I want you to load those crates of eggs your ma washed up so we can sell 'em this morning," Omer ordered his sons. "We might trade 'em for some meat with the butcher or grocer."

Omer and Clara walked toward the car shed to see their boys carefully placing four crates of eggs into the back seat of the sedan. The car was pushed outside to give the boys more room to open the doors and pack the egg crates.

"With this big list, it'll be noon or after before we get back now," Omer complained as he put his watch back into his pocket.

William smiled. Lester cranked up the Maxwell, and it sputtered to life. He stood aside and gave his dad a thumbs-up. As Omer was shifting the vehicle into gear, Duke appeared from the behind the barn and ran to the rear driver's side of the car, lifted his leg, and urinated all over the wheel.

"Git that damn dog away from my car!" Omer yelled. "You'll be washing that off when I get home, Kleeman!"

The assembled workers waved good-bye to the elder Streeters as they pulled away and left for their day-trip to Redwood Falls. As Duke chased the billowing cloud of dust the car made as the elder Streeters drove away, William stopped waving and started directing.

"Men," he said seriously, "I need your help, and I need it somethin' bad."

William explained the urgency of getting his buggy painted. If they all worked together, he said, it could get done right quick.

While Lester felt they should start painting the shed first, William insisted that the buggy get done immediately.

"Lester, I need that paint to dry, and your pa will string me up if he knows that I'm lollygaggin' with the buggy instead of the shed," William pleaded. "I gotta get that buggy done."

The usually silent John Streeter worked up enough gumption to pipe up in defense of William. "I'll w–w–work right fast," he promised. "Let's h–h–help Willie."

"All right, you two," Lester conceded. "You got me talked into it."

The three scurried around the yard, preparing for the task at hand. William's buggy was pushed behind the shed to conceal it from anyone entering the yard. The ladder was found to get them to the top of the shed's peak, and the necessary supplies were gathered and deposited into the work area. As the paint buckets were opened and stirred, William wiped any loose paint and dust off his buggy with an old rag.

"I owe you boys a lot," William told the young brothers. "I'll take this big brush and paint the buggy body with the black lacquer. You guys take the two smaller brushes and get goin' on the spokes and wheels."

The painting went surprisingly fast. Drops of paint were splattering all over the ground as they worked. The breeze was moderate, and the sun rose warm, making it perfect drying weather for the paint.

"Be careful," William admonished. "Your pa might see that paint slopped on the ground and wonder what happened."

"We're making good time," Lester said as he smeared the blood-red paint between each spoke. "This buggy will be done in no time."

Just then, Lester saw a small light-green snake slithering away from the grass.

"Yuck, I hate them snakes!" he yelled. "There's another one!"

Soon a dozen snakes were writhing in all directions. They were harmless garter snakes, but they still made the boys uncomfortable.

"I know you ain't much for snakes, but they ain't gonna bother you, Lester," William said with a smile.

William stared down at the scaly animals and glared for a moment. The snakes suddenly moved together in a bunch and in unison slid toward the trees and away from the painting.

"I guess they won't bother us, Willie," Lester said with a smile. "They decided to hightail it outta here."

John smirked and diligently painted along each crevice in the wheel he was working on. He knew just how important this job was to impressing Maud Petrie—and he wanted to help out his fun-loving mentor, William Kleeman. In less than two hours, the boys had finished painting the buggy. William buried the black paintbrush to hide it from Omer Streeter. He kicked dirt and grass over any spilled paint and admired the buggy.

"You boys done made me a brand-new buggy!" William exclaimed. "Maud Petrie will think I'm worth my weight in gold when she see this rig!"

William pulled out his pocket watch. He estimated that Grace and Omer would be returning in a couple of hours. It would be wise to get the shed painted as soon as possible.

"Lester, can you check on the feed and water for the livestock?" William asked. "I think me and Johnny can get movin' on paintin' this shed."

Lester nodded and headed for the barn to start inspecting troughs and pens. William placed the rickety wooden ladder up against the south side of the shed, facing the sun that was moving higher in the sky. The ladder was twelve feet in length and barely reached the top of the peak, but it would suffice for this simple job.

"Johnny, you afraid of heights?" William asked.

John Streeter had never climbed a ladder before. When jobs required ladders, it was Lester or Omer who performed the task. However, John would do anything for William, and he volunteered for the task.

"I c–c–can handle i–i–it, Willie," he said confidently, grabbing a red pail and brush.

He mounted the ladder carefully. William was uneasy as John slowly inched his way up the dilapidated ladder, one step at a time, while clinging precariously to the paint pail and brush.

"You all right up there?" William hollered, squinting to see John over ten feet in the air, struggling not to spill any paint.

John nodded without a sound. The dilapidated ladder creaked as he ascended higher, rung by rung.

"Well, I best get to paintin' down here."

He grabbed the other red pail and Lester's brush to start on the far west wall. He didn't want splatters of paint falling on him from John's brush above. William recalled the fun he'd had on Saturday and started humming dance tunes to himself as he slopped red paint on the first board.

Suddenly, he was startled by one of the wandering garter snakes. It was abnormally large and eating dirt next to his heel.

Crack! Thud!

William heard the ladder slide off the south wall and crash to the ground. He dropped his brush and raced to the front of the shed to see little John Streeter lying flat on his back, with eyes closed. He was silent and immobile, with blood running from his nose.

"Johnny!" William called while slapping his face. "C'mon, buddy, say somethin'! Open your eyes!"

The fifteen-year-old was completely still with the sun glistening on his skin.

The snake turned and slithered back a few feet.

CHAPTER 13

OFF TO CLEMENTS

MAUD PETRIE WAS BECOMING INSUFFERABLE as she prepared for her Saturday carriage ride.

Frank had already been at their place early to get morning milking finished early on Friday morning, and Clara had a scrumptious breakfast prepared. Because Frank and Henry were hauling two steers into Clements for butchering, they decided to make extra time to travel.

"Daddy, which one of these broaches looks better on me?" Maud asked as she held up alternating broaches that almost looked identical. "Which brings out my eyes the most?"

Henry knew that the next day and a half would be unbearable. Placating his daughter's demand to make a choice, he pointed to the broach on the right.

"Definitely that one," Henry stated, while rolling his eyes. "It just makes you look superb, my dear."

Maud grinned and quickly scaled the steps to her room.

"Clara," Henry said with a murmur, "I don't know how much of this I can handle."

"Oh, Henry, she's a girl in love. Let her enjoy this," Clara chastised.

Frank came in with a wicker basket containing two small, brown eggs.

"Sorry, Mrs. Petrie," he said apologetically. "This is all I could find."

"Henry, either we have to buy some fall chickens or get by with only two eggs a day," Clara stated. "The two hens can't keep up. We use ten eggs just for breakfast every day."

"Perhaps Frank and I can find some in Clements today when we finish selling the steers," Henry answered. "How many hens should we get?"

"I think at least a dozen or two," Clara said. "We might want some extras for chicken meat too."

"My folks have some extra chickens, Mrs. Petrie," Frank interjected. "I'm needin' to be home for a visit soon anyway."

While Frank was much closer to the Petrie family than his own kin, he did try to make periodic visits to his home farm a few miles away near Wabasso.

"We'll look in Clements today and then ask your folks if we can't find any, Frank," Henry replied. "I think it might be a good idea to have some extra chickens this year."

"I'd be willing to go into town and skip school today," Claude interrupted as he sat down to breakfast. "I'm all caught up on my subjects."

"I'm sure you would," Henry answered with a smile. "But your education is too important to be playing hooky today."

"Does that mean I don't have to help you and Frank load up those steers this morning?" Claude asked with a grin. "I don't want to be late."

Henry knew that to be consistent, he had to let Claude get to school on time. He and Frank would have to struggle with loading the animals without him.

"Claude Petrie, it's your lucky day," Henry answered with a slap to his son's back. "Frank and I will load the steers on our own."

Frank raised his eyebrows and remained silent. Clara was planning to bake bread on Saturday, and the week's egg supply was running low. They hadn't been to the general store in Rowena to get supplies yet this week either. She gave the men extra oatmeal and had five eggs for everyone to share, scrambling them to stretch the unusually small amount. The new eggs Frank retrieved from the coop were included in the count.

"Henry, since you and Frank are going to the butcher in Clements, can you please stop by Raddatz's and get some groceries?"

The Raddatz family owned the grocery and dry-goods store in Clements. They were distant relatives to Frank. The store was located on the main intersection in Clements and provided area families with many fine choices of food.

"I'd be happy to, Clara," Henry answered. "Can you make a list of things we need?"

Frank, Henry, and Claude quickly finished breakfast as Maud stayed in her room, picking through makeup, jewelry, and various colored ribbons for her hair. She had already determined that she would wear her red dress, since she didn't want to wear the exact same outfit that she had worn when she had first met William the previous Saturday.

Clara scribbled out a list of items she needed, including sugar, flour, baking soda, yeast, oatmeal, coffee, lamp oil, and a new broom.

Because the Petries kept a huge garden and orchard, they had a massive supply of vegetables and fruits. Their meat was from the farm, and because they didn't keep many pigs, they often traded beef for pork at the butcher shop to keep a supply of bacon and pork chops. The large icebox that stood in the corner of their basement, as well as the dank basement itself, kept items cool. Meat was often packed away in crocks, and vegetables were sealed in jars for later use.

Claude picked up his books and metal lunch box and left for school.

"Let's get those steers loaded, Frank," Henry said anxiously, finishing his last sip of coffee.

The men hurried outside and maneuvered the team of workhorses backward toward the side fence, running along the west side of the large red barn.

"Whoa!" Frank called to the horses as the cart they were pushing in reverse met the open door.

Henry opened the inside gate that held the cattle, and Frank jumped the fence to push two brown steers toward the open gate. It took a time and patience to get the irritated animals to leave the security of their pen and walk onto the awaiting wagon, only to be carted off to certain death. Henry ordinarily shied away from having to step into the deep manure, but he knew Frank needed help. He slopped through the dung with his heavy work boots and grabbed an old broom handle, getting behind the cattle and jabbing them in the rear end to prod them into the wagon. After much yelling, slapping, and shoving from the men, the animals finally made their way onto the awaiting wagon, and Frank slammed the gate down, trapping them inside. As the steers bellowed in their tight quarters,

Henry closed the inner gate and Frank moved the horses forward so the outside door could be shut.

"Well, we'll be eating some good steaks next week, Frank," Henry said with glee, wiping his hands off with a ragged handkerchief. "These boys will be hamburger soon enough. It's time to get going to Clements."

"Do you have that supply list, Mr. Petrie?" Frank reminded his boss. "Mrs. Petrie will be madder than a wet hen if you forget."

"Good heavens, thanks for reminding me."

Frank mounted the primitive springboard seat and gently slapped the reins to move the livestock wagon forward. Henry walked quickly to the house and retrieved the list from Clara, who was trying to pick which hair ribbon best matched Maud's dress.

The slow horse-drawn trip to Clements reminded Henry Petrie how blessed he was to have a powerful Buick to travel with. Henry was especially proud to do business in Clements, having sold the original quarter section of land that allowed Peter O. Clements to plat out the city. He was well known in the community and enjoyed the notoriety. Frank patiently whistled to the horses, periodically flicking the reins to keep them moving with the heavy cart. The two steers plus the weight of the wagon and passengers made for a heavy load, and Frank didn't want to overwork the team of horses as a result. After spending an hour traveling the seven miles to Clements, Frank and Henry arrived at the butcher shop.

Frank waved to Adolf Messerschmidt, the German-born butcher who was famous for his spiced meats, homemade sausages, and customer service.

"Hello dere!" he called out in his broken English. "You back dhat cart in here!"

Henry had patronized Messerschmidt for years. Both he and Frank knew the routine for unloading the livestock at his shop. Several men with bloodstained aprons arrived to help open the filthy gate and prod the impatient animals off the wagon. Henry rarely helped with unloading. He visited with Messerschmidt as Frank and the butcher's men took care of that challenge.

"I'd like to trade a few pounds of bacon and chops for whatever comparable amount of beef it would be worth, Adolf," Henry bargained. "I know you'll treat me right."

"Der beef is more money than pork now, Henry," Adolf answered. "I vill give you two pounds of pork for one pound beef."

"Very fair, my friend," Henry replied. "Can I take the pork today?"

"Yes, dere is too much pork in der shop, so you are helping me," Adolf responded. "My men get it weighed for you."

The two businessmen shook hands and promised future commerce.

"I'll be back next week to pick up our beef!" Henry called out to Adolf as the empty wagon pulled away. "You can look at my new Buick!"

"Dhat's fine! *Auf Wiedersehen!*"

"Adolf said there are some fully grown chickens for sale over at Bloedow's place, so we should go there right away," Henry told Frank.

Frank Bloedow operated a farm store that dealt in seed, feed, fertilizer, and other miscellaneous goods. As the creaky wagon pulled up in front of Bloedow's Feed & Seed, Frank and Henry could hear some chickens cackling in the back of the building.

"Henry Petrie, good to see you in town," Frank Bloedow called out. "How can I help you today?"

"Hello, Frank," Henry replied as he climbed down and brushed himself off. "Adolf sent me over here. We need some full-grown laying hens."

"The Lord has answered my prayers," Bloedow said in an animated fashion, staring up to the sky. "Have I got a deal for you!"

Bloedow led them to the rear of his building. More than thirty white chickens were scratching in the grass, held in a makeshift fence that was staked into the dirt.

"I traded these dumb things for some seed oats, and I really don't need them, Henry," Bloedow said in a frustrated voice. "What'll you give for them? Thirty-one of 'em total."

Henry generally bought his chicks in the spring from the hatchery in Redwood Falls. Clara assisted with the purchasing, and he usually paid little attention.

"How about twelve dollars for all of them?" Henry said, knowing he was going to be getting dozens of eggs per day and lots of chicken meat.

"Sold!" Bloedow called out. "My men can help load 'em in your wagon, if you want them today."

"Wait a minute, Frank," Henry said. "Won't they fly out the top? The sides are fine, but they can fly."

"I've got some chicken wire to roll across the top. That'll keep them in," the clever merchant replied. "You can drop it off next time you're in town."

"I'll pay cash today," Henry said as he turned to his hired man. "Frank, help load those hens in the wagon."

The transaction was made, and the angry chickens clucked loudly as the wagon moved a block north and across the street to the Raddatz Grocery Store.

"I best stay out here with the wagon, Mr. Petrie," Frank said calmly. "Ain't much for stores."

Henry hopped down from the wagon seat and entered the store. An immense red coffee grinder with huge flywheels sat on the counter. Henry scanned his list.

"Rosa," he called to the shopkeeper, "I need two pounds of coffee ground up and bagged."

The store owner's wife scooped coffee beans from an aromatic bin and dumped them into a silver hopper at the top of the grinder. She started cranking the massive flywheels to operate the burrs that chopped the beans into ground coffee.

"Hello, Henry," called out Bill Raddatz. "You have a list for me?"

Henry handed over the note to the store owner.

"I'll get this filled right away." Raddatz scurried around the store, placing sundries into a wooden box that was a leftover from the previous week's shipment of bulk goods.

The glass counter had a variety of colorful candies displayed next to the large brass cash register.

"I'll take a small sack of horehound candy, along with a sack of peppermint, and one of lemon drops, please," Henry requested of Rosa Raddatz.

She nodded and began scooping the sugary treats into small brown-paper sacks.

By this time, Bill returned with the groceries and wares on Clara's list, packed neatly into two large wooden boxes.

"Can you put it on my account?" Henry asked. "You know I'm good for it."

"Of course, Henry," Raddatz answered. "We've been happy to have an account for you since the day this store opened."

Several other customers had distracted Mrs. Raddatz and were eyeing some goods on the top shelf.

"Peter!" the shopkeeper called to the back of the store. "Come help!"

A slim, redheaded boy of about eleven appeared sporting a shop apron and prominent freckles.

"Take these boxes out to Mr. Petrie's rig," the elder Raddatz ordered. "Just follow him out."

Henry took the lighter box and moved to the front, nodding to Mrs. Raddatz on his way out the door.

Frank and the team hadn't moved since Henry entered the store. The chickens had tempered their anger and huddled into a group that was clucking periodically.

Henry set his box on the wagon platform, near Frank's feet.

"Put that box next to the other one," Henry told the young Raddatz. "Thanks for your help."

Henry took out a shiny Indian Head penny and placed it in the boy's sweaty palm. The boy studied the coin and was a little surprised to receive it.

"I appreciate those that work hard," Henry whispered. "You work, you get paid something. You don't work, you don't get paid."

"Thanks, Mr. Petrie!" the boy said enthusiastically. "You have a nice day!"

Henry smiled broadly and climbed onto the wagon. Frank clicked his lips and slapped the reins to call the horses forward. It was a successful trip to town on a fine Friday.

CHAPTER 14

———————

A SURPRISING FALL

WILLIAM STARTED TO PANIC. John Streeter, the son of his boss, lay bloodied and quiet after falling from a ramshackle ladder that William should have climbed himself. The painting job came to an abrupt halt. Lester, John's older brother, was nowhere in sight, having gone to the far side of the farm to check on livestock troughs. William kept begging for John to wake up, with no success. He mopped up the fresh blood dripping from John's nose with an old kerchief.

"Johnny! You're my boy," William said in desperation to the lad. "I love you."

William caught himself in the realization he had not uttered those words to anyone other than his mother, and that was before he was ten years old. But it was the truth. Little Johnny Streeter offered William a deep brotherly love that made them true friends. William was starting to panic and couldn't bear the thought that John might not wake up. John's skin was turning from tan to pale.

As he held his ear to John's heart, William spied the large garter snake writhing behind him, attempting to nip at his heel. A sudden calm settled over William as he drew a deep breath. He closed his eyes tight, then opened them to glare directly at the snake's bulbous eyes.

"Not this one," William whispered to the serpent.

A shadow blocked the bright sun that had been warming the men all morning.

Lester Streeter stood over his brother, John, and a panicked William. John suddenly turned to his side and started to cough, blood and mucus splattering from his mouth.

John blinked rapidly, then focused his eyes on William and smiled. The snake turned and darted toward the grove, disappearing for the day.

"What in tarnation happened here?" Lester yelled as he glanced at the tipped-over ladder. "What's wrong with Johnny?"

"I–I–I'm all right," John responded with a hoarse voice as he leaned forward. "Just sore."

"He fell off the ladder! Go fetch some water—right quick, Lester," William ordered. "Run!"

Lester raced to the main well and grabbed a wooden pail and metal cup that was hanging nearby, pumping the handle feverishly to fill the pail with water. William felt John's body with his trembling hands, searching for cracked or broken bones.

"You don't seem to have busted any bones, Johnny," William said, sniffing periodically. "Can you stand up?"

John took William's hand and slowly stood erect, looking around in a daze.

"No broken b–b–bones." John smiled as his skin turned from a pasty white back to its usual tan hue. "Th–th–thank you." John grabbed his mentor and hugged him tightly as tears streamed down both their faces.

"I thought we might have lost you, buddy," William said as he released him from the embrace and started to mess up John's hair. "That was quite a scare."

Lester returned with the water. He gave the tin cup to John, who gulped the water down. John took the cup away from his lips and turned to his older brother.

"Not a w–w–word to P–P–Pa, Lester," John admonished as he stared seriously into his brother's eyes. "Promise."

Lester looked at his brother with tears in his eyes. He knew John loved William as much as himself. There would be hell to pay if Omer Streeter found out that his youngest boy nearly got killed because he climbed a dangerous ladder under their supervision.

"Promise," Lester replied softly. For the first time since their grandfather died seven years earlier, the brothers embraced.

The painting resumed, with all three of them pitching in. William scaled the ladder after a brief argument with Lester about who would climb it this time. They finished the job with only minutes to spare before Omer and Grace Streeter returned from Redwood Falls. The three men kept the secret until the days they died, never telling a soul about John's fall and brush with death.

CHAPTER 15

THE CARRIAGE RIDE

THE BIG DAY HAD FINALLY ARRIVED. William Kleeman dressed up the best he could before he left to pick up his romantic interest, Maud Petrie. He nervously hitched up his black team of horses and admired his freshly painted buggy. Peering toward the sky, he was relieved to see no clouds since his buggy lacked a top to protect the riders from rain. John Streeter arrived to help William with the harnesses.

"This woman is a real looker, Johnny." William beamed. "I ain't got a worry in the world if she'd take me on as a serious suitor."

John silently reached over to grab the weathered harness and pulled it across the aging horse's back. It was apparent that William would be taking less time with him in the coming weeks if the carriage ride worked out.

The black steeds stamped their feet and swished their tails as William and John buckled the harnesses and attached the buggy hitch. As they finished hooking up everything, William put his arm around John.

"I'll let you know how this whole thing turns out today," he whispered. "I ain't expectin' to do much other than talkin' and maybe sneak a kiss."

John blushed slightly and patted William on the back.

"Good luck," John replied without his customary stutter.

"C'mon, I'll give you a quick ride back to your folks' place and then head over to see Maud," William offered with a broad smile.

He hopped onto his buggy, and John scrambled up next to him. William pulled the rig around the yard and turned north to drop off John at the Streeter home farm. When they arrived, Lester waved to William from the barn. But there was no time for conversation, so William quickly pulled the buggy over, and John shimmied down the passenger side.

"I'll be seein' you soon, Johnny," William called out as he snapped the reins and turned down the driveway.

William thought about what approach to take with Maud. Should he try to move quickly and sneak a big kiss or be more gentlemanly and bide his time?

Meanwhile, the Petrie household had been an insufferable mix of anxiousness and anticipation all day. Claude, Henry, and Frank had kept their promise not to scoop manure that day and stink up the yard for the new couple. However, Maud's fussiness over her hair, makeup, and dress had driven the men to the far northwest corner of the farm to saw wood. They couldn't handle Maud's moodiness, which was combined with glee and wonderment, so they left it to Clara to tend to her every need.

"Mother, I've tried on every dress. I think that this red one shows best," Maud said. "I can't bear the thought of picking the wrong one."

"You look beautiful. And anyway, he'll be looking at those blue eyes, not your dress."

Just as Maud was puffing on a light amount of perfume, they heard the jingle of harnesses and the clopping of hooves. Her heart raced, and she could feel her arteries open up to pump blood faster. "He's here!" Maud shrieked as she looked out the window.

Maud raced down the stairs and cracked open the porch door, leaving her mother shaking her head and smirking at the top of the staircase.

"William!" Maud called from the front porch. "I'll be right out!" Then she turned back to yell up the steps, "Mother, we'll be back in a while!"

"Aren't you going to introduce us?" Clara yelled back.

"No time for that now, Mother!" She raced to the awaiting buggy, letting the white screen door slam behind her.

William jumped down and gently took Maud by the left arm.

"Let me help you up," William said as Maud anxiously placed her unsteady foot on the iron buggy step and hoisted herself onto the seat. She quickly slid over, but only partially so she'd be sitting close to William. William jumped up and moved close to his date.

"Do you want to go anywhere in particular?" William asked as he grabbed the reins.

"I thought we could just go west somewhere," Maud replied sheepishly.

"How about Daubs Lake, north of Wabasso?" William stated confidently. "I go fishin' there with friends. The drive will give us some time to talk."

Maud was admiring William's handsome face and blue eyes while purposely brushing up against his arm. "That's a wonderful idea," she said, batting her eyelashes.

The Petrie men and Frank Schottenbauer had seen the buggy come onto the yard. They stationed themselves behind a shed to spy on the activity while Clara peeked out the kitchen window.

"Good-lookin' guy," Claude said plainly as Frank stood by jealously and helplessly watched the flirting. Both men were guarded and suspicious.

"By all accounts, John Wilkes Booth was a handsome man too, Claude," Henry retorted.

The buggy moved slowly and turned south, then went to the first mile road to head west toward Wabasso and the oversized slough named Daubs Lake.

The conversation flowed smoothly as the young couple sat tightly together on the leather seat.

"I ain't stopped thinkin' about you since that dance in Redwood," William blurted. "Sure glad you took me up on this ride."

"William, I was so hoping you were going to call on me," Maud said nervously. "I haven't had much experience with men. I just want you to know that as we start. My family and I expect you to be a gentleman."

Maud recalled the awkward conversation she'd had with her mother only an hour before his arrival. Clara had warned her about the temptations with a man at that age.

"I'll respect you, and I hope you can trust me," William replied.

The two traveled lazily to the lake and parked their rig near the shore to watch some ducks and other fowl swimming nearby. As they sat on an aged blanket teasing and flirting, William craned his head to kiss Maud. Then he quickly pulled away.

"I hope you ain't feeling like I'm not bein' a gentleman right now," he said to Maud with a wink.

"I've not been kissed before. It's wonderful," Maud said as her heart raced. "But this can be the extent of our affection for the time being."

William knew that the prudish Maud wasn't likely to relent further, so he respected her wishes and kept his advances at bay, knowing that for Maud's sake he could wait until their wedding night.

After an hour of giggling, storytelling, and periodic kissing, the couple returned to the Petrie farm, where Henry had been pacing the floors.

"I just get so nervous about Maud," Henry said with a worried groan. "She's just so naïve about things."

Claude and Frank didn't want to deal with the return of Maud and William, so they decided to take the Buick to Rowena for a few supplies that Clara needed.

"Henry Petrie, I had a good talk with our daughter while you men were sawing wood. She knows the temptations, and I told her how to handle herself."

As Clara was finishing, they heard the buggy pull up in front of their house. The Petries scrambled to the kitchen window to catch of glimpse of action. William dismounted the carriage and assisted Maud to the ground. Henry burst out of the front door as William walked her to the house.

"Why, Daddy," Maud started nervously. "I thought you were cutting wood."

"We finished up for the day, and the boys went to town to get some supplies. Who do we have here? I'm Henry Petrie."

"Name's William. William Kleeman, sir," William said in a friendly manner as he stuck out his right hand.

Henry shook his hand and looked the attractive young man over top to bottom. He could tell why Maud was swept away.

"You got a great young gal here, Mr. Petrie," William said with a toothy grin.

"William was a perfect gentleman, Daddy."

As Clara came outside, William looked her over.

"My mother, Clara Petrie," Maud said proudly.

"I see where Maud gets her good looks," William said in a playful manner. The Petries were uncomfortable with that kind of familiarity from someone they'd just met. Henry moved toward Clara and put a possessive arm around her, as if worried that William might somehow seduce her.

"Oh, William, you are such a tease," Maud said as she hit his bicep.

"Would you like to come in and have something to eat?" Clara asked with Minnesotan politeness.

"I really have to get back and help with chores over at the Streeter place, where I work," William replied quickly. "Maybe another time?"

"William, we'll be looking forward to many visits so my folks will get to know you much better," Maud announced as Henry scowled.

William escorted Maud to the front door as the Petries stood to the side. To Maud, he whispered, "I'll be callin' on you soon."

With that, he spun around, nodded to Henry and Clara, and marched to his buggy and mounted the seat. He waved to Maud and winked at her as his team trotted toward the road.

Henry and Clara could see that their girl was in love.

CHAPTER 16

HENRY RUNS FOR SHERIFF

WEEKS PASSED, AND MAUD SPENT AN INORDINATE amount of time with William in the early winter of 1909 into 1910—and less and less time with her parents. The small house William rented south of Redwood Falls was only a few miles north of New Avon Township, where the Petries lived, so it was convenient to visit. Maud never learned to drive a car and rarely drove a team, so she was at the mercy of William Kleeman's schedule picking her up from the farm and returning her home. While five miles wasn't a long trek in her father's Buick, it was too far for Maud to walk. Periodically, Claude would sneak her a ride to William's shanty in a spare horse and buggy when Henry and Clara were gone visiting with neighbors.

At the same time as the Petrie-Kleeman courtship advanced, Henry Petrie had decided to seek the Republican nomination for sheriff in Redwood County. While Henry and Clara had briefly discussed his possible candidacy the night Maud and William met, the idea was shelved until the spring of 1910 was dawning.

"Henry," Clara chastised, "why on earth do you want to be sheriff when you don't have much experience as a lawman?"

"This world is full of two kinds of people—those who violate the law and innocent people who obey the law. I'm determined that no one who possesses evil should carry out their deeds in Redwood County."

As a politically savvy conservative, Henry had dual reasons to seek the Republican nomination. Redwood County had proven to be a fertile territory for the Grand Old Party. He drove from town to town in his Buick, campaigning at newspaper offices and on main streets. The political battle proved to be uphill since he was seeking to oust an incumbent. Just weeks before the September primary election, Henry took out front-page ads hawking his candidacy in every newspaper in the county.

Unlike any other candidate for county office that year, Henry paid extra to have his picture included with his statement: "I hereby announce that I am a candidate for the office of sheriff of Redwood County subject to the decision of the Republican primaries Sept. 20, 1910. Henry Petrie."

His advertisement certainly gained attention over other candidates for the various offices, including incumbent sheriff B. C. Schueller. The incumbent's advertisement stated: "I hereby announced to the voters of Redwood County that I am a candidate for the Republican nomination for sheriff at the primary election to be held September 20, 1910. Your support will be appreciated. B. C. Schueller."

During his courtship of Maud, William had been overly polite to the proper Clara Petrie. Nonetheless, his flirtatious attitude toward

Maud in her presence made Clara suspicious about his out-of-bounds behavior when the couple was alone.

When he dined with the Petries on Sunday evenings, William was never in the house to say grace and often ate his food quickly, exiting before the Petries could have a thorough conversation with him.

"Henry," Clara warned after they were alone one Sunday night, "there is something about this Kleeman. He is *too* good looking. He's rude and sly. He's a rogue. How could a boy like him not end up being a philanderer?"

"Ma," Henry replied, "you know that daughter of yours better than anyone. She is right set on lovin' him and runnin' off into the sunset. No one, not even us, can stop that now."

Ironically, it was the protective father who turned the tables on the historically generous mother when it came to accepting their daughter's love interest.

CHAPTER 17

WILLIAM'S BIG DECISIONS

WILLIAM DECIDED IT WAS FINALLY TIME TO ASK Maud Petrie to marry him. He still periodically attended dances and other functions where pretty girls gaped at his handsome face from afar, but it merited little return attention from William. His buddies Art Davis and Forest Van Sant marveled at how disciplined he'd become in passing up various opportunities to be with other women. Of course, William brought Maud along to most dances, where he took advantage of every opportunity to hold her close as they danced.

In order to really impress Maud, William thought it was time to purchase the long-awaited automobile he'd been eyeing in the Sears Catalog since the fall. He carefully saved money over the winter and spring, cutting back on his purchases of everything from Christmas presents for his parents and siblings to beer for himself and his friends. As spring planting began, he visited again with his closest confidant, John Streeter.

"Johnny, I've got enough money saved for that car I've been wan-tin'," William proclaimed as they sat by the shore of Daubs Lake with fishing poles dipped into the water. "I just need to mail the cash to Chi-cago, and Sears will ship me a car to the railroad depot in Redwood Falls. If you study what they call economics, it shows the best time to buy anything is last year. I want to get a car before it gets more expensive."

John blinked at him and tilted his head. "Do we d–d–drive it off the train c–c–car?" he asked. "You don't w–w–w–want a Maxwell car?"

"We'd have to put the car together at the rail station. I can't afford cars like your Maxwell or the Petries' Buick, Johnny," William answered. "But I only need to save a little more money to own a brand-new Sears car. Once I get it, I'm gonna ask Maud to marry me."

John felt a lump in his throat. He suspected that time was com-ing, because William was spending more and more of his free time with Maud and less and less with him. That meant William would move away somewhere, since there was no way Maud would live in the ramshackle house William was renting from his father. A tear rolled down John's face as he stared straight ahead. William noticed the heartfelt emotion. He knew John had been a little jealous of Maud taking more time away from him.

"You'll b–b–be happy with her," John said quietly. "I ain't gonna f–f–find no one to spend my l–l–life with."

William put his arm around John and tipped his hat.

"A good-lookin' guy like you will have to fight those women off," William teased. "Remember that waitress back in Redwood when we bought the horses?"

"It's OK, Willie," John replied. "I'll m–m–manage."

"Well, we can still go fishin', huntin', and special things, all right?" William said with a smile. "You're one of my best friends. I mean that. I tell you what, if we don't get together for somethin' at least once every other month, I'll let you snap my suspenders as hard as you can."

"You p–p–promise?" John asked, surprised.

"We keep our promises to each other, Johnny," William said seriously. "We've never told a soul about when you fell off that ladder, right? Besides, I'll get tired of Maud and need to get away from the house, especially when she's got her monthly. That means I'm probably gonna be pestering you once a month."

John nodded, not really understanding what William meant about Maud. At least William would always be there as a true friend for him as time continued on. William wouldn't be around as much when he quit as the Streeters' hired man and he got hitched to Maud Petrie.

Just then, John felt a tug on his fishing line. He jerked the rod, and a medium-sized bullhead emerged from the water.

"Got yourself a good one! You used the bait I told you to use, and look what happens!" William shouted. "I'll help take him off."

"Y–y–you're my b–b–best friend, Willie," John said quietly, while looking at the fish. "M–m–maybe my only f–f–friend."

"You follow what I do to the mark, and I think you'll be all right, Johnny," William said with a grin. "Not just in fishin' either."

William mussed John's hair and enjoyed the sunshine that the bright Minnesota day offered at the serene lake. John tried to emulate William as best he could, but he knew they were different people.

Several familiar snakes, slithering at a distance from the shore, watched the two men fish together all morning.

CHAPTER 18

GETTING THE FIRST CAR

Two weeks later, William, Lester, and John arrived in the Streeters' car at the Redwood Falls train station and sought out the depot agent. A large train was billowing steam from its side and smoke from its top as it waited for people to board and leave. Men were working to unload boxes and packages of varying sizes. Several pieces of farm machinery were carefully being slid down a ramp off one of the rear flatbed cars.

"I've got a special shipment comin' from Chicago," William told the depot agent. "I got one of those Sears cars comin'."

The agent looked at a clipboard and flipped through the inventory of arriving materials. "Yes, we have a large shipping crate on the flat car that's right in front of the caboose," he said. "I can have one of my men find it and to help you three get it unloaded."

The agent signaled a young man who was wearing work gloves and standing off to the side. "Right this way," the young man said as he darted alongside the train, passing the coal, baggage, and passenger cars as they moved down the railroad tracks. Finally, they reached the last flatbed railcar, which was parked next to an unloading ramp.

"This here is it," the young man said. "I'll help you slide it down the ramp."

A large wooden crate was marked WILLIAM KLEEMAN, REDWOOD FALLS, MINNESOTA in large, black lettering on the middle of the crate and SEARS, ROEBUCK & CO., CHICAGO, ILLINOIS stamped neatly along the bottom. The four men carefully slid the crate down the ramp and onto the awaiting platform.

"What are we supposed to do with this thing?" Lester asked. "I thought you bought a car."

"I did, Lester. We gotta put it together. The catalog said we could do it right at the depot. That's why I brought all those tools along in the back seat."

"Well, we can't put a car together on the railroad platform with all these people walkin' around," Lester responded. "Let's push the crate over to that landing."

Lester pointed to a flat area of grass that dropped off slightly from the edge of the railroad platform. The four men grunted and groaned as they slid the massive box across the wood platform and pushed it onto the ground below.

"Bring your car around to this side of the depot, Lester," William ordered. "We'll have all the tools to do what we need, and then me and Johnny can follow you back to the farm."

Lester pulled the car around as John and William stared at the huge shipping container.

"Let's unload all the tools, so we can get to work," he told John, who immediately went to the back of the Maxwell to pull out a hammer and crowbar.

"You c–c–can open the box while Lester a–a–and I bring the t–t–tools over," John stammered.

"You read my mind, Johnny," William said with a beaming smile. "Thanks, buddy."

William pried open the side of the box that was stamped OPEN HERE and set the panel off to the side.

Onlookers and waiting passengers started to gather around to watch Lester, John, and William pull four large wooden wheels out, along with the car body, which had the engine attached. Since William was too cheap to buy extra accessories, they didn't have to bolt on fenders, a top, or side curtains.

"Looks like a buggy with an engine underneath," Lester said, scratching his head. "Should be simple to put this thing together."

Lester was very mechanically inclined and had a natural curiosity about cars and machines. He helped William operate his father's farm machinery and enjoyed it immensely. The men carefully, but quickly, did the necessary work to attach the high red wheels and prepare the engine, periodically consulting the owner's manual that was included with the car. The box even contained oil and some basic tools.

After less than an hour, the new car was fully assembled, facing the Maxwell car that Lester parked nearby. It was much smaller than the Streeters' vehicle and probably half the size of the Buick that the Petrie family owned.

"Sure looks smaller than what I was thinkin' from the picture in the catalog," William said as they stood to admire their handiwork. "But it's still a new car."

Looking at the large wooden crate, William signaled the young depot clerk and asked if they could use the container that the car was shipped in.

"My boss would probably pay you a dime for it and either use it for shipping or kindling in the stove that sits in the waiting area," he said while looking over the large dimensions.

"We'll leave it here for you," William said with relief. "A dime will still buy a beer at the saloon."

The boy left, and William turned back to look over his new car.

"We got the oil put in. There's a can of gas on the floor of the Maxwell," William said as he lifted up the seat, exposing a gas tank. "Go fetch it, Johnny."

John returned with the small, red gas can and poured it into the awaiting car while William and Lester studied the crank in the front. Several men circled around in the background, watching the scene with curiosity.

"All right, men," William said. "I think we're ready to start this thing and go home."

He pushed in the crank and spun it a few times with no success. He took a rest for a few seconds and spun the engine over a few more times.

"Did you choke it, Willie?" Lester asked. "Ain't gonna start if you don't get gas in the engine. We gotta make sure the spark lever is set right. It's that little handle by the steering tiller. You just need a few things to make this motor work: gas, spark, and compression. Get those three things timed right, and you got yourself a runnin' engine."

The clerk returned with a silver dime and plopped it in William's sweaty palm. "Here's your dime for the crate, mister," he said with a smile. "Nice car."

Lester went to the right side of the car and adjusted a small black lever that stuck up by the tiller steering lever. He returned proudly to the front of the car and pointed out a small metal ring that stuck out next to the crank. When pulled, the mechanism choked the engine. Lester pulled the ring and looked at William.

"Try crankin' it again, Willie," Lester instructed. "We'll get it goin'."

William cranked vigorously several times, and the engine chugged to life. The assembled group of onlookers behind them cheered and clapped. Some had been standing around watching them assemble the car since the box was popped open.

Lester and William studied the manual again quickly to make sure they had enough basic information to drive the car safely home from the depot—how to engage the transmission and how to stop the car, for a start. John stood close by, knowing that he'd be able to catch a ride with William in the new vehicle.

"I think we're ready, Lester," William said with a grin. "You lead, and I'll follow. Look back every so often to make sure it ain't quit on me."

"Johnny, I need you next to me, buddy," William told John with a wink, who nodded and trotted around the car to mount it.

William climbed up on top of his new car while Lester got his parents' car cranked to life. Lester started to slowly pull away as William gave him a thumbs-up. William pulled the large transmission lever back and adjusted the throttle, and the car moved out of the railroad depot and fell in behind the Maxwell. The car looked primitive for its time, especially behind the Streeters' Maxwell, which had four cylinders, a steering wheel, pneumatic tires, and a large back seat.

Other than almost rear-ending Lester at the first stop sign after they left the depot, the virgin drive went surprisingly well. While the car was unsophisticated, it was indeed brand new and gave William a huge sense of pride. He finally owned his own team of horses with a buggy, and now he owned a brand-new automobile. It was time to ask his gal to marry him and live happily ever after.

CHAPTER 19

POPPIN' THE QUESTION

WILLIAM CONTINUED TO COURT MAUD, chiefly on Saturdays and Sundays. Their interludes were passionate and unbridled, but Maud still wanted to keep their passion in check until they would fully consummate their relationship when they were married. It had become extremely frustrating for William, who wanted to show the nubile Maud Petrie that he indeed meant to marry her. However, he respected her wishes and refrained from pressuring her too much. Maud had fallen head over heels for the attractive young man, and she refused to be a winter spinster for another season. Maud had hinted on more than one occasion that she wanted to get married, but respecting his right to ask, she patiently waited.

William finally decided that he'd propose to Maud near the waterfall at the park in Redwood Falls. The forty-five-foot falls were picturesque. They'd provide a perfect setting for their engagement.

On a cloudy Sunday afternoon in April, William Kleeman proposed to Maud Petrie with a simple and inexpensive ring that he had purchased at the jewelry store in Redwood Falls for cash. His Sears car was unreliable on the steep driving paths in the park in Redwood Falls, so they parked the car at the top side of the park and carefully walked around small trees, weeds, and craggy stones to a rocky platform near the falls. He swept off the loose dirt and got down on one knee after they watched the water a few minutes. Not surprisingly, his words were awkward.

"Maud Petrie," he said abruptly. "I'd be happier than a lark if you'd be willin' to be my wife."

"Yes! I'd get married tomorrow if we could," Maud gushed. It wasn't an unexpected proposal. She'd been thinking about the possibility often, and she immediately started planning the wedding. "When and where should we do it? As you know, Momma's the organist at Holy Communion, so we'd have to get someone else to do that." Maud's thoughts were outpacing her words.

William had few requests, but when necessary, he let Maud know what areas he felt required attention. That was especially true regarding the timing and circumstances of their marriage ceremony.

Since William worked as a field hand chiefly for Omer Streeter, but periodically for other area farmers, the summer of 1910 would be a busy one. July through early September would be dominated by cutting and shocking grain and loading bundles. Then they'd be engulfed by the threshing season.

"Maud, I ain't havin' no church wedding," he scolded. "It should be a right-quick service, and we can honeymoon with my relatives over in Janesville after. I want to do it after threshin' season is done."

Maud was taken aback. She'd been a dedicated member of the Church of the Holy Communion since she was small. Her parents and Pastor Joss would be terribly disappointed if they didn't get married in their church. It would be all right to visit his relatives in Janesville, since she'd only met his parents and siblings by Gilfillan Station a few times.

"William, I know you aren't much for churchgoing, but this is important to me," Maud pleaded, setting up their first argument since getting engaged. It had been less than five minutes since he'd asked the question. "I understand the timing with your work."

"I won't be changin' my mind, Maud. We can get married at the courthouse or my folks' place, even though it's small."

"All right, William Kleeman," Maud conceded. "I'll try to explain to Momma and the pastor why we can't get married in the Episcopal church, but since my folks' house is a lot bigger, I think we ought to get married there. Pastor Joss will have a hard time with this. I don't think he'll marry me outside of the church building, so we'll have to find someone else in the Protestant faith to do it."

"That'd be OK, if your folks are good with it," William replied, a little surprised Maud wasn't more resistant. "Their house is mighty fine. We'd just have my family and a couple of friends from my side."

"I am the happiest woman in Minnesota," Maud bragged, hugging William tightly. "My parents can host the wedding at their home in the morning, followed by a grand breakfast afterward."

Maud's train of thought couldn't keep up with her mouth. Dozens of thoughts streamed through the newly engaged girl's mind. As with any young gal in love, her wishes were monumental. But unlike most, hers could be financed by her parents. Henry and Clara Petrie had proven to be more than patient and very generous with their only daughter.

"I want to get married as soon as we can after threshing is done," Maud asserted. "When will you finish?"

"Well, we were finished about mid-September last year."

"Then let's pick a date right now," she beamed. "The second Saturday of September is the earliest we could do it. That's the date we should announce to our folks."

William didn't argue with his anxious fiancée. He was as antsy as Maud to get hitched and start their married life. Maud was excited to get the wedding done. She was determined that her parents wouldn't be allowed to object to her plans.

As they slipped and climbed their way off the rocky ledge, a familiar oversized garter snake slithered behind Maud's right heel.

CHAPTER 20

CONVINCING THE FOLKS

MAUD PETRIE, AN ONLY DAUGHTER WITH A GIFT for persuasion, convinced her protective mother that the marriage should take place the second Saturday in September. William would be finished with the threshing season, she told her mother, and they'd agreed it would be an ideal time. It would also be convenient for William's relatives, whom they planned to visit in Janesville on their honeymoon.

"Mother, William proposed to me at Ramsey Falls this afternoon, and I accepted!" Maud proclaimed that evening in the kitchen. "We want to get married as soon as threshing season is done!"

"He didn't ask permission or inform your daddy first?" Clara asked with astonishment. "Just dropped you off here without talking to us at all?"

"Mr. Streeter wanted him home to help with chores, and he was already running late, Mother," Maud said, defending her fiancé. "We plan to sit down together on Saturday and discuss everything, but William and I already planned out some things."

"Maud, this is so sudden," Clara warned. "You just met that boy a few months ago. It wasn't like you went to school or church with him like that Churchill boy."

"Mother, I knew from our first dance in Redwood Falls that he'd be my husband. It's my destiny to be with him."

"I know there won't be any talking you out of this, Maud, but there's somethin' about that boy," Clara said with reluctance. "He's not quite as polite as he should be. I'm concerned that he's too much of a charmer."

"If by 'charmer' you mean he's extremely handsome, I think he has to plead guilty," Maud said with annoyance. "It's one of the reasons I'm marrying him. Life will be an adventure with him, Mother, not just the daily drudgery."

"Like I said, Maud," Clara retorted, "your mind is made up, and I'm not goin' to change it."

"We decided that the second Saturday of September would be ideal, since he'll be finished threshing by then," Maud said. "We'd like to get married here."

Clara stood up and grasped her daughter's shoulders.

"You what?" Clara asked in astonishment. "You already picked a date, and you're not going to get married at our church?"

"Mother, I originally thought Holy Communion would be a good place for the ceremony, but William doesn't want that," Maud explained with a quivering lip. "The date is in stone. I wouldn't go to my own funeral that day."

"There are two problems, young lady," Clara said in a harsh tone. "That date is right before the Republican primaries, and your father is running for sheriff. He's been workin' hard on the race. This will make a mess of his plans."

"Mother," Maud argued back, "this the rest of my life. A marriage with the man I love. Daddy's conflict is just politics."

"I'm going to have quite a time explaining this to him," Maud said with a sigh. "The bigger issue might be the location."

"Honestly, I tried to convince William that Holy Communion would be a wonderful place for the ceremony, Mother. He just wouldn't have anything to do with it. He said it wasn't negotiable."

"You said he isn't much for churchgoin', Maud," Clara snapped back. "But usually the bride and her family determine the location of the ceremony."

"I know, Mother," Maud replied quickly. "This is my fault. I told him we could host the wedding here and that Pastor Joss probably wouldn't marry us unless it was in church."

"Well, Pastor Joss certainly will be gravely disappointed in all of this," Clara said, looking down at her shoes. "I'm sure you won't want to explain it to him."

"Mother, I think we could get another Protestant minister to marry us. Maybe the Presbyterian pastor in Redwood," Maud explained. "I told William that a judge would simply not do."

"It just makes me wonder," Clara responded quietly. "He hasn't stepped foot in Holy Communion, and the few times we had him for supper, he's not around to say grace. It's just not something I like to see."

Maud nodded. It wasn't an ideal situation. Other friends had to battle "mixed marriages" of Protestant and Catholic, but this situation was even more unusual. Whenever she brought up the subject of William reading the Bible, saying a mealtime prayer, or coming to

Holy Communion Church with her, he resisted quickly and aggressively. It was just something that would have to be tolerated.

"All right, Maud Petrie," Clara conceded. "I'll carry the burden of telling your pa we're hosting a wedding in this house, without our Episcopalian minister, and that it will be less than two weeks before this big election where his name is on the ballot."

"Mother, I owe you everything," Maud said, hugging her mother tightly. "You know Daddy will listen to you before he takes my side on these matters."

Maud had her mind set, and so did William, apparently. Clara decided that it'd be best to take her daughter's side and be stubborn about it, even if Henry resisted.

———

"Are you out of your mind, Clara?" Henry demanded when his wife informed him that Maud insisted on being married on September 10, 1910, at their home. "I'm in the middle of campaigning for sheriff. I need that time. It's right before the primary!"

"I don't care if President Taft himself is coming to the train depot for your political campaign, Henry Petrie," Clara scoffed. "This is our precious child, and she will be married on *that* day in *this* home. You told me yourself that there was no changin' your daughter's mind."

Henry slumped into his large wooden rocking chair and brooded. He knew it was a losing battle to fight Clara, but winning over both Clara *and* Maud would be impossible. Maud's insufferable stubbornness would win out. He knew the best way to end an argument was to keep his mouth shut.

"Fine, Clara," Henry conceded unenthusiastically. "I'll just work around it."

The pandering to Maud continued, damning any possibility that a time-consuming wedding wouldn't impede his campaign schedule. Still, as his campaign progressed, Henry worked hard, visiting community events and newspaper offices across Redwood County.

In his occasional moments of distraction from the campaign, Henry was giving some consideration to where his daughter and her new husband would live after they were married.

"Maud," her father stated calmly over a weeknight supper in August. "Your mother and I intend to make Frank's place available for you and William to live in."

It was a generous offer, but it would also allow the protective Petries to watch over their daughter.

Clara chewed her bread as she awaited a response from her daughter. The Petries had already discussed the arrangements for the small home down the road in New Avon Township with each other, but not with Frank Schottenbauer, their hired man, who had lived in the home for several years. Maud stirred her stew and welled up with excitement.

"Daddy!" Maud cried in a thankful tone. "Thank you for helping us get a start. I'd love to live next to you!" She paused. "But what about Frank? Where will he go?"

"I wanted to see if you were comfortable living there with William first," Henry answered. "Frank doesn't know, but we'll have time to find him a place. Your mother and I thought perhaps he could live upstairs."

"After the wedding is done, William and I will be spending a good amount of time with his relatives in Janesville. I haven't met any of them, and he thinks it would do us well to stay there and become acquainted." She had no expectation about how long a honeymoon should last. Some couples took extended tours, she knew, but most local folks kept the event brief and close to home, if a honeymoon was taken at all.

"William tells me we can board with relatives in and around Janesville during that time," she stated. "If we pay to board at a hotel, it would maybe be for the first night only." Maud grew flustered and a bit flushed as she realized she was talking to her parents in a round-about way what was to happen on her wedding night.

The following Sunday, she told William about her parents' generosity in offering the farm next to theirs.

"Maud, we're gonna be livin' next to your folks?" William lamented. "For how long?"

"I'm not sure, William," Maud responded defensively. "I think it's very kind of them to rent that place for us."

"It sure is, but I was thinkin' we'd live here," William said despondently. "After all, we'll be newlyweds and might be makin' babies."

"William Kleeman," Maud scolded, "it's not as if we're moving into their house. They'll still be almost a mile away."

"Not sure it's right expectin' them to pay for so much," William said with a guilty frown. "Rentin' that place, payin' for most of the wedding, the meals—"

"That is their business," Maud said defiantly. "I'd rather have it that way than them not doing anything at all."

"Doesn't their hired man live in that place now?" William asked. "How is he takin' this news?"

"Daddy wanted to know we were fine with the idea first," Maud assured. "He said he'll find another place for Frank. They might board him upstairs in my room. Besides, aren't you planning to farm with Daddy anyway?"

"Well, I was thinkin' about that, Maud, but we've been so busy over at the Streeters', I haven't had much time to talk to your daddy about these things. I told Mr. Streeter that I'd be with him through our weddin' and then I'd let him know. Johnny and Lester are gettin' so experienced that I won't be needed as much after threshin' gets done."

"From what I know, Daddy is thinkin' that you'll be helpin' him out, along with Frank and my brother Claude," Maud said as she pulled her shawl tighter. "We wouldn't have to pay any rent, and we'd get most of our food from the garden and the barn."

"I sure hope your hired man is gonna be fine with this, Maud," William replied as he stood up and looked at his watch. "This'll be a big change for him. I'm not sure he likes me much to start with."

With the sun setting, they shared a passionate kiss, and William started his Sears car to take Maud to her parents' home.

They arrived while it was still light outside, which was good, since the oil headlamps shed very little light to travel by on the gravel roads. Frank Schottenbauer looked out the barn door to see the giddy Maud Petrie and attractive William Kleeman dismount from his primitive car. He stared with a broad scowl across his face.

"Maud, we just finished supper, but we have some food left for you," Clara said sweetly. "William, you're welcome to join us."

"Thank you, Mother," Maud replied quickly. "We'd love to have some supper. I'm starving."

"Thank you kindly, Mrs. Petrie," William said with a wink and exaggerated expression. "Mmmm, that smells right good."

Clara had grown tired of William's flirtations and sophomoric antics. While she fully acknowledged his attractiveness, she also dropped hints to Maud that she had concerns about his maturity and discipline.

Two place settings were put on the table by Maud as Clara stirred up the fried potatoes that had chunks of minced onions mixed in. Two pork chops were left, which had been designated for Henry and Frank to eat for lunch the following day, but now would be consumed by the young couple instead.

"Let me open the windows and air out this kitchen," Clara said as she lifted the wooden sill.

"Frank!" Henry called out the window as he spotted the hired man walking nearby. "Make sure you get the eggs gathered up before dark."

While Clara Petrie was the one who most often battled the hens to gather eggs, Frank usually took on the task on Sunday nights.

"Maybe we should say grace before eating?" Clara suggested to Maud and William.

"Excuse me, ma'am," William quickly replied as he stood up from the chair. "I need to use the outhouse right quick. Go ahead without me."

He raced out of the room and went straight to the outhouse, slapping the porch door behind him. Clara scowled at Maud.

Breaking the tension, Maud launched into a prayer. "Dear Lord, bless our food and family. We thank you for your many kindnesses and ask that this wedding be free of trouble. We ask these things through Jesus Christ, our Lord. Amen."

"Needin' to use the outhouse when it's time to thank the Lord," Clara muttered under her breath. "Never saw bowels get so irritated when it's time to pray."

Henry looked around and whispered to Maud, "I want to bring up you livin' at the neighboring place. It's time to have that talk."

Everyone heard the porch door bang as William hurried back into the kitchen from the porch.

"William, I hear that you and Maud are comin' along on your wedding plans," Henry said as he adjusted his chair closer to the table. "You know we're happy to host."

William sat down quickly and started forking food into his mouth.

"Maud's in charge of all that," William said as he gobbled the food. "Like most everything else, as you know," he added with a smirk.

Henry and Clara never appreciated William's attempts at humor as much as Maud did.

"Oh, William," Maud interjected, giving William a light slap on the arm. "I don't want to bore you men with details you don't need to worry about."

"Well, Clara and I have been talking. We think it might be best if you and Maud would move next door after you get married," he said. "We'd plan to cover the rent, our way of giving the two of you a start in the world."

William, who had just discussed the matter with Maud, pretended not to know that his fiancée had already informed him of the likely move.

"That would be mighty generous of you, Henry," he said as he slurped out of his cup of water. "What about your hired man? Don't he live over there?"

"It's something we need to address," Henry replied with a sigh. "We'll make it work."

Frank had noticed the outhouse door had been left open. He went to close it so the wind didn't catch it and stress the hinges. On his way, he was walking past the kitchen and heard the conversation.

A den of coyotes yowled their familiar cries in the distance.

CHAPTER 21

CHANGING FRANK'S LOCATION

THE NEXT DAY, AFTER DELIBERATING WITH CLARA at bedtime, Henry decided that he needed to discuss the changes around the farm with Frank. Asking him to move off the neighboring farm after years of staying in the house and tending the livestock plus the addition of William around the place would be difficult for him to hear. Clara, who loved Frank dearly and thought of him as a member of their family, suggested it might be best to have Frank take Maud's room upstairs. Frank had worked for the Petries for so many years, they thought he'd be comfortable enough to share living quarters with them by now.

Henry found Frank in the larger barn. He'd just fed the workhorses some oats and started scooping manure away from their stalls.

"Frank, good morning," Henry said with forced good cheer. "Lots of work to do this week."

"Mornin', Mr. Petrie," Frank responded. "We can go over all the week's chores that need to be done while I'm workin'."

"Very good. Let me grab a fork and help you."

Frank sensed something a bit out of place, since Henry rarely wanted to work with the daily manure chores and infrequently helped when they did the main barn cleaning on Saturday mornings. It was usually up to Frank and Claude to carry out the dirty work.

"You'd be spendin' a lotta time on that weddin', Mr. Petrie?" Frank asked calmly. "Seems like Mrs. Petrie is right busy."

"Yes, the wedding and my campaign have kept me very busy. You've been doing extra work as a result. I do appreciate that."

"It's all right," Frank answered as he scraped the dirty floor with his fork. "You know I enjoy workin' for you."

"I'd keep you forever, Frank, and you know that," Henry said with a genuine voice. "But with the wedding, we think that there has to be a little change to the living arrangements."

Frank kept scraping manure to the side and replacing it with fresh loose straw as he listened, not showing any reaction.

"We've decided that we'll continue to provide a place for you to live, Frank, because you're such a good worker. But it can't be in the place you're at now. We think it'd be best if Maud lived in that house with her new husband. And he could do the chores there."

"What are you thinkin'?" Frank replied as he suddenly stopped scooping. "There ain't no other place close enough to here for me to do the chores here. I enjoy walkin' over here, bein' it's so close."

"Well, we're thinkin' of having you move upstairs, Frank, with us. Claude is mature enough now, and Maud will be gone. We'd like to pay you an extra dollar per week as well."

"I don't know what to say, Mr. Petrie," Frank said with tears welling up in his eyes. "Just now, I thought you'd just throw me out and send me over to Wabasso or Clements to live."

"Oh, Frank," Henry responded with a quivering voice. "You're like an adopted son to Clara and me. We'd never do that."

Frank wiped his eyes with his handkerchief quickly and started spreading the fresh straw under the horses.

"Mr. Petrie, I'd be honored to be over here," Frank answered between sniffs. "I'm not sure how I'll be likin' your new son-in-law quite yet. Matter of fact, I think it'd be best if I did chores on the day of the weddin' and then go somewhere else."

"Well, I respect what you want to do on the wedding day. As far as William Kleeman goes, I think the jury is out for all of us, Frank," Henry responded. "I've only known him a few months—"

"He's a looker, and that might be a problem, Mr. Petrie," Frank said sternly, cutting off his boss. "I've seen his kind before."

"Maud's got her heart set on him, and there isn't much we can do at this point," Henry responded. "He'll be helping on the farm, and we'll plan to rent a few more acres next spring to keep them busy. We'd share machinery, but I wouldn't expect you to do work on his land, Frank. You'll still work under my direction, not his."

"Thank you, Mr. Petrie. I'd just as soon be workin' for you only. My little brother can still help when we got big jobs to do like threshin' and pickin' corn. He's gettin' bigger all the time."

"That's the way it'll be then, Frank," Henry responded with a broad smile. "I'm honored to keep you on. We need your help."

"Mr. Petrie," Frank added as Henry started to turn away, "I'm only gonna say this one time."

"It's all right, Frank. Go ahead and speak your piece."

"I think Miss Petrie done deserve better," he blurted out, looking Henry straight in the eye.

"I know," Henry said quietly. "I know."

CHAPTER 22

GETTING THE MINISTER

THE MATTER OF GETTING A MINISTER was a vexing one for the young couple. With William refusing to be married in a church and Maud unwilling to be married in the courthouse by a judge, the choices became limited. William had started to pack a few things from his house into boxes, with the occasional assistance of John Streeter. His sparse belongings didn't require a lot of work, but Maud felt she needed to help clean the house so the Streeters could rent it out to another tenant.

"My folks won't care one way or another who marries us, Maud," William said in an exasperated voice as he swept the kitchen floor. "It's just so much easier to have a judge do this."

"William, I will not hear of it," Maud said with a flushed face as she wiped the bottom cupboard with an old rag. "My daddy is not in the mood to ask another minister when Pastor Joss would do it."

"You said he won't marry us unless it's in his church. Did you confirm that?"

"I asked last Sunday, and he flat out said he wouldn't do it," Maud said. "Not unless it's in the Church of the Holy Communion."

"What's acceptable then?" William asked through the dusty air. "How about if you can't find anyone, I'll go get Judge Laudon to do it."

"We may not have a choice," Maud said as she swiped her cloth across the top of the counter. "The Presbyterian minister is Reverend Ehrstein, and Daddy said if I want him, I have to go ask. Would you go along?"

"I'll take care of it if we get Judge Laudon, but I ain't much with ministers, Maud," William replied with a flushed face. "You'll have to ask him with your pa."

"If we had a telephone in this hut, I'd call him right now. But that isn't the case," Maud responded in a frustrated voice.

"Any way you cut it, might be awkward," William said with a smirk. "I'd be up for running away to get married."

"William Kleeman. My parents would kill me, and then my daddy would have to investigate himself if he wins the sheriff's race!" Maud said, laughing. "I'll find a minister if I have to drive to every Protestant church in Redwood County."

The next day, Maud convinced her father to let her ride with him on a campaign swing to Redwood Falls. She didn't give him a direct reason for asking, which was cause for some suspicion, but he decided her presence would show him to be a family man if the newspapermen at the *Redwood County Sun* and *Redwood Falls Gazette* saw his adoring daughter tagging along.

"This is a marvelous idea," Henry said as he drove the Buick into Redwood Falls. "Everyone loves a family man."

"Daddy, I have a favor to ask," Maud said sheepishly. "Could we stop briefly at the parsonage for Reverend Ehrstein over at the Presbyterian church?"

"Maud Petrie," Henry scolded, "you're hitchin' a ride to town for your own purposes, aren't you?"

"I still want to help you campaign, Daddy, but I also want to arrange for a minister to marry me. It means a lot to me—and to you, I know—that I get married by a minister and not just a judge."

"You're right," Henry responded with a sigh. "I'll go with you. We'll get this taken care of today."

The two decided that it would be best to stop at the parsonage first, in case Reverend Ehrstein wasn't home. Perhaps they could set up an appointment with his wife had he been called away. They dismounted the Buick and looked at the grand home that was located right next to the church.

"Beautiful home," Henry said as they got out of the car. "I know him a bit, Maud, so I can start."

They approached slowly, and Henry knocked loudly to make sure they heard him. A tall, silver-haired gentleman answered the door, wearing ordinary clothes. Henry immediately recognized him as Pastor Ehrstein.

"May I help you?" he asked, looking at Henry with a hint of recognition.

"Good morning, Reverend Ehrstein, I'm Henry Petrie, and this is my daughter, Maud. Do you have a few moments?"

"Ah yes, Mr. Petrie. You're one of the candidates for sheriff, I believe," Reverend Ehrstein said with enthusiasm, extending his hand. "It's good to meet you. Saw your picture on the front page of the paper, as a matter of fact."

"Well, this isn't a political visit, although I'd appreciate your vote," Henry said earnestly. "I'm just going to be honest, Reverend. My daughter here is getting married in September at my home. Pastor Joss is pretty set on doing the ceremony at Holy Communion, but my daughter's fiancé isn't interested in getting married inside a church building, so we need a man of the cloth to marry them at our home. As you are a fellow Protestant, we'd really like you to do it."

Ehrstein looked Maud up and down while Henry was speaking. Their family had a good reputation in town. He knew his fellow clergyman Reverend Joss had a tendency to be scrupulously doctrinaire.

"It would be a bit unusual for me to marry a couple where neither is a member of our church, Mr. Petrie. Wouldn't you say?"

Henry looked at him and blinked. He agreed, without question. "I know it might be unusual, Reverend," Henry replied as he looked over at Maud. "But she is a faithful girl, and we are believers. My wife plays organ almost every Sunday morning, and when she can't, this girl does."

"Getting married by a judge doesn't seem right. We really should have a man of the cloth," Maud pleaded. "Would you at least consider it?"

"Your reputation precedes you, Mr. Petrie. I hold you and your family in high regard, as do many of our parishioners. And as you know, the Presbyterians are a cousin of the Episcopal faith. Please step in, and we'll see what we can do."

Henry and Maud walked into his home to work out the dates, location, fees, and other details. It was indeed a successful trip to Redwood Falls that day, at least for Maud Petrie.

CHAPTER 23

GETTIN' HITCHED

WEDDING PREPARATIONS CONTINUED as time spilled forward.

Maud and Clara planned to have a breakfast for their guests on Sunday after the wedding and before the newlyweds would board the train to Janesville. It would certainly add more fussing and expense to an already stressful weekend, but Henry knew it would be futile to object. He let the women plan the details and stayed out of their way.

Soon enough, the wedding day dawned. The Kleeman family arrived in the morning, asking the perfunctory questions about helping clean, cook, or otherwise assist with preparations.

"I am so proud of William," Minnie Kleeman told Clara Petrie, whom she considered upper class in comparison to her own humble ways. "He's as handsome as ever today."

William was striking, wearing a dark cloth suit, pure white shirt, and a black tie. He'd always been one of his mother's favorites, from a young age parlaying his handsome looks and confident demeanor as ways to manipulate his mother.

"How is dhat race going for sheriff, Henry?" asked the father of the groom, August Kleeman.

"We shall know in less than two weeks," the annoyed candidate and father of the bride replied. Henry didn't need any more reminders that he was stuck off the campaign trail today.

"Mother!" Maud shouted from the second story. "You need to help me with my dress."

Clara hastened upstairs at her daughter's call. The exhausting preparations had worn everyone's nerves thin, especially the candidate, who was confined to his own home, hosting relatives who either lived outside Redwood County or were already casting their votes for him.

As friends and relatives continued to arrive, Frank Schottenbauer finished the daily chores and quietly left by buggy for his parents' farm, boycotting the wedding ceremony. It would be best not to see Maud that morning, and he especially didn't want to have anything to do with the new groom. For his part, William only invited his parents, his two brothers and three sisters, his buddies Forest Van Sant and Arthur Davis, and the Streeter family. The house was large enough to host his family, as well as a few neighbors and relatives of the Petries, including Julia Christensen, who had accompanied Maud to the dance where she and William first met.

Reverend J. J. Ehrstein arrived in a small Oldsmobile with enough time to meet the groom, with whom he still wasn't acquainted. Henry and Maud had warned the minister that William's preference was for a judge to marry them and that he wasn't much for attending church or formally praying.

As he dismounted his car, Reverend Ehrstein caught a glimpse of the extraordinarily handsome groom visiting with his father, August, and his soon-to-be father-in-law, Henry Petrie. Ehrstein was wearing a simple black shirt with a Roman collar and black pants and carrying a small Bible.

William spied the minister getting down from the car. He swallowed hard and braced himself for an uncomfortable discussion.

"Reverend Ehrstein, glad to see you," Henry said heartily, extending his hand. "We appreciate you going out of your way for us today. This is the groom, William Kleeman, and his father, August Kleeman."

The pastor looked at William's bright blue eyes and felt a swift, cold breeze that sent a sudden shudder down his spine. His stomach was churning.

"Pleased to meet you both," Reverend Ehrstein said with a nod. "Excuse me. May I ask where your outhouse is located, Mr. Petrie?"

"Yes, it's right around the south side of the house," he responded, pointing in the proper direction.

The minister quickly moved away from the three and rushed to the restroom in time to relieve himself.

"That pastor didn't look so good," William said with a smirk. "Might be a short ceremony today."

"We just need him to get through the basics and sign your wedding certificate," Henry replied, bothered by William's sense of excitement that the nuptials would be brief. "I'll find out if he's all right."

August and William continued to visit while Henry walked toward the outhouse, only to find Reverend Ehrstein mopping his brow with his handkerchief in a deep sweat.

"Are you all right, Reverend?" Henry asked as he stood next to him. "Have you taken ill?"

"I don't know what's the matter, Mr. Petrie. I've been fine all morning, but when I stepped out of my car, I started to feel nauseated. It's a bit better now. To be safe, I'd better shorten the ceremony. Will your family understand?"

"You're doing us a great favor today by being here to conduct the ceremony," Henry answered. "I'll let Maud and Clara know you aren't feeling well. They'll understand. No one else needs to know."

The Streeters arrived in their Maxwell, showing great pride that their hired man was going to get married. The usually stoic and grumpy Omer Streeter surprised even his own children.

"Kleeman, you're a lucky man," Omer gushed, smiling the broadest smile William had ever seen from him. "I saw your wife when I went to town the other day, and she looks like a good woman."

Lester and John patted William on the back. John was feeling a little bittersweet about the day, knowing that Maud would now take William's full attention away.

"When I get back from Janesville, we're still goin' fishin' over at Daubs Lake, right?" William said as he put his arm around John. "You can come too, Lester, but you can't hold a candle to Johnny on catchin' fish."

"I–I–I would like th–th–that," John responded as Lester frowned.

"I saw your house and was impressed by how clean it is," Grace Streeter interjected. "No doubt your new wife was helpin' get it ready."

Omer Streeter pulled William aside as the boys and Grace looked over the farm and moved toward the house.

"We vould still like you to call on us, Kleeman," Omer said in a serious tone and a quivering voice. "Johnny took a likin' to you, and Grace will cook for you anytime. You could still work for us during threshin' and corn pickin'.'."

"Mr. Streeter," William answered with a smile, "it's been an honor workin' for ya. Johnny is a special man, and you need to treat him that way. I'll be farmin' over this way, but I think there'll be time for me to come over. I'm hopin' every month or so."

Omer pulled a ten-dollar bill from his shirt pocket and pushed it into William's palm. His eyes were welling up with tears.

"You take this money and treat your new wife on honeymoon. Grace has other gift for you too, but I want you to have this. Don't tell her I give you this money. You know how tight she can be."

William felt a tear well up as he gave Omer a half hug, laughing and smiling. It was the first time he'd ever embraced his old employer. The stodgy and ultraconservative farmer would never part with a ten-dollar bill unless he really appreciated someone.

"Thank you, Mr. Streeter," William answered, swallowing hard. "You have a special set of boys, and I will be callin'. Can't be with the woman all the time, you know."

Omer turned and caught up to his family, which was nearing the house. August Kleeman came to fetch his son. The ceremony was about to begin.

"William, the minister ain't feelin' too good, so stand back a bit and know that the vows will be right quick," he whispered as cattle mooed and chickens scratched in the background. "I'm very proud of you, my son."

"Thanks, Pa," William replied with a grin. "Let's get this done."

They entered the house and went to the large living room to see Maud in a beautiful yet simple white dress, standing next to Clara and Henry Petrie. Claude, her younger brother, was standing behind them, with Julia Christensen, her maid of honor, and her parents off to the side. Other relatives and neighbors rounded out the rear corner of the room. Frank Schottenbauer was noticeably absent.

August joined his wife, Minnie, on the other side of the room, near their three daughters and two other sons. The Streeters stood near Forest and Arthur, gathered in the back corner. Lester Streeter, a big man, eyed up the husky Julia Christensen, who wore an expensive dress and beautiful hairstyle.

Reverend Ehrstein conducted a brief ceremony, standing back a bit in case he got suddenly sick. Clara Petrie had placed a wooden bucket close, but out of plain sight, in case he needed it for vomiting.

After each newlywed said, "I do," and briefly kissed, the minister ended the ceremony and exited to his car. The entire matter took less than fifteen minutes, which William could tolerate.

After the ceremony, a fine breakfast was served by several of the Petries' neighbor ladies, with assistance from William's sisters. The day was cool, but not unseasonably cold, with a light breeze and bright sun.

CHAPTER 24

LEAVING FOR THE HONEYMOON

As guests departed, Maud and William realized that it was time to be dropped in Clements for the afternoon train that would take them on their honeymoon to Janesville.

"Daddy, we have our bags packed for Janesville," Maud said wistfully. "We'll be back in a week."

"My darling Maud," Henry said with tears in his eyes, giving her a long hug. "I am losing my little girl."

"Daddy, I'll always be your little girl," she said with a sniff. "William will take good care of me."

They descended the stairs to see a few guests still milling around and visiting with Clara and Claude. William was saying good-bye to his own family.

"You greet all the folks and relatives for me," August said. "Ve don't get back like we should. They'll be excited to see you."

"Willie," Minnie Kleeman said over sobs. "Please come callin' to us when you get back, and let us know how everything went."

"I will," he answered as he gave her a hug. "We'll ring you on the telephone as soon as we get back."

William put their bags in the massive trunk that was bolted to the back of Henry's Buick. They'd decided it would be best if Maud wore her lovely wedding dress on the trip instead of changing clothes. William would also stay in his snappy black suit. With a few relatives and friends still milling about, the newlyweds bid farewell as Henry climbed into his car and blew the horn. He circled over to the front door to pick up Clara, who was still visiting with guests.

"Clara, we have to get these kids to the depot in Clements or they'll miss the train!" he hollered.

Henry got out and escorted his wife to the open car door, partly out of chivalry and partly to hurry her along. The Buick chugged its way out of the driveway, with the guests waving frantically as Henry tooted the horn. The family visited on their way to the Clements depot, which was busy with activity. Henry pulled into the ramp, where a giddy William Kleeman was ready to unpack the luggage from the trunk and get tickets bought for Janesville. He raced into the depot terminal and pulled out the ten dollars that Omer Streeter had given him hours earlier.

"You'll be switching trains in Sleepy Eye, and then again in Mankato," the ticket seller told William as he gave back his change. "Make sure you keep your luggage with you or in the baggage car."

William nodded, took the tickets, and slipped them in his pocket, returning to see Henry and Clara bidding farewell to his new wife.

"We'll be back next week, Daddy," Maud said with a mix of emotions. "The schedule says that the train from Mankato will arrive here at four o'clock in the afternoon."

"I might throw in some campaign time at the depot and come early to get you," Henry replied, reminding everyone that he was turning his focus back to the primary campaign for sheriff in Redwood County.

"We'd best be going, dear," Clara said to the group. "We have company at the house, and your train is leaving soon."

Henry and Clara embraced Maud, followed by courteous handshakes for William.

"I'll take good care of her," William said quietly to Clara.

"You'd better," Clara snapped back sternly.

The train conductor called, "All aboard!" The train bellowed out a long whistle, alerting everyone to hurry.

William and Maud scurried to get their luggage to the baggage car and handed it to a young man who was loading the last items. They proceeded to the passenger car, which was about half-full of people taking their seats isolated in the rear corner, so they could snuggle close together and have privacy.

"I'm so excited to meet your relatives in Janesville," Maud told William. "I feel like it's a whole new adventure for us."

The two discussed their new living arrangements and how the immediate future would look.

"Daddy and Mother are switching out Frank's items at the house with everything from my bedroom while we're gone," Maud said, imagining her belongings in the farmhouse instead of in her bedroom at her parents' house. "They're going to clean it up too."

"My brothers and the Streeter boys are moving my things out of that shanty I was in and over to our new place," William responded, proud that he also had others to do the tedious work. "I ain't got much to move. Lester knows how to drive my Sears car. Him and Johnny will figure out how to pack everything and get it to our place."

"What are they doing with that old shack of yours?" Maud asked.

"Last I heard, Lester is going to move over there. He's old enough to be on his own, and he's hankerin' to get in right quick. That's how I got him and Johnny to agree to move my things to our place. I saw him takin' a likin' to Julia at the wedding."

"Their father seems quite gruff," Maud said as she reflected on her few interactions with Omer Streeter. "I was a little surprised that they came to the ceremony."

"He's strict and can be a downright ass," William replied with a smile. "But he paid for our train tickets and the hotel we're stayin' at tonight, so he can't be all bad."

"He what?" Maud interrupted with a stunned amazement.

"Old Man Streeter, tighter than a drum, slipped me ten dollars before we got hitched this mornin', and that's no lie," William responded, straightening up in his seat. "Never would've predicted that in a million years."

"We're staying at the Janesville Hotel tonight. Mother and I made arrangements last week. It's just a short distance from the train depot. It was nice for Mr. Streeter to pay for it."

"I'm looking forward to tonight. I have been for a long time," William said with a smirk.

They held hands tightly as the train steamed toward Sleepy Eye. After switching trains twice, the new couple finally arrived in Janesville after hours of riding. The stops provided time to use the water closets and to stretch. After arriving in Janesville, they carried their bags to the hotel and had a fine meal befitting a newly married couple. Since it was after seven o'clock before they ate, they were famished and ate heartily of the soup, salad, and steak. A slice of pie each rounded out the meal before they retired to their room.

Before they returned to their home in New Avon Township later the next week, Maud would be pregnant.

CHAPTER 25

THE NEWLYWEDS RETURN WHILE THE RACE FOR SHERIFF IS SETTLED

To AVOID LAYING WASTE TO AN ENTIRE CAMPAIGN DAY—and never failing to seize an opportunity to get his name in the paper—Henry made sure that the wedding announcement published in the *Redwood County Sun* included a mention of his candidacy: "The bride is the daughter of Henry Petrie, candidate for sheriff, and a young lady who has many friends in that part of the county."

Clara and Henry discussed the matter as they drove to Clements to pick up their daughter and new son-in-law from the train depot on the Saturday before the primary election. Clara and Claude had spent a good part of the week cleaning out the rented farmhouse next door while Frank and Henry placed items in the wagon and the Buick to get Frank's belongings moved to the Petrie farm. Henry worked in several campaign stops throughout the week, knowing that time was running short.

"I'm not sure talking about your candidacy in Maud's wedding announcement was appropriate, Henry," Clara Petrie complained. Her friends clipped the article from the *Sun* and teased her as a result. "It was her day, not yours."

"Well, I didn't choose to have her marriage ceremony less than two weeks before election day. I lost campaign time last Saturday, plus most of Friday, helping you get the house ready for the ceremony. That doesn't include moving Frank's items to our place."

Soon, they'd arrived at the Clements train depot.

"How was the honeymoon?" Clara beamed as she greeted her daughter and son-in-law.

"It couldn't have been better," Maud replied, excited to see her mother after the weeklong absence. "It's good to see you. I haven't been away from home for this long in my life."

"Henry Petrie, running for Redwood County sheriff. I'd appreciate your vote on Tuesday," Henry said loudly as he clasped a stranger's hand at the depot waiting room, not far from the ticket window.

"Can't vote for ya, mister," the man replied. "I live over in Brown County."

Henry eyed the crowd. Womenfolk weren't worth pursuing because they couldn't vote, nor could anyone under twenty-one years of age. That ruled out two-thirds of the crowd in the depot, but made it easier to identify the potential voters.

"Hey, you," a uniformed man called from the ticket window. "No campaigning inside the depot. You'll have to step outside and do it on the platform."

"Sorry, sir. First I heard of that rule," Henry called back, half apologizing in his tone. "I'll go outside."

Henry looked around the platform and saw Clara visiting with Maud on a bench near the luggage car.

"You got my vote, Mr. Petrie!" a familiar voice chimed behind Henry.

Henry spun around to see his new son-in-law smiling at him and extending his hand. He held out his hand and shook it vigorously.

"Welcome back, son," Henry said. "I thought I'd get some campaigning in, but it's tough. I can't shake hands inside the depot, where most people are getting out of this wind, the women and young folks can't vote, they have to actually live in this county, and then I have to find Republicans only, since it's a primary vote on Tuesday."

"Sounds like you're lookin' for hens' teeth, Mr. Petrie," William said as he looked around, trying to find anyone he might know in order to introduce his father-in-law.

William spied the Buick parked in a prominent spot near the depot landing. A homemade campaign sign was festooned on the car. It was an old white cloth tied to the back door with black paint that simply said PETRIE FOR SHERIFF on it.

"Good campaign trick with the car," William teased his father-in-law. "I like the sign."

"I've been driving around this county for months. I'm relieved the election is going to be done on the twentieth," Henry said in a weary voice. "Schueller is working hard too."

Clara and Maud made their way across the depot platform to find their husbands.

"Daddy, I'm anxious to get back to the house," Maud said as she looked at the crowd still streaming out of the train's passenger car. "Do you *have* to campaign anymore?"

"Just a few more tries and we'll be on our way, Maud," Henry replied with a worried look.

He darted toward two men who were gathering their bags from the luggage car.

"Hello there," he said heartily. "Henry Petrie, running for sheriff! I'd appreciate your vote in the primary next Tuesday!"

"Democrat, Farmer-Labor, or Republican?" the older man asked flatly, eyeing Henry up and down with suspicion.

"I'm running in the Republican primary," Henry replied confidently, knowing that Redwood County was dominated by members of that ilk.

"You're outta luck. I ain't got no use for any damn Republicans," the man retorted with a scowl. "They're just for the rich bugs and the high muckety-mucks. Go find someone else."

The man grabbed his bag and stormed away as Henry stood helpless with a dejected look on his face. The man's younger companion lagged behind and whispered to Henry, "Sorry about my daddy's behavior. He's pretty much a Farmer-Labor man. I'd be thinkin' of votin' for ya, but I'm only twenty years old and can't."

The young man turned and walked quickly to catch up to his father.

"Just my luck," Henry muttered to William, who was standing behind him. "The only non-Republican in these parts and I had to waste my time with him. Then his kid, who might give me a chance, is too young to vote. It's time to leave."

As he walked toward Maud and Clara, three middle-aged women pushed past. Knowing that they didn't have the right to vote, Henry essentially ignored them, just giving a tip of the hat as they scurried away.

"No luck, Daddy?" Maud asked as she witnessed the exchange from a distance.

"The older one is Farmer-Labor, so not voting in my primary, dear," Henry said in a despondent voice. "The younger one is a year short of being able to vote. I spent over two hours here and probably didn't get more than one vote that I didn't already have when I came to town. We should get women's suffrage passed in this state so I could get you ladies to vote for me."

"We'd love to vote for you, but I'm not sure suffrage will happen in my lifetime. Not everyone is going to vote for you, Henry," Clara said kindly, knowing that he was clearly frustrated with hunting down eligible primary voters in his quest for the nomination for sheriff. "Though I know you've worked very hard and deserve to win."

"It'll be dark soon enough, and I want to have a good supper with my family," Henry replied, clearly relieved that the election would be finished on Tuesday. "No campaigning on Sunday, so after church tomorrow, we'll get caught up with arranging things at your house, Maud."

In the primary on the following Tuesday, Henry Petrie would only carry a handful of precincts against the popular Republican incumbent, B. C. Schueller. Henry's hard work wouldn't result in a successful nomination for sheriff. Given that Henry lost the primary by a margin of more than three hundred votes, it was unlikely that an extra day or two of campaigning would have made the difference. The wedding didn't ruin the election after all, nor did the election ruin the wedding.

CHAPTER 26

NEW KIDS AND A NEW CAR

BEFORE THE WEDDING, WILLIAM LIVED next to the Streeters on a farm three miles south of Redwood Falls, ideally located between where his folks lived near Gilfillan Station and where his new in-laws farmed, near the tiny outpost of New Avon. As planned, after their return from honeymooning in Janesville, he and Maud moved into the farm next to the Petries, who helped by providing the rent payment and other assistance. The Streeter boys had moved all of William's meager belongings to the new house. Frank Schottenbauer had moved his items to Maud's old room at the Petrie farm and essentially switched places with her.

While William would do chores at their new rented farm, it was agreed that he'd have just a limited number of black cattle, along with his dog, Duke, who'd been cared for by John Streeter while William and Maud were on their honeymoon. The chickens and any other livestock would be housed at the main Petrie farm, where Frank would have easy access for chores. That included the handful of hogs that the Petries kept for pork.

William wasn't poor, nor was his family. However, his tightwad father had instilled similar German frugal tendencies in his son. Hard work was to be appreciated, and labor-saving devices on his farm could wait until money came along to pay cash. He wasn't a fan of large credit bills, which had stymied both his and his father's desire to own their own farm and stop the never-ending cycle of renting farms and land.

August Kleeman offered an example to William by leasing rich Redwood County farmland from the Gilfillan family. That opportunity from the Gilfillans had presented itself many years ago, and that's what resulted in his choice to uproot Minnie and their family from the Janesville area to start with. The Gilfillans owned thousands of acres of land and were, by far, the wealthiest family in Redwood County. Their large estate had its own grain elevator, a servants' house, and a number of hired men. Entire families were allowed to rent, lease, and eventually buy farmland from the Gilfillan family. That was August Kleeman's goal. He knew that the farmland in these parts produced large yields for corn, oats, and wheat. It was an attractive place to settle for those interested in working hard to produce large crops.

Nine months and two days after their wedding day, William and Maud's first child, Gladys Kleeman, was born at home. It was June 1911, an exciting time for both extended families as they welcomed the first child of a new generation. With Clara and Henry Petrie close by, they provided essential help with the young couple's needs in child-rearing. William and Maud proved to be very fertile and produced babies quickly. Lois, the next child, was born in

November 1913, and their only son, Gordon, arrived in March 1915. The deliveries of all the Kleeman children were done at the house, with Clara assisting the doctor in whatever needs arose. With three children under the age of four, the small, two-bedroom home near New Avon was cramped, and their Sears car was insufficient.

Although time was increasingly scarce, William always kept his commitment to John Streeter and made fishing trips, hunting excursions, and car rides a monthly event for the two of them. William could air complaints about his problems, and John could get quality time in with his mentor. Oftentimes, William and John could squeeze in a few hours of relaxation on Sunday mornings after chores while Maud and the children were at church with the Petries.

William didn't want to rely on his generous in-laws for every expense, so he'd been saving privately for a bigger and newer car. His small two-cylinder Sears car was almost outdated from the day he and the Streeter boys assembled it at the Redwood Falls depot in the spring of 1910. By the time Gordon was born, William knew he needed a newer, larger, and more reliable car, but it would have to be as cheap as possible. In looking around at different types and styles, it was common sense that a Model T Ford would be the smartest investment for his family.

"These cars have been selling left and right, Willie," Gerhard Landkammer told the young father as he looked at several black Model Ts parked near the Hopfenspirger Implement in Clements. "If you've got young'ns, I'd get a sedan."

William looked the models over carefully. More and more people were buying the cars, and the price kept coming down. Glancing down the street of Clements, more than half the cars, which were still interspersed with horse-drawn wagons, were Model T Fords.

"What's the bottom line on the price, and what I can get for my car in trade?" William asked as he pointed to a four-door touring model. "I'm likely to put the car in the shed for the winter and use the horses through the snow, so we probably don't need the hardtop."

"It's going to be about four hundred ninety dollars for the touring car, and nine seventy-five for the full sedan with the hardtop, Willie," Gerhard said with a smile. "I think I know which fits your budget better. I'm going to be honest on your Sears car. We'd give you twenty-five bucks for it, and I'm not sure why I'd be givin' you that much."

"Don't you think a kid startin' out fresh would want it to get around in?" William asked in astonishment. "It's gotta be worth more than that in trade."

"We're pretty firm on the Fords, Willie," he responded with a pat on his shoulder. "They make 'em as cheap as they can so Henry Ford can get everyone on the road. Your problem is that the Sears is basically a wooden frame and wooden wheels with a small engine under it. Even the scrap price is poor because it's mostly wood, not metal. The farmers can't really pull out and use that two-cylinder opposed engine for farmwork either."

"I actually thought about that," William confessed as he looked at the shiny, new Ford. "The engines on these bigger cars can get put on a cart and used to grind feed or somethin'. Not my Sears."

"If you want to sell that Sears privately, you're welcome to keep it. I'd sell you the Model T straight out for four hundred ninety dollars," Gerhard teased. "Don't make no difference to me either way."

William tried to seduce Lester and John Streeter into buying the Sears, but neither was interested. He conceded to trading in his old wooden-wheeled Sears car that had served him fairly well for five years. His growing family and the impracticality of having a motorized buggy on wheels was proving somewhat embarrassing for Maud, who was used to riding in her father's higher-class automobiles. The Kleemans had only used the more primitive Sears from late spring until late fall, knowing that the harsh Minnesota winters, with massive amounts of snow and cold, would raise havoc with the car. It was much more practical to hitch up the team to either a wagon or sleigh from mid-December through early April. Surprisingly, the black team of horses was still serving William well, even in their advanced age.

"You can keep the Sears, and I'll give you four hundred sixty-five in cash for the Model T," William said in a relieved voice. "Do you have a touring car ready, or should I be comin' back for one later?"

"This is the only model we have, Willie," Gerhard said, knowing that the cars were selling fast. "I'd expect the next one in by Monday. Take your Sears home and we'll trade in a few days. Let's sign some papers and get the deal finalized. You're a cash buyer, right? Not buyin' on time?"

William nodded, and the deal was struck. His would be one of the many families across the country getting into a brand-new Model T Ford that year.

As William and Maud's small, rented farmhouse filled with new family members, an opportunity arose for Henry to purchase his own farm site and land closer to Redwood Falls. Henry had been renting the current two farm sites as a package, though, so his land purchase meant Maud and William would have to move as well, hopefully to a larger farmhouse that would still be close enough to the Petries' new place for regular visits.

Henry Petrie broke the news to William and Maud that their farm would have to be vacated and a new farm found to either buy or lease. Knowing William's hesitation to buy anything substantial on credit, Henry searched for farms that could be rented and that had larger farmhouses on them.

CHAPTER 27

CHECKING OUT THE NEW PLACE

HENRY PETRIE HAD KEPT IN CONTACT with his old friends and neighbors in the Clements area ever since he'd sold the quarter section of land to plat out the city in 1901. When he discovered the old Holmer Johnson place two miles north of Clements had been sold to an Illinois landowner named Ambrose Hollenbeck, he contacted him by wire and asked to rent it. It would be a good location for his daughter and her family to settle on an established farm site. William, Maud, and Henry decided to look at the place after being granted permission by the Hollenbecks.

"Daddy, I am anxious to live in a larger home," Maud told her father. "We enjoy living near you, of course, but now the house is just too small."

"I think it was the right decision to purchase land close to Redwood Falls," Henry replied. "The small railroad line went through

Clements to Rowena and Wabasso, and the other line runs from Morgan to Gilfillan to Redwood Falls. New Avon got missed. It'll cease to exist in a few short years. I think it'll go the same way Sundown did south of here. It's time for us all to move—for a variety of reasons."

Sundown was the name of the township directly south of Three Lakes Township, but it was also the name of an unincorporated village south of Clements. At one time, it boasted the county's largest creamery, a music instructor, and some buildings. By 1915, it was becoming a ghost town, much like New Avon was.

"We have an appointment to look over the old Holmer Johnson place," Henry declared. "We can arrive anytime this afternoon. Nelson is the name of the current renter."

After finishing a delicious meal prepared by Clara, the Kleemans and Henry headed toward the car shed that held Henry's massive blue Buick. As usual, William offered his hand to Maud on the passenger side and allowed her to sit next to her father in the front seat. He stepped up the running board and sat in the roomy back seat. A quick crank at the front and the Buick sputtered to life.

"We'll be back soon enough!" Henry called to Clara, who waved from the open kitchen window. She had care of her three young grandchildren to let the others have a more peaceful visit to the prospective farm.

Henry surveyed the familiar land as they drove east. "This is some of the most productive farmland in these United States," he declared with good reason. "The neighbors are friendly, and there's a schoolhouse close by for when the children grow older."

A dirt road that ran straight to Morgan was the turn they needed. A schoolhouse, pump, and outhouse sat in the corner on their immediate left. After passing the north-south intersection that ran between Clements and Redwood Falls, the long driveway was on their left.

"That driveway looks really long, Daddy," Maud complained. "Hope the place is worth the distance."

While William wasn't afraid to speak his mind, he hesitated to say much to his father-in-law in this case. Henry helped them pay bills when needed and had always been gentlemanly to William, despite the latter's crude humor and lack of formal education.

The Buick pulled into the yard where the current renters were packing up to move. A tan, mixed-breed dog barked a friendly greeting from a distance and met the Buick as it entered the yard. They quickly scanned the yard. A dozen white chickens pecked the ground near the granary. An enormous barn was the centerpiece of the whole place, with the head and tail sections of the barn aligned on a north-south axis. A small workshop sat on the northwest side of the main yard. Several farm implements were lined up north of the barn. Most of the machinery was still horse drawn.

A young farmer dressed in dirty overalls and work boots greeted them. Unlike the clean-shaven William, he sported a short beard and mustache. Suddenly, as the Buick approached, the dog spotted William sitting in the back seat. His friendly demeanor immediately turned vicious. He violently barked and snarled at the back seat, ignoring the front passengers. The dog foamed at the mouth and jumped toward the rear running board.

"Michael!" the farmer called out. "What in tarnation has gotten into you?"

He pulled the growling and snapping dog to an isolated tree on the northwest corner of the farm and tethered him with an aging length of rope.

"Sorry about that dog," the farmer apologized. "He never acts like that."

"Good morning, sir," Henry called after shutting off the Buick's engine. "I'm Henry Petrie, and this is my daughter, Maud, and son-in-law, William Kleeman. The Hollenbecks said we could look at this place for rentin' in the coming year."

The farmer tipped his hat to Maud and smiled. He looked about William's age, but Maud and William weren't familiar with him or his family.

The dog kept incessantly barking and growling.

"Shut up!" the farmer yelled at the anxious pup. "You go lay yourself down now!"

The dog settled down and lifted his hind leg, urinating on the tree. He crept down slowly in the warm sun that was illuminating the yard from the south. He faced the opposite direction from where William was standing.

"This is a mighty fine place," the renter continued. "I've been rentin' this place since the Hollenbecks bought it off Old Man Johnson's relatives a few years back."

"Is there something wrong that we should be aware of . . . I'm sorry, I didn't get your name," Maud asked politely.

"Name's Nelson, Joseph Nelson." The farmer grinned. "Hollenbeck told me there'd be some people lookin' at the place. Get on down, and I'll show you around."

Ignoring Maud's initial question, Nelson mentioned how rich the land was for crops and how large the barn was to provide care to his animals.

"There's a couple of hundred acres of ground with this place. The north part can get wet, and there's always plenty of rocks that need pickin' up," Nelson warned. "But overall, a great farm."

"I'm sorry," Maud interrupted again. "This seems to be a fine place, but if so, why are you leaving?"

"My folks have a place north of here, and there's some Gilfillan land coming up for sale close to their place," Nelson replied, yielding to Maud's persistence. "We think it's time to be owners and not renters. Wife's in the house with my young'ns. She can show you the house while us menfolk are in the yard."

Henry, William, and Joseph turned and walked toward the massive barn, by far the largest building on the site.

"This barn has to be twice the size of the one we got now," William said. "Show me how you have it set up."

The dozen brown steers that Joseph kept on an exterior fence had been watching the men ever since the car pulled into the yard. However, as William came around the corner, they suddenly shuffled off to the far south part of the barn, pushing each other to be as far away from the conversation as possible.

"There's an oats bin on this side of the barn," Joseph explained, pointing to the northwest corner. "We put wheat on the other side and straw for bedding in the middle. I drop straw down from the haymow, and the oats I don't feed the horses get sold off the next year for cash."

William appreciated the modern layout of the barn. There was room for an array of animals, and he could grow his farming operation to include more livestock than what he and Maud had right now. William could envision a modern farm with everything that they needed: horses for work, cows for milk, chickens for eggs, beef cattle and pigs for meat.

While always engaged in farming, Henry was considered a gentleman farmer who shied away from the dirtiest jobs. "This barn will provide enough room for milk cows, horses, and maybe even some pigs," he called out to William from the door as he and Joseph went in to view the animal pens up close.

Nelson kept a team of horses in separate stalls behind a wooden door with large metal latches.

"My team's in here, right below one of the small bins for oats," Joseph explained. "That way, I just pull a small board out and the feed drops down in their bunks. They call it one of them there gravity feeders."

As William entered the room where the horses were kept, they suddenly began to whinny loudly and kick the stall doors with their heavy hoofs. One reared up and acted as though it had seen a snake.

"What on earth has gotten into you animals?" Joseph questioned. "Ain't used to strangers, I guess."

William and Joseph turned to exit. After they left, the animals calmed to their earlier demeanor.

While the men toured the outbuildings, Maud peered around the farm site and stayed near the car after the initial conversation. Her main interest was the house, not animal pens, barns, and sheds, but she hesitated to intrude on Mrs. Nelson by herself. She looked at the house's size from the exterior and judged that it was much larger than their current home. It was painted white, but a bit faded. Like most absentee owners, the Hollenbecks had neglected to have the house painted since they had bought it from the Johnson estate several years earlier. Maud thought the aging facade would need attention in coming years if they were to stay. A small porch at the entrance to the house was open, but it provided an additional place for spare boots and unused tools and a place to greet visitors.

She finally decided to take Joseph Nelson's advice and start up a conversation with his wife. On her way to the porch steps, she overheard the dog whining and yelping. Maud took a deep breath and gave a polite knock. Elizabeth Nelson appeared at the door. She was visibly pregnant and looked haggard for her young age of perhaps twenty-five. The noise of young children fighting in the house permeated the background. She smiled sweetly and invited Maud to come in.

"My name is Elizabeth," she said to Maud, relieved to see another woman on the place.

"I'm Maud Kleeman, and we're here to look at your place," Maud said politely. "We may want to rent it for the coming year."

"Me and Joseph and our four boys have been here for about five years now," Elizabeth explained. "We moved here right after gettin' hitched."

Just then they were interrupted by two unruly young boys with messy hair and filthy overalls. The ragamuffins came barging through and chased out the door, screaming at the top of their lungs. They both obviously needed their noses wiped and their hands washed. The women looked out the door to see the boys chasing and playing.

"Bang! Bang!" one urchin yelled as the other screeched a war chant in reply.

The children circled the yard, and the oldest boy stopped and stared right into William's eyes. For one brief moment, the yard was quiet.

The moment broke, and the boys continued to chase each other, with chickens flying out of their way to avoid the commotion.

"Bang! Bang! You're dead!" the older boy teased.

The younger boy fell to the ground and pretended to be shot as the older one stood over the top of him, kicking his thighs. Soon the ordinary tomfoolery had turned too rough, and the younger boy shrieked for his older brother to stop it as he brutally kicked his brother harder and harder.

"Matthew!" Joseph commanded the older boy. "Stop that *right now!*"

While the children had played rough before, the severity of the abusive blows had never occurred previously.

"You OK, Mark?" his father asked kindly as the young boy grimaced in pain.

"Yeah, Pa." He winced, rubbing his bruised and aching muscles. "Just playin'."

"You get outta here! The both of ya!" Joseph hollered. "Don't let me see that kind of rough horseplay again."

Maud witnessed the violent display from the doorway and frowned. While she had young children, she had only one boy, and Gordon wasn't two years old yet. Her more civilized offspring wouldn't be allowed to turn into such ruffians, she thought.

"Boys will be boys," Elizabeth said with a sigh as she peered around Maud to witness the aftermath of the ruckus. "They've lived on this place their whole lives, so the move might be tough for them. But we'll be closer to their grandparents, and that'll help out a lot."

Four children, with the oldest being six years old at the most? Maud quickly calculated the boys' estimated ages and the time they were living on the Johnson place. Like Maud, Elizabeth must have been pregnant or delivering a baby almost every year since they were married. The young women moved to the kitchen, where Elizabeth spent much of her time.

"This is John," she said proudly, pointing to a baby propped up in a creaky wooden high chair that was pushed up to a simple table.

Maud looked around the modestly sized room. Tin plates and cups were unwashed and stacked by the sink, which had a shiny red cistern pump popping up on its left side. A large wooden icebox sat in the corner, keeping the family's food cool, as needed.

"I wonder what's gotten into Michael," she said as she heard the mutt snarling through the open kitchen window. "That dog is usually such a gentle soul."

"How did you arrive at Michael for the name of a dog? Our dog is named Duke."

"He's named for Michael, the Archangel. This dog is our protector. Perhaps not against the wickedness and snares of the devil as the real Michael, but all the same."

Maud was taken aback by the intense religious overtones and thought the explanation was a bit dramatic for an inquiry about a dog's name.

"Joseph let me name him," Elizabeth continued proudly. "He named all the children, and I got to name Michael."

"How far along are you?" Maud asked, trying to change the subject. "Looks like you're with child."

"I'm about six months along, according to Doc Adams," Elizabeth replied as she patted her swollen belly. "Nothin' more innocent or precious than these babies."

The men rounded the farmyard after their inspection of the barn. A small work shed to the north could serve as a place for William to fix machinery. It was small by most standards, but ample enough to suit his needs. The granary was wooden and had two slatted bins to hold ear corn on each side. The Nelsons' Model T Ford was parked under the middle of the building, providing it some shelter, even though there were no doors on either end of the building. A large wooden fanning mill, a machine that separated chaff from grain, was on the other side of the car. Joseph pointed out additional storage for small grains like oats and wheat that were mainly sold to the Clements elevator for cash in the spring to help pay bills.

"The neighbors around here are mighty fine too," Nelson bragged. "We help each other with threshing and shocking in the fall—we form a crew to get everyone's work done."

William was all too familiar with that part of farming, having worked every autumn harvest since he was a child. Mid-July to early September was dominated by first running a grain binder to cut oats, walking behind the machine to shock the grain into small tepees to dry in the sun, followed by loading all the grain bundles by hand onto horse-drawn wagons that were brought to a large threshing machine that separated the straw from the grain. It was exhausting work that lasted for almost two months straight in the hot Minnesota sun. Knowing the value of mechanical help with the harvest, William grew excited.

"Someone in these parts owns a threshing rig? I ran one for my old boss by Redwood Falls for a few seasons. Who is it?"

"Carl Otto, kitty-corner across the way. He has a rig with a tractor and the whole works," Joseph boasted as he pointed to the southwest. "He's a gem of a guy."

As they exited the granary, William was startled by a rat's long tail slinking along the edge of the corncrib.

"You got a lot of rats and mice around this place?" William asked, pointing to the rodent scurrying away into the ears of corn.

"No more or less than what other folks got," Joseph said plainly. "We get the single-shot .22 and blast 'em when we see 'em. That one will pay the price if he comes out again."

Henry clicked his pocket watch closed with an audible snap.

"I think it might be prudent to look at the house so we can respect Mr. Nelson's time," Henry said, moving the conversation to an end.

"That'd be dandy," Joseph said with a smile. "Things are a bit messy with us movin' and all, and we ain't exactly fancy housekeepers at the best of times."

Henry, William, and Joseph walked past the Buick and headed toward the house. They followed Joseph up the aged wooden steps and waited at the house's entry. A large wicker basket holding a mountain of soiled cloth diapers was on the far end of the porch. Henry, who stood closest to the rancid pile, winced at the stench and held his breath as they waited for the tour.

"Ma!" Nelson hollered into the house. "We got company!"

Just then, the dog eyed William at the door and reawakened. He started snarling and jumping. The older two boys continued to play in the yard and began to throw sticks toward the dog, teasing him incessantly.

"Come on in," Joseph called to Henry and William after spying Maud conversing with his wife. "You want some coffee or cookies?"

They politely declined the offer and followed Joseph into his home. Some primitive, homemade wooden toy guns were scattered on the floor, modeled after the real shotgun William observed hanging above the coat hooks in the entry room. Henry and Joseph entered and moved to the opposite corner of the kitchen.

William popped his head into the doorway and caught a glimpse of Joseph's pregnant wife. As Elizabeth's gaze met his, her unborn child jumped in her womb.

"I–I need to sit down," she stated suddenly. "Joseph, can you get me some cold water?"

"Tarnation, is that baby pestering you?" Joseph asked seriously. "You haven't had a difficult birthing season yet, so don't start with this one."

He vigorously pumped the small cistern handle up and down, bringing a tin cup underneath to catch newly spilled water from their well underneath. He handed the cup to Elizabeth, who groaned.

"I think you might do most of the tour, darlin'," she told Joseph. "This home has been big enough for us," Elizabeth said to the assembled group as she wiped the baby's face with a rag. "The two oldest boys' room is upstairs, and the two youngest are in the room next to ours. Joseph can tell you about the rest of the place."

The kitchen was comfortable and would potentially provide enough cupboard space to house the Kleemans' assortment of dishes and kitchenware. A pantry off to the side provided storage for canned goods, crocks of meat, jars of fruit, sugar, coffee, and the other supplies needed for a growing young family. The Nelsons had fastened a rumpled tan curtain to separate the pantry from the living space.

"What's that hole in the ceiling?" Maud asked, pointing to a gaping eyesore that was between the main kitchen and dining area, not far from the door.

"That there hole was left over from the Johnsons," Joseph replied. "Looks like they had a smaller stove at one time, and the old chimney pipe used to stick up through there. There wasn't nothin' in that hole since we moved in a few years ago. Not sure what it could ever be used for again."

Maud knew that the home wouldn't be perfect. She thought she could tolerate a hole in the kitchen ceiling.

"Don't wake up Luke," Elizabeth cautioned as the group moved out of her view. "He's sleeping in the second bedroom."

Joseph moved quietly down the hall and pointed to a bedroom containing a crib, a small, metal-framed bed, and one small dresser. It was the room for the youngest two children. A young boy, about three years old, lay napping on the bed, slumbering through the racket outside his door. The group shuffled around the house, inspecting the sizes and shapes of the rooms. Maud took more aggressive mental notes as to room dimensions and potential furniture arrangements than the men. She examined the hall, with filthy handprints on the walls, cobwebs hanging from the ceiling, and worn hardwood flooring.

"This is the biggest bedroom," Joseph said, pointing to the largest bedchamber. "The infant just moved from our bedroom to that room across the hall a few months ago. Had to get busy makin' more babies." Joseph grinned to William with a lascivious smirk.

William winked back at Nelson with an equally prurient grin. Henry and Maud were not amused.

The larger bedroom had a modest closet and a tall, thin window, providing light from the southern sun. The frequently abused full-size bed was unmade and covered with soiled linens that obviously hadn't been laundered in ages. A plain wicker basket lay in the corner containing one pair of filthy overalls and one dress. Maud thought the room smelled a bit ripe, but airing out a home would be little work. A small homemade rug lay frayed and limp at the foot of the bed. Henry and Maud conferred on the closet size as William slowly made his way across the hall from the other room.

Henry surveyed the walls. A framed wedding certificate from 1909 was nailed above the bed and a simple wooden cross was nailed to the opposite wall. Other than those two objects, the closet door, and the single window, the walls were entirely bare.

William moved into the room and scanned the surroundings. Upon seeing the cross, he quickly fled to the hallway and waited for Joseph and the others to join.

"Makes for a good birthin' room, ma'am," Joseph stated. "Every one of my young'ns was born in this here room."

Like most women on the farm, Maud too had given birth to her three children at home. She appreciated the room's size as compared to the relatively cramped bedroom she currently occupied. As with all the other rooms in the house, it would need a good cleaning and sweeping to suit her tastes.

"My sons' names are Matthew, Mark, Luke, and John," Joseph proclaimed proudly.

"Nice names," Henry replied flatly.

"See anything they might got in common?" Nelson asked rhetorically.

"Yes, saints," Maud answered politely. "I'm appreciative of that, Mr. Nelson."

"By the time my woman and I are done, we ought have all the apostles and then some," he said with a toothy grin.

The group exited the bedroom and strolled down the hall, which opened into a large living room that boasted an immense plate-glass window, a fireplace hearth, and unpretentious furnishings. A tattered red velvet rug took up most of the floor space.

Maud envisioned that the family room, with its fireplace to keep them warm, would provide a space for the children to play and for her sewing in the brutal Minnesota winters. William found an excellent location for a large grandfather clock that he'd splurged on in his younger years.

"Some of these here items were left here by the Johnsons, and the Hollenbecks didn't care about them, so here they are. This here rug and that old piano in the corner are part of the deal."

A modest upright piano covered in layers of dust sat with its accompanying wood bench in the southeast corner of the room. It looked like the instrument had been neglected for some time.

"No one knows about playin' the piano around here, other than those kids bangin' on it all the time," Joseph huffed. "Damn kids and that piano, worst combination."

Maud and her mother both knew how to play the piano, and she was excited to think they might get one for free.

"Would you leave the piano here, Mr. Nelson?" Maud asked anxiously, hoping to inherit the untidy instrument from the Nelsons.

"Tarnation, woman, I'd pay you to take that blasted thing. We ain't got no use for it; plus it weighs a ton."

William spied a Bible sitting atop a wooden shelf on the north wall. He moved to the opposite side of the room, toward the steps leading to the second story. Just then, the group heard the baby crying loudly. They knew Elizabeth would continue to have her hands full.

"You can leave the piano and rug, Mr. Nelson, but we'd want everything else out of here. Everything on the walls, the books, and such. We don't need those things."

"Suit yourself, Mr. Kleeman. Might have left some real treasures for ya, though," Nelson teased.

"The house seems solid and has some nice craftsmanship," Henry noted, pointing to the fireplace and the oak crown molding that hugged the top of the walls and ceiling.

Henry, William, and Maud tried to ignore the obvious cleaning the house needed. Firewood kindling lay in the living room, with peeled bark and wood chips scattered around the floor. Dust, spider webs, and clutter were in every room. With the number of children and the farmwork that needed to be done, they understood that housecleaning probably wasn't a top priority for the Nelsons. With proper cleaning and organization, it would make a fine home, William and Maud concluded.

"Looks twice the size of what we got now," William murmured to Maud, who nodded in reply. "There ain't nothin' wrong, other than it's dirty."

Maud and the men trekked up the narrow set of stairs that led to the second floor, led by Joseph Nelson. A good-sized closet was at the top of the steps and contained a long rod, with ample storage.

"This here room works out for our older boys," Nelson said as he kicked a homemade wooden hobbyhorse to the side with his filthy boot. "Just the right size room for them, but they're a little young to be up here on their own. When storms come, the little scaredy-cats all pile in the living room with blankets next to the fireplace."

"Our children often join us in our bedroom during storms," Maud said politely. "It helps calm them down when the thunder rolls in."

"Well, me and the woman got adult-like things going on quite frequent in our room. We don't need no kids bein' witness to that," he said, elbowing William in the ribs.

William smirked while Henry visibly rolled his eyes.

"Is it cold up here?" Henry asked, changing the subject. "I see one small furnace duct."

"Colder than hell up here in the winter, mister," Joseph answered honestly. "We pile the young'ns up with blankets a mile high. I saw frost on that there window over two inches thick last year."

The room had one simple bed with an iron headboard, but it was ample enough for the two small boys to share. Two scraggy pillows and a shabby brown blanket adorned the unmade bed. A modest pine dresser and tiny closet rounded out the room. It had a single window, smeared with countless little fingerprints, that stared out across the grove of trees. The walls were entirely bare, other than assorted dirty handprints and some cobwebs hanging in corners. A mixture of dust, hair, and grime were rolled into a small pile in one corner of the room. The boys had followed the example of their parents when it came to housekeeping. Maud thought it might eventually be a good room for Gladys and Lois to share. Little Gordon didn't really need to be separated from the girls at this young age, and they could all stay in the secondary bedroom on the main floor together until the girls grew a bit older.

The group was interrupted by the two boys chasing up the stairs and bursting into their isolated cove.

"Hey! This is *our* room!" the older boy yelled. "Scram!"

"You show a little respect to your elders," Joseph warned sternly. "Now go outside and run off some of that energy. Get!"

The boys spun around and let out alternating shrieks as they banged down the steps and retreated outside to the yard.

As they moved around the Nelsons' house, both William and Maud could visualize their growing family moving to this place. Even though they would be renting, perhaps the Hollenbecks might relent and sell the farm site and possibly the land. It made Maud giddy to think she would have such a large home to call her own. It was all too premature to predict now, but the place satisfied their needs and exceeded the size of their current home. The group made their way down the steps to see Elizabeth holding the baby, but now with a two-year-old clinging to her right leg, rubbing sleep from his eyes.

"Plannin' to get out of here by the end of next month," Joseph announced. "We're putting together one of them there Sears houses that the catalog advertises."

William nodded, knowing that the Sears catalog offered many treasures for the rural resident to purchase.

"We got that catalog over in the outhouse," Joseph declared. "We could fetch it and show you the house we ordered."

Maud visibly flinched, knowing the unsanitary conditions of having feces-stained hands that undoubtedly had pawed over the catalog many times over. Henry, sensing it was time to leave, politely declined the offer.

"We really must go, Mr. Nelson," Henry said quickly as the group exited the house. "You've been more than generous with your time."

As he finished speaking, the two older boys, who had mysteriously disappeared for a few quiet minutes, came darting off Henry's Buick and shot across the yard.

William and Maud edged toward each other and began to talk quietly about the new farm they might be able to rent.

"You boys had better not have ruined nothin' on that car!" Joseph yelled across the yard. "I'm right sorry if they messed with your car, Mr. Petrie. It sure is a looker. What a nice shade of blue. We get around in a plain ol' Model T."

Henry was especially proud of his automobile. A Buick was one of the top-end cars, bested only by Packard and Cadillac. Its size, power, and color made it stand out from the more common black Fords that dotted the landscapes across Redwood County. Henry had bought his first new car in the fall of 1909 and used it frequently to campaign across the county when he ran for sheriff. His first model was traded in for this newer one just last year.

"It looks like they didn't bother the car much, just put the transmission in gear," Henry replied as he jerked a lever on the floor loose. "They're just being kids."

"Did you know the Sears catalog offered a car for a few years?" Joseph asked. "They came out around the time we got hitched. It was basically a buggy with an engine on it. Nothin' like the Ford. We've had ours for two years. The Redwood paper offers the Chalmers cars all the time, but it don't seem like people are buyin' much."

"Actually, my son-in-law over there had a Sears car when they first came out," Henry answered, showing he could speak mechanics with the best of them. "Wasn't very good."

William and Maud continued whispering with each other while Henry and Joseph discussed automobiles and farm machinery.

"Excuse me, Mr. Nelson," Maud interrupted. "If anyone is to bother you about renting this place, tell them it's taken. We're very interested, and we'll inform Mr. Hollenbeck accordingly."

"All righty," Joseph quickly replied. "You folks will take a likin' to this place. Hopin' you'll stay long enough to die here like Old Man Johnson."

Henry and the Kleemans bid farewell, and the Buick roared to life. The high wood spokes turned their way south down the driveway. Unbeknownst to the passengers, they were chased halfway to the road by the older boys and the farm dog.

CHAPTER 28

―――――――――

HOME FOREVER

WILLIAM AND MAUD WERE HOPING their relocation would be permanent. They didn't want to move more frequently than needed, especially with so many children. An additional advantage with this new place was that Sunrise Schoolhouse was located conveniently across the way. Their three young children would live closer to school than any other child in the township. They'd have an easy walk to school. William wouldn't have to hitch up a team or start a car to take them, unless there was horrific weather.

Their first year at the new place, 1916, proved to be an adequate year for farming. William had to make do with a limited amount of machinery since he'd just moved to the new place. With two hundred rented acres, he had more land to cultivate than the average farm in the area.

"I could really use Gordon to grow up right quick," he'd often tell Maud after a hard day's work in the field.

William's neighbors were helpful and offered assistance when he needed it. They noticed that William would often rely on his dad or a brother to come help when he was struggling with the livestock or needing help with planting. Periodically, John Streeter would come and stay overnight to help with farmwork that required two grown men. The neighbors shared a threshing machine that would separate the small grain from the stalks. It was one of the few times a tractor pulled onto the Kleeman farm.

Carl Otto, the Kleemans' neighbor to the south, farmed two hundred eighty acres of land, a sizable farm that was equipped with modern equipment, including a large tractor, a threshing machine, and multibottom plows. Otto was the friendly neighbor that Joseph Nelson had mentioned on William's first visit to the farm site.

Otto would often tease William when they saw each other at the saloon in Clements or even in their fields across the road from each other. "Villiam, ve are in de twentieth century!" Otto called out with his German accent. "It is time to get a tractor."

William knew he was a little behind the times with new technology. He had waited to get a car but had given in to impress Maud with his Sears Motor Buggy when they were engaged. Tractors were a rare commodity when he was a teenager, but now a vast majority of his neighbors and friends owned one. In fact, he'd been the main operator of the large International Harvester tractor that Omer Streeter had owned when he worked as a hired man. But he didn't have the luxury of a tractor on his farm.

On a sunny spring day, William was struggling with his team of black workhorses as he tried to harrow a particularly rough patch of soil on his farm. Across the south road, Carl Otto manned an immense International Harvester tractor he'd purchased at the

Hopfenspirger Implement in Clements. The local clientele patron-ized the Hopfenspirgers heavily and kept their dealership busy by obtaining the newest farm machinery available.

Otto slowed his tractor to a halt, pulling back the massive clutch to stop the machine's transmission. He dismounted it and waved at William, who was embarrassed by his primitive apparatus next to Otto's advanced, labor-saving tractor.

"You know, I move twice as fast, till three times more ground, and never have to stop and feed oats to my tractor," Otto counseled. "Dis tractor is a lifesaver—and remember, I'm a German too. Ve're too tight to spend money, but dis machine saves you money. Think about it. I may get a new tractor next year, and I could sell you this one cheap."

The word *cheap* resonated with William. He had a large family, and it was always growing. While they could raise chickens for meat and eggs, cows for milk, cattle and pigs for meat, and a massive vege-table garden for produce, it always seemed to be a struggle for money. But Carl Otto had a large family too, with more land and more chil-dren than he had.

"I'll think about it, Carl. Your tractor is a lot like that one I used over at the Streeter place when I was their hired man," William said. "Let's talk next spring before planting gets started. We like to pay cash, so the price has to be right."

"My sons will bring the tractor over when I finish here, and we'll help you get done," Carl responded kindly. "You only need to give me a little money for gas if you can handle dhat."

Carl gave William some advice on how deep to set the harrow and how to manage the horses when they hit thick patches of soil. William's father wasn't around daily to guide the young farmer, who'd just reached thirty this year, so the advice of an experienced neighbor was a great help.

Farming his own place was a great amount of responsibility that strained the body and the mind. Crops could get chopped down by hail, could be drowned out, or could dry up; animals could get sick and die; the weather could prevent planting or harvesting at the ideal times; vegetables needed weeding and attention; butter needed churning; wheat and oats had to be threshed; animals needed to be butchered and dressed into slabs of meat. The work never ended.

Three Lakes Township was a six-square-mile area named for three lakes that sat immediately north of William's land. Local farmers had started draining the lakes a few years earlier to make way for more tillable land, but the remnants provided a fishing hole for William when he sought some fish to eat and time to relax away from the daily demands of the farm. His old fishing hole—Daubs Lake, where he and John Streeter would dip their fishing lines—was now a little too far for a quick break.

In addition to the piano the Nelsons left behind in the house, William and Maud also inherited plenty of varmints from the farm's previous residents—including a family of black crows that nested in the large cottonwood tree by the barn, a den of garter snakes next to the toolshed, the numerous rats in the granary and wooden corncrib, plus a menagerie of stray raccoons, skunks, and foxes.

CHAPTER 29

SEEKING A NEW MEMBER
OF THE FLOCK

THE REVEREND ALOYSIUS ABERNATHY was a stolid and conservative
Lutheran minister in Clements. His small white church, located on
the east side of town, attracted many of the German Lutherans in
the area who shared backgrounds similar to the Kleeman family's.
His tall, thin frame contained a fire-and-brimstone pastor who wasn't
afraid to proselytize to the unbelievers.

Abernathy heard from a member of his congregation that William Kleeman, a baptized Lutheran, was rather successful and popular in the area, so he reasoned that William could set an example for
other young German Lutheran farmers by joining his congregation.
He hitched up his single-horse buggy and rode out to the Kleeman
farm, which was exactly two miles north of his church site.

William spotted Abernathy coming down the driveway, clad in black minister's garb, a wide-brimmed black hat, and wire-rimmed spectacles.

"Oh no," William groaned. "Someone comin' that doesn't belong here."

Duke, who had been chasing the chickens, gave a welcoming bark.

As Abernathy drove onto the farm site, he caught a glimpse of William standing outside the work shed. A cold breeze suddenly appeared, and he felt a jolting shiver down his spine.

The minister slowed his rig to a crawl and regained his composure. His horse, which was ordinarily well behaved, started to whinny loudly and protest as he drew closer to the yard and caught sight of William.

"Whoa, boy," Abernathy soothed. "You be calm now."

The unexpectedly temperamental horse turned its head away from William and toward Reverend Abernathy, fixing his gaze to the minister.

"Top of the morning to you," Abernathy said politely to William as he pulled his horse around the front of the yard. "You must be William Kleeman. I'm the Reverend Aloysius Abernathy from Clements."

"I'm guessing you aren't here to pick up my cream and milk for the Clements Creamery? I'd be William Kleeman."

"I've been told you may share my faith as a member of the Lutheran Church. We're looking for upstanding members to grow our congregation, and you've been recommended as a possible candidate."

"Well, whoever told you I was upstanding must not know me very well," William teased with a grin. "I ain't much for churchgoin', but guess my folks said I was Lutheran back in the day. They've been Methodist since getting to Redwood County. Not sure I claim any church, Reverend. And I'm plannin' to keep it that way."

Reverend Abernathy, still sitting high atop his small buggy, wasn't amused by William's explanation. He sat there stone-faced, feeling a cold chill that he'd never felt before. Given the less-than-encouraging start to their conversation, he decided not to get down from his buggy.

Abernathy cleared his throat and continued, "We're only two miles away. It would be so convenient for you and your family to attend services every Sunday, Mr. Kleeman. The flock I shepherd are good, God-fearin' folks, and it would do you well to meet them."

"Well, I get to town to have some beer at Schmidt's saloon and play the one-armed bandit from time to time," William baited. "Otherwise to sell grain, milk, and cream. Don't make it to town on Sunday much since everything is closed."

"Mr. Kleeman, our church is not closed on Sunday. And you must know drinking and gambling are deeds of the devil."

"I don't do it too much, Reverend. Just enough to have a little fun." He knew just how to pester the devout man of the cloth.

"Perhaps your wife and children are interested. We have a very good Sunday-school program."

"My wife goes with her folks in Redwood, so she wouldn't be interested."

Abernathy cracked his reins as William was finishing. His horse turned his head straight ahead and looked away from William, still avoiding catching his eye.

"Mr. Kleeman, you were correct in the beginning of our conversation," the reverend pronounced. "I don't believe you'd be an upstanding member of our congregation. If you choose to seek the ways of our Lord, I will be available to you."

With that, he pointed his horse south and drove his rig down the driveway, turning right on the dirt road to trot his buggy back to Clements. William swallowed hard and ambled up the steps to the house.

"Who was in the yard, William?" Maud asked.

"Some Reverend Abernathy. I had a little fun with him."

"William! I hope you didn't insult a man of the cloth. Leave it to you."

"Well, he don't appreciate me drinkin' a beer with Schmitty or throwin' a nickel in the bandit, so we agreed to disagree," William lied. "Let's just say I ain't much for religion."

It frustrated Maud that William wouldn't allow any religious symbols to be hung in their home. If the Bible were ever to be read to the children, he wouldn't stay in the room, and the book always had to be returned to the enclosed cabinet William never had call to open.

"We've talked about it a hundred times, William. You could join me and my folks as an Episcopalian," she offered hopefully. "The Church of the Holy Communion has few members. We'd love one more."

"Maud, you know better. There's a reason we got hitched at your folks' house and not in a church."

Maud decided to change the subject rather than further engage in an argument she knew she wouldn't win. "I've got laundry to finish. May we please get a gas engine to run the machine, so I don't have to pull that lever endlessly?"

"Someday, Maud," William said with a sigh. "When the crops come in at a good price, we'll have a wash-machine engine for you.

And I'll get one for outside to saw wood, grind corn for the livestock, and run the cream separator. I'm thinkin' we'll get one this comin' year sometime when an auction might have one cheap. They save a lot of time and work. Maybe Old Man Streeter would even sell me his old ones."

CHAPTER 30

―――――――

THE SCHOOL BOARD
ASKS A QUESTION

SPRING AND SUMMER CHORES DRAGGED ON for the Kleemans as they filled their newly rented farm with implements and household items needed for their growing family. On a hot August day, William heard Duke barking as a stately Hudson automobile pulled into his driveway. It held three men, all leaders of the school and neighbors to William. One was his closest neighbor, Carl Otto. He recognized Ed Volk, the neighbor immediately across the road who owned the land Sunrise Schoolhouse sat on.

"Morning, William," Carl called. "Today is a real barn burner."

William didn't understand his neighbors' and relatives' need to constantly talk about the weather, even on a plain day. "Hello, Carl. Sure is hot. You men don't need to be recruitin' me for church membership, 'cause I ain't interested."

The three men got out of the vehicle as Duke sniffed their trousers.

"Villiam, I think you know Ed Volk. This here is Villiam Parker. Bill is chairman of our school board. We ain't here for church business, just school business."

"Nice to meet you, fellas," William answered as he wiped his brow. "My daughter Gladys will come schoolin' across the road next year. Sorry, men, she's not quite ready yet."

Maud pulled the curtains back and peered out the window. She was too busy with Gladys, Lois, and Gordon to come out and listen to the conversation with the menfolk.

"Villiam, I'm gonna just come out and ask you," Carl said, looking William straight in the eyes. "The three of us are all on the school board, and we're hirin' a new teacher who'll start teaching in early October when harvest is done."

"Ain't no question in that," William said with a broad smile. "I ain't needin' no schoolin' no more."

"She needs a place to board for the year. Ve always start with the closest place to the schoolhouse to ask about boardin'. Since you're across the road, ve thought we'd ask you first."

"She don't have no place to go, Mr. Kleeman," Volk added. "We're in a pickle."

Miss Gertrude Griffin, the homely teacher from the previous school year, didn't room with the Nelsons due to their filthy housekeeping and large brood of children. She'd decided to leave the difficult task of teaching the students at the one-room school; she'd resigned when the 1915/16 school year concluded. Known as Sunrise Schoolhouse to the locals, the building was situated in Section 16 of Three Lakes Township, District 106, just west of the Kleeman farm.

Holmer Johnson, who initially homesteaded the farm the Kleemans occupied, was a member of the original school board. The school was authorized in 1904 and was now a fully established building—one of only two in the township that served the rural students.

"Shoot, this is just all of a sudden," William replied, scratching his head. "We got three little ones, and the doc just said Maud is pregnant again."

Carl stroked his beard. He knew the Kleemans wouldn't be expecting the request, but they had to ask. The new teacher didn't own a car or team of horses, and long walks to the school through the brutal Minnesota snow and cold would be difficult.

"William, I know we're just droppin' this on ya," Carl continued, wiping sweat from the tip of his nose with a soiled handkerchief. "But we need help. Our small houses are plumb full of kids too, and we live farther away. Think of this woman walkin' through the snow this winter."

"Well, what's she like? Where's she from? Maybe she could help with the young'ns."

"Her name is Mary Snelling, and she's with her folks in Mankato right now," the chairman added. "She's a wonderful gal. She'll be a good boarder, I'm sure. She could help prepare your kids for schoolin'."

"I rule the roost, but I'd want to ask Maud about something like this. When do you need an answer?"

The men huddled briefly and whispered quietly. Carl Otto stepped out of the group. "We know she'd like to come visit once in September to meet the family she'd be livin' with. She'd come later with all her things right before school starts in early October."

"In addition to her helping your children and wife with some work and chores, you'd get nineteen dollars cash per month for your trouble," Bill Parker added. "And you'd be expected to provide meals on days she's here."

"I used to joke with old Holmer Johnson that if we had our own little town here, it'd be called Sunrise," Volk said with a smile. "We got a school, but too close to Clements to start a store or anything."

William thought the chance to earn some rent money should be considered. It could be a winning situation. Maud had three children under the age of five to care for, and another coming. The school-teacher could help her with meals, cleaning, the kids, and maybe even some other chores.

"We'll do it," William said with a grin. "We could use the help, and I think we won't want her stompin' through that snow too far this winter."

"Do you want to ask your wife about it?" Volk asked, squinting tightly in the hot sun. "It will be a big change for her."

"I think she'd be likin' the help with the young'ns," William replied confidently. "She'd have some female company too, more than just her ma. Ain't got no sisters."

"I'm sure it'll work fine," Carl said quickly. "Lord knows the womenfolk need company from time to time."

William shook each man's hand as they discussed arrangements for payment and a scheduled visit.

"I'll write Miss Snelling in Mankato and inform her that we've found her a place to stay," Parker said with a cheerful smile as he bent over to crank his car.

"Thank you so much, Mr. Kleeman," Volk added. "We owe you a lot for making this year one of the best we'll have at the Sunrise Schoolhouse."

The men jumped into the Hudson, excited that they were able to convince their first-choice candidate, William Kleeman, to board the new teacher at his home. They really had no alternatives if he'd turned them down. William waved good-bye to the men and jogged to the house, which was sweltering in the day's unbearable heat.

He was excited to share the news with Maud, even though he had a touch of apprehension about not consulting her on the life-changing decision first. "Maud! I got some news."

He could hear Gordon crying from the smaller bedroom. Gladys and Lois were playing with wooden blocks on the living room floor. As he'd told the visitors, Maud was pregnant again, due in February 1917.

"Here!" Maud shoved a cloth diaper soaked with urine at him. "Take this out to the porch and dump it in the diaper pail." Having three young children and being several months pregnant at the same time on a hot and humid day wasn't pleasant.

Maud had aged immensely since their wedding day. Her face was graced with several new lines, and her frame carried thirty additional pounds. For his part, William barely looked any different from his youthful, boyish self. Maud's daily routine was tiresome, and the chores never ended. It had seemed so much easier for her mother when she was growing up—although the losses of two of her younger brothers was emotionally challenging. Her daddy also had a hired man, and Frank took on some of the chores that her mother may have been stuck with, had he not been employed by the family. In addition, her younger brother Claude was extremely helpful for both farm tasks and housework that her parents needed done.

Maud was expected to cook three meals daily, do all the laundry by herself, keep the house and dishes clean, can vegetables, change diapers, feed and care for the children, and more. Her house lacked electricity or running water, so she used chamber pots to toilet train the children. They tried to keep the house cool by opening the few windows that actually would open to allow a periodic breeze to enter.

"Please dump the apple peels down the outhouse hole. It helps with the smell!" Maud yelled to William. She'd just set a pan of them on the table for him to take.

When William returned from depositing the soiled diaper on the porch, he was focused on steering the conversation to the decision he had made about bringing in a boarder.

"Maud, I have some news," William said, smiling. "I'm hopin' you like it."

Maud finished dressing Gordon and held him in her arms.

"William, I have to get dinner ready. Let's talk in the kitchen," she said with an irritated look. "The girls should go outside to run off some energy soon."

"Maud, the men on the school board want us to board the new teacher," William said while pushing a fork around in the apple skins. "It'd mean nineteen dollars cash a month, and she could help with the kids and cookin'."

"And you told them we'd take her in without asking me first?" Maud asked, already knowing the answer. "Lord knows I'm not consulted about anything."

"Maud, they really wanted to know today, and I knew you were busy fussin' with the kids in here," William said defensively. "I told them we'd do it."

"William, we were going to move the girls upstairs sometime this year," Maud said with a grim look. "I suppose it can wait nine months until the school year is over."

"You have to think about how this will help *you*, Maud," William pleaded, wiping the sweat off his forehead. "Think of help with cookin', cleanin', and the kids. She'd only be here until early June if it ain't workin' for us."

Maud lifted Gordon into the wooden high chair. She grabbed a tin cup from the cupboard and operated the cistern pump to get a cool drink of water that she finished in two slurps. Then she wiped her entire face with her apron.

"William Kleeman, I work my fingers to the bone around here. I'm pregnant almost every year. I have cookin' and cleanin' and washin' and chores to do all day, every day!" she said in exasperation. "It's a good thing I might get some help, but it isn't right you decided this without me, William. I know we womenfolk can't vote, but it'd be nice if I had a little say in this house."

William turned on the charm that had seduced Maud from the beginning and put his left arm around her. He smiled wide and slow, putting his right hand up to her quivering chin.

"You deserve better, Maud Kleeman," he said romantically. "This teacher comin' here will be the best thing that happens for you, I promise."

Maud's heart melted, just as it had when she danced with William in the fall of 1909. She pulled William closer and smiled back.

"You are a wicked ladies' man, William Kleeman," she said coyly. "We can manage the next nine months with this teacher and see how it works."

William gave her a gentle peck on the lips and turned away to throw the bucket of apple peelings down the outhouse hole as Lois and Gladys tore through the yard to chase Duke.

CHAPTER 31

—————————

THE NEW TEACHER
TAKES A LOOK AROUND

ON A BRIGHT SEPTEMBER DAY, A LIVERY RIG from Morgan pulled a small buggy down the Kleeman driveway. Carl Otto had informed William and Maud that the new teacher would be arriving this day to meet them and the children, work out arrangements for her living quarters, and negotiate the expectations for her chores.

William had been working in his toolshed and stuck his head out the door when he heard Duke barking near the driveway entrance. The livery driver got out and offered a hand to Miss Mary J. Snelling, the newly hired teacher for the Sunrise Schoolhouse. She was twenty-one years old and tall, with a thin body and appealing curves. Her silky, light-brown hair glistened in the sun, and her bright blue eyes matched her new dress. She had applied a moderate amount of makeup, which enhanced her fine cheekbones and white teeth.

William looked Mary up and down as he approached the livery rig. He'd expected an aging and bespectacled schoolmarm who was homely and plump. Of course, the school board members had made no mention of her looks, nor had he asked. That wouldn't have been appropriate. Nonetheless, he was stunned to see his new boarder.

"Mr. Kleeman, I presume? My name is Mary Snelling. I'll be your boarder for the school year."

William swallowed hard and took off his work cap.

"Pleased to meet you, ma'am," he said, extending his hand. "You can call me William."

"All right then, William. You may call me Mary. May I see your home?"

"I'd be honored," William said, catching himself exaggerating his response awkwardly. "My house is over here, Miss Snelling."

Mary turned to the livery driver as William plopped his hat back on his head.

"I should be finished in less than an hour, driver," she said politely. "Will you wait here during that time?"

"Yes, ma'am," he answered as he looked over the yard. "The horses may need some water, though."

"There's some buckets over by that well," William said, pointing to his large cast-iron pump. "Feel free to water 'em as much as they need."

The driver fastened blocks on either side of the buggy wheels to secure the wagon and went to get the empty buckets. The black steeds calmly waited for their cool drinks as their tails swept away pestering flies.

"Right this way, Mary," William said, taking unexpected pride in his new, voluptuous boarder. "I'll show you the house."

"Maud!" William yelled as they entered. "Our new boarder is here."

"Shhh!" Maud admonished as she finished putting the last clean dish into the cupboard. "The children are all napping."

Maud turned to the doorway and saw Mary Snelling. Just as William had done minutes earlier, she looked over the beautiful young teacher top to bottom. Immediately, she saw herself as an old woman. Her giddy and still youthful husband stood several feet away—closer to Mary Snelling.

"Uhh, pleased to meet you. I'm *Mrs.* Maud Kleeman," she said with an overly polite tone. "Please excuse the mess. We've just finished dinner."

Mary shook her hand lightly and quickly.

"Good to meet you, Maud," Mary answered, purposely using her first name without asking permission. "I'm Miss Mary Snelling. Thank you for allowing me to stay here this year."

"Mary here, she's wantin' to see her room," William said, with a hint of nervousness. "Should I show her?"

"The children are asleep, so we can *all* go upstairs," Maud said as she threw her dish towel on the table. "Follow me, Miss Snelling."

The three went through the house, with Maud briefly giving a description of the rooms as they passed. They climbed the narrow and creaky steps to the upstairs bedroom, which held a single bed with simple linens, a small dresser with an oval mirror, and a straight-backed oak chair. The room had only a small closet, but the larger closet at the top of the steps would be for Mary's use as well. It was the spare room that had been used by John Streeter when he stayed to help William with farmwork.

"This would be your room," Maud said. "It isn't very big. I hope it meets your expectations. We try to keep everything clean and comfortable around here."

Mary looked the room over carefully. She really didn't need a large room or fancy accommodations. The room might be modest in size, but it had all the furnishings she required.

"This is very nice. It will suit me just fine," Mary said quickly. "I may bring a couple of items, outside of my clothing."

"That big closet at the stop of the steps would be yours too," William added.

"Do you have accommodations for a bath?" she asked Maud. "I tend to bathe more than once a week, which I know is the habit among countryfolk."

William tried to prevent his leg from twitching. The tension in the room was thick.

Maud's first reaction to Mary's question was to wonder where her husband would be during these frequent baths. She chose to ignore the backhanded insult of her family's personal hygiene. "We have a large tub that gets brought in by the fireplace downstairs. You can use it as much as you want. Water has to be heated over the stove first, though, and you'd be responsible for that."

"I think we can look downstairs now," William interrupted, trying to change the subject. "We have other things to discuss."

The women descended the stairs and stepped carefully through the rest of the house to avoid waking the sleeping children. They ended their procession in the kitchen.

"We were told by the school board that you'd be willin' to help with chores around here like cookin' and cleanin'," William said in a boyishly innocent voice. "After your bookwork is done, of course."

"I'm happy to help with whatever I can," Mary answered genuinely. "When grading, lesson plans, and other schoolwork is completed, I'll be available to help in many ways, including caring for your children."

"Too bad you can't meet them—Gladys, Lois, and Gordon," William said with a frown. "Not that you'd know, but we are expectin' another baby early next year."

"I'm confident the children will be a delight. Don't disturb them on my account. We'll have plenty of time to get to know each other."

"We plan to have all three kids in the smaller room down here, and the new baby will be in a cradle in our room," William explained, pointing out the rooms in question. "We'll respect your privacy best we can."

"I'm sure it will be fine," Mary replied as she smiled sweetly. "My things won't take up much room. My father will accompany me when I arrive the last Saturday of September, and then he'll return to Mankato. I'll be happy to cook and clean here. I help my parents with those things now."

"Is there anything we can do to prepare for you, Mary?" Maud asked, trying to be a bit more polite. "I hope the room upstairs will work."

"I'd like to do my laundry on Saturdays. Otherwise, I think we can manage. As I said, I'll help with things in the house and the kids as time allows. I should really be going now, though. My driver has been waiting patiently, but I told him I wouldn't be too long. After I move in, I'll look forward to seeing more of the property and meeting the children. I'll have much more time then."

"They'll be likin' you a lot, Mary," William assured her. "I can just tell."

"Well, I really must be going." She stepped toward the door. "I need to sign my contract with Mr. Otto before I go back to Morgan to catch the train."

The three moved outside, and the driver escorted Mary up the buggy step to her seat as the summer sun blazed down on the black surrey.

"I'm lookin' forward to havin' you back, Mary," William called from the side of the buggy.

"Thank you for your kindness," Mary replied with a sensual smile, staring directly at William and ignoring Maud.

The buggy slowly pulled away. As it moved down the driveway and onto the road, small dust clouds formed in its wake.

The black crows in the old cottonwood cawed loudly as they stirred in their nest.

"What on earth was all that!" Maud shrieked as soon at the buggy reached the connecting road, nearly a third of a mile away. "How humiliating!"

"What in tarnation are you talkin' about, Maud?" William snapped. "I was just bein' nice."

"You were eyein' her up and down like a one-pound porterhouse steak, William Kleeman!" Maud yelled back. "And she was lookin' at you the same way!"

The two refrained from reentering the house, so as not to wake up the napping children.

"What was I supposed to do—ignore her, be rude? Maybe I'll just have you talk to her, and I'll run the other way when she shows up!"

"You agreed to her comin' without even so much as talkin' to me, so it doesn't really matter. Did you meet her first? To see if she's got the looks of a show girl?"

"I never saw her until today!" William hollered. "Ain't never seen her once!"

"We will discuss this at another time," Maud said, calming suddenly. "I want to check on the children." She spun around, marched into the house, and slammed the porch door behind her.

"Why is she in such a bad mood, Duke?" William asked his faithful dog as Duke sniffed around the area that the buggy had been parked. "She ain't had her monthly three times in a row, so there ain't no blamin' that."

Duke whimpered and looked up at William with his ears raised, as if to sympathize.

CHAPTER 32

THE BOARDER TAKES UP RESIDENCE

THE HOT SUMMER WEATHER DISSIPATED as August and September melted away. William worked with Carl Otto to get his grain shocked and threshed, and in return, he helped Carl and his other neighbors with their farmwork. William's younger brother Fred came to help for a day when the tractor and threshing machine were at the Kleeman farm. But because he was also a hired man at a farm near Gilfillan Station, he couldn't help longer than that. John Streeter came to help for two days, getting dispensation from his father to help William when the threshing rig came to the Kleeman farm.

By the end of the September, William and Maud had negotiated how he would behave around Mary and what types of chores would be expected of their new boarder. Maud also had William screw crude hooks into the living room ceiling so an old bedsheet could be attached when baths were taken in front of the fireplace, thus giving privacy to the bather and creating less anxiety for other members of the household.

On a sunny Saturday afternoon, a large black Packard sedan pulled into the Kleeman yard. It was Mary Snelling, driven by her father, Jacob Snelling, from Mankato.

"Looks like our new boarder is riding here in style," Maud said as she pulled back the curtain and observed the large luxury automobile sitting in the yard. "What kind of car is *that*?"

William stood next to her shoulder and peered out. "Looks like one of them Cadillacs or Packards," he said in wonderment. "Pretty high end. One bought by the high muckety-mucks."

Maud and William exited the house and greeted the Snellings.

"Hello there," William called. "Welcome."

"I'm Jacob Snelling, Mary's father," said a tall, thin man with a moustache and sharp clothes. "Pleased to meet you."

He opened the back seat to reveal a variety of clothing, shoes, and personal effects that engulfed the entire compartment.

"These are just some of the items she brought for starters," he said with a grin. "She has more that will be sent to Morgan by rail next week."

"What is all this?" William asked in astonishment. "Looks like you got a dress for darn near every day of the week."

"Actually, I do, William," Mary said as she came around the side of the car. "I'll make room for them in that closet at the top of the steps."

William grabbed a suitcase as Mary's father held her dresses and moved toward the house, nodding to an apprehensive Maud as she waved from the front door. Maud had promised William she'd forget about the uncomfortable initial meeting with Mary.

"Come in, sir," Maud said to the man to whom she hadn't yet been introduced. "I just put on some coffee."

"I'm Mary's father, Jacob Snelling. Pleased to meet you. Sorry my wife couldn't make it."

Clara Snelling was older than her husband. She'd been married before, but lost her first husband when they lived in Wisconsin. Clara preferred not to travel in general and also periodically took ill, as was the case for this trip. So Jacob made the trip across two and a half counties on his own to deliver their daughter to her new teaching job.

Mary entered the house carrying a cloth bag of personal items and a few books. Her 1916 college yearbook from Mankato Normal School, the *Mankatoan*, slipped out of the bag and fell to the ground. William picked up the book and thumbed to her picture, next to which was printed: "Mary Snelling, Mankato. She thinks much good and speaks little ill of her neighbors." He grinned, thinking she'd fit right into their household.

Gladys and Lois darted outside to chase Duke into the grove, laughing and skipping all the way. They didn't stop to meet the new boarder.

"William can show you all upstairs," Maud said in a relaxed tone as everyone entered the kitchen. "We're very excited to have you here."

Mary was relieved to discover less tension than during her first visit. Since then, she'd been telling herself to be more understanding, to loosen up and realize the Kleemans weren't from a large city like Mankato. She was joining their household now, and she'd need to adjust to their ways.

"I'm so looking forward to getting started at school and getting settled in to your home. Please let me know how I can help. I'm planning to do my own laundry on Saturday mornings, since you tend to do laundry on Mondays."

Mary's dresses and other personal effects were stashed away in her room and closets. William and Maud had swept and wiped down the room so it was clean and presentable. They'd put fresh linens on the bed and removed everything from the large closet at the top of the steps.

"I'm afraid I need to ask where your outhouse is after that long ride," Jacob asked politely. "We stopped in Sleepy Eye on our way, but that feels like a long time ago."

"Sure, it's around back," William replied quickly. "I'll show you."

"I imagine I'll need to know where that is eventually too," Mary said with a wink.

Smiling, William and Maud led Mary and Jacob outside. The group made a sharp right and walked about fifteen yards to find a small, white building with wooden shingles and a loose-fitting door.

"Thank you," Jacob said with a nod as he strode to the outhouse. "I'll be right back in the house for that coffee."

Maud and William followed Mary back to the large car and retrieved the rest of her belongings—more books, another bag of personal effects, an extra pair of shoes, and a work smock.

After carrying the last load to her room, they went to the kitchen settled in for a visit.

"Gordon is taking a nap, and the girls are outside playin'," William said as he poured a cup of coffee for Mary. "I'll get them right quick."

Jacob came inside and sat down with a glum look on his face. "I'll miss you, Mary," he said as Maud poured his coffee. "The house will be a little empty."

"Well, I'm not a little girl anymore, Father. And you still have Esther at home," Mary answered, referring to her younger sister.

"It's just not the same. But it's time for you to make your way in the world, I guess."

"She'll be just fine," Maud reassured him. "We'll take good care of her."

"That's right," William added. "We'll make sure she gets everything she needs, and the schoolhouse is just across the road."

"Yes, we actually stopped and looked around before we came here," Jacob responded. "We dropped off some books, tablets, and pencils to save time later."

Gladys and Lois ran into the kitchen as Jacob was speaking and were stopped by Maud.

"Gladys. Lois. This is Miss Mary Snelling," she explained, kneeling down to face the girls. "She is the nice woman who's going to live with us. Remember, we've been telling you about her."

"Hello, Miss Mary," they said sweetly in unison.

"Pleased to meet ya," Gladys continued.

"You are just darling," Mary said as she bent down to their level. "I'm a teacher, and I *love* children. We're going to do some reading and storytelling sometimes, so when you get to school, you'll be the smartest children in the bunch."

"We'd love that," Gladys replied with a smile. "Momma's taught us some letters and numbers."

"Not as much as you should know," Maud interjected. "Miss Mary here knows much more than I do."

Mary blushed as a baby started crying in the smaller main-floor bedroom. Little Gordon's nap was over.

"I'll get him," Maud said as she turned to exit. "Gordon will be excited to meet you."

She returned moments later with a clingy eighteen-month-old who was rubbing sleep from his eyes. He had noticeably blue eyes, much like his father and mother. His neatly trimmed hair had a cowlick on the right side.

"This is Gordon," Maud introduced. "He'll be two in March."

"What a handsome young man you are," Mary said as she pinched his cheek. "We'll have a lot of fun together."

Gladys and Lois started tickling their little brother, prompting the sleepy toddler to smile broadly.

Jacob pulled out his gold pocket watch and clicked open the protective case. "I don't like to drive in the dark. If I leave now, I might make it," Jacob said as he finished the last of his coffee. "I'm glad to meet you. I think Mary will have a wonderful time here."

"We do too," William responded with a smile as Jacob snapped shut the watchcase. "We'll make sure she stays out of trouble."

The group moved outside and stood near the massive car, where Duke was sniffing the tires.

"Mighty fine automobile, Mr. Snelling," William said, looking over the car and shooing Duke away. "Must be top of the line."

"I bought it used from one of the bankers in Mankato and got a good deal on it," he replied, somewhat embarrassed at the large size and modern styling. "I'd never buy a car like this brand new."

"Does it have one of those starting motors on it, so you don't have to crank it? I've never seen a car with a starter."

"Why, yes, it does. If you have a good battery, you're all set."

As the Kleemans backed away to give them a bit of privacy, Jacob gave Mary a hug and bid her farewell. Jacob mounted the car, and for the first time, William and Maud saw a car start without a crank. Jacob pressed a large button on the floor, and it started right up.

"I'll be dang'd," William said, amazed at the new technology. "No needin' to crank-start a car!"

Jacob tooted the horn and swung around the yard, making sure to avoid Duke and the children, who were now chasing each other near the barn. He waved good-bye to his daughter, confident that she was in good hands.

The family of crows who nested in the large cottonwood tree watched intently as Jacob left, cackling as he turned onto the road.

CHAPTER 33

SCHOOL STARTS

WILLIAM, MAUD, AND THE CHILDREN made Mary feel welcome, and everything was organized as needed to make her stay comfortable. Monday would be a big day: the start of the 1916/17 term at the Sunrise Schoolhouse.

Mary spent a good chunk of Sunday afternoon and evening preparing her books and lesson plans. She liked to be organized, and she wanted to make sure her record book was meticulous for anyone who wished to check it later. In reviewing the previous years' records, she was astounded at the inconsistent attendance of the students. One student had attended just twenty days of school, whereas the record for best attendance was tied between Ardelia Ewald and Lewis Meeks at one hundred fifty-six days. While she knew it would be difficult for some parents to understand, Mary wanted to stress attendance to improve literacy. Attendance was often spotty, especially for older boys, since it was common for parents to feel more formal education was unnecessary once the students could read, write, and figure.

As part of her teaching contract, Mary had agreed to a pay stipend of five hundred twenty dollars for the year. The contract required her to keep accurate records and teach the children a curriculum as directed by the school board. She was also bound by a "moral turpitude" clause that she stated she wouldn't behave in an immoral fashion in or out of school, that she'd use appropriate language, and that she'd refrain from the consumption of alcohol and abstain from tobacco. In addition, she was responsible for keeping the schoolhouse fire lit as needed, with wood provided in a pile next to the building. Various chores could be assigned to the students—such as sweeping, pounding chalk dust from the erasers, and general cleaning.

Butterflies filled her stomach as she walked down the driveway alone and turned right to face west directly toward the Sunrise Schoolhouse. On Monday, October 2, 1916, the weather was chilly. In this rural area, schools often started later and continued into June, since many children were needed at home during harvest and plowing. They helped pick corn, among other vital chores, through September.

"My name is Miss Snelling, and I'll be your teacher this year," she started out sweetly to the thirty-three students who crammed into the one-room schoolhouse. "I'll go through the roster of names, and I'd like you to raise your hand when called upon."

Mary had organized her attendance record by last name, clustering families together, starting with the five Blake children and ending with Frieda Zamzow. Every child in her school lived on a farm. Though she was a "town kid," as her students frequently reminded her, Mary grew to respect the walking distance many traveled and came to understand the need for families to have older children home for farmwork.

The students ranged in ages from six years old all the way to fourteen. Many were siblings, and everyone was a neighbor of some sort. Mary felt it would be easier if the older children helped the younger students with their work and then phased into their assignments, which helped her maintain some order.

Mary liked to get to school by eight o'clock each morning. On cold days, the extra time allowed her to prepare a fire in the cast-iron stove that sat in the corner. She could also finish preparing lessons for the children. Every day, she rang the large bell five minutes before the nine o'clock start time. Most children had to help their parents with farm and household chores in the morning before school, so Mary had grown accustomed to the smells of cows, pigs, chickens, and sweat when the schoolhouse filled up with her students. Because most rural farm families kept a routine of taking weekly baths on Saturday in preparation for Sunday church, the children were ripe for bathing by the end of each week. Friday was an especially challenging day of mixed aromas in the schoolhouse air. When the outside temperature allowed, she would open all the windows to allow fresh air to pass through and carry out the smells.

Without a car or a team of horses at her disposal, Mary didn't get to Mankato to visit her folks very much. She became dependent on the Kleemans or friendly neighbors to get her to Clements to ride the train home, although the two-mile walk wasn't impossible to accomplish. Her return trips home became infrequent.

As for her part at the Kleeman household, Mary was immensely helpful with the children, even helping change Gordon's diapers. She brought in firewood, warmed water for baths, and read to the children almost every night. She had a series of picture books that amazed the children. The books had many colorful illustrations and large-type print, so it was easy for Gladys and Lois to see and help read along. When mealtime preparations were needed, Mary often helped peel potatoes, prepare the vegetables and meat, pump water, and bake bread. Her cheerful demeanor and helpful attitude were a positive addition to the Kleeman household. She not only endeared herself to Maud, who was only too grateful for an extra pair of helping hands, but also to the children.

While Mary did take baths twice a week instead of just on Saturday like the Kleemans, the system of rigging up the bedsheet in front of the tub with the utilitarian hooks dangling from the ceiling worked fairly well. Usually, William was given a signal from Maud that he should go to their bedroom and read when the metal bathtub was pulled in front of the fireplace on Tuesday evenings. Mary was extra careful to make sure the children were all sleeping and that Maud was comfortable with William being exiled to their private room, not to be allowed out until he was told it was clear to do so.

Mary was often occupied at the schoolhouse after school hours with reading, grading, and the other teaching responsibilities. Between her school obligations and the duties at the Kleemans' to earn her room and board, there was little time for making new friends and socializing.

The family and their boarder settled into a routine after a few weeks, and mutual respect was earned as time went on. Periodically, William would peer up the stairs and catch an occasional glimpse of the attractive boarder as she changed clothes in her room with the door slightly ajar. But he kept his curiosities in check, mostly because a vigilant Maud kept a strict eye on her handsome husband.

William did find Mary to be something of a wonder. Her patience with the children contrasted somewhat with Maud, whose frequent pregnancies only added to the irritability caused by the stress of child-rearing and heavy household work. Mary was young and slim—unblemished by childbearing and the physical and emotional pressures of motherhood. Her sweetness and charm were genuine, not intentionally flirtatious as he'd believed when they first met. The uneasy mental peace Maud had made early on about the potential temptations between William and Mary gave way to more confidence. After weeks of successfully sharing the same space, the probationary period of distrust ended.

CHAPTER 34

BREAKING THE
MORAL TURPITUDE CLAUSE

Periodically, Maud and the children would visit her parents near their new farm by Redwood Falls. The Petries thoroughly loved the long stays, with Clara cooking and entertaining the brood of grandchildren and Henry spoiling them with stories and candy. Frank always made sure he'd purchased extra peppermint drops at the general store in Rowena when he heard the Petries' grandchildren were coming to visit. The visits provided a welcome respite for Maud, who needed an occasional reprieve from responsibility that Mary or William couldn't provide at home.

The children weren't old enough for school, which meant William could deliver Maud and the children to the Petrie farm on a Friday. They could stay the weekend, attend Church of the Holy

Communion in Redwood Falls on Sunday, and then be retrieved by William. He'd join them for a dinner prepared by Clara and then drive his family home. The periodic long stays had ended with Mary's arrival in late September, but Maud grew comfortable that there was enough household trust to plan a weekend visit to the farm near Redwood Falls sometime between Thanksgiving and Christmas.

Steadfastly continuing his resistance to attending church, William always had an excuse for why he couldn't accompany Maud and the children: the livestock needed to be tended, especially milking that had to be done twice a day; he wasn't feeling well; he had field work to do; or another of the apparently endless stream of other objections. With the moral guardian of the house gone for the first time in months, William decided it would be fun to spend a little time with his old chums at the saloon in Morgan.

"Ring me the Arthur Davis residence by Redwood Falls, please," William said to the switchboard operator anxiously that Saturday morning. The telephone buzzed as he waited.

"Hello, Davis residence," Arthur's mother answered.

"Hello, Mrs. Davis. This is William Kleeman. Is young Art around?" Since Arthur was named for his father, William always made sure to be clear about which man he meant when he called over to their farm.

"Yes, Willie," she said quickly. "Let me get him."

Moments later, his old friend was on the line. "Willie, how are ya?"

"Fine, Art, fine. I guess you're still bach'n it at home," William teased.

"Yep. Seems easier." Arthur, who was several years younger than William, had still not married, although he had come close several times. "What's on your mind?"

"Art, Maud and the kids are at her folks' place. Wonderin' if you'd like to meet up at the saloon in Morgan tonight," William said in a hushed voice, hoping Mary wouldn't overhear from upstairs. "We could get some beers with Forest and catch up on things. Maybe play some poker."

"Me and Forest were already gettin' together, Willie. We were going to do chores early and meet at six o'clock to have a little supper. Why don't you meet us there?"

"I can buy the first round of Schell's," William offered. "I know you'll want more than one."

"We'll take you up on that, Willie. See you at six."

William put down the telephone's earpiece and looked at his watch. Perfect timing. He had just enough time to do the milking and the few other chores that needed doing before he left. Since the bar always smelled heavily of tobacco smoke, he thought it might be best to take his bath after he returned home or in the morning. Maud and the kids were gone anyway.

The weather was chilly, but the Model T was still running fine, so that simplified the six-mile trip into Morgan. William thought he could get by with using the car until the first major snowfall, then park it over winter in the shed. They'd have to use the team of horses and sleigh to get around the rest of the season.

"I'm goin' to town for a while, Mary!" William called upstairs after he'd scurried to do the chores. "Not sure when I'll get home!"

"Have fun!" Mary yelled from her small desk on the second floor, where she was working on lesson plans for the next week.

Before he left, William changed into his town clothes and put some large chunks of firewood into the hearth and stirred the red-hot ashes. He knew it was getting chilly in the house at night. He added extra pieces of kindling to the living room stash from the woodpile along the side of the house to make sure Mary had easy access without going outside.

William cranked up the Ford, settled himself in with three lap blankets to stay warm, and started down the driveway. The sun had already set, so there was a considerable bite of cold in the air, and he needed the headlights to navigate the country roads.

As William turned onto Main Street in Morgan, many cars and teams of horses were lining the sides of the boulevard. William looked for a place to park and found one in the extra-wide middle of the street. Morgan was well known for allowing cars and teams to park not only along the sidewalks but also in both directions along the middle of the street. He made it into the saloon, where the piano was playing and laughter was loud. The place was crowded, smoky, and smelled of sweat. Two familiar faces grinned as he pushed his way to the back of the saloon.

"Willie!" his old friend Arthur called out. "How's our married man?"

"He's thirsty for beer," William said as he plopped in his chair and waved to the waitress for a round of Schell's for the threesome. "Smart of you two to be sittin' right by the stove to stay warm."

"How's that young schoolteacher workin' out for ya?" Forest asked with a smirk. "She's a mighty fine-lookin' woman."

"She helps around the house a lot," William answered, trying to be serious. "It's a treat to have her."

"I *bet* it is. Last time I saw her, I was thinkin' she was a treat too."

"You ain't kiddin'," Forest chimed in. "I caught a look at her when we were at your place helpin' with the cattle that one Friday in October. She's a looker. Maybe you could get us acquainted sometime?"

The waitress delivered their beers. "What do you boys want to eat? You look hungry. Man cannot live by beer alone."

"I'd like a bowl of soup and that ham sandwich," Arthur said as he looked up at the menu board. "That's it."

"Give me that there pork chop and beans," Forest added with a broad smile. "And let me know where you might live."

The waitress frowned. "You ain't gonna know where I live if you're the last man on earth."

The three laughed heartily, and Arthur punched Forest in the arm. Their lack of maturity didn't impress the waitress.

"What would you like, good-lookin'? I could tell *you* where I live if you want."

"Bowl of soup and a pork chop," William said with a reddened face. "I ain't needin' to know where you live."

"He's got two women at home already," Forest said, laughing. "Three might be too many."

The waitress winked at William and walked away to the kitchen, which was billowing with smoke.

William looked straight at Forest. "Shut yer mouth," he said quietly, looking around the room. "People might hear you."

The three finished their first beers quickly and ordered a second round, which was paid for by Forest.

"Hope you boys came out OK with your crops this fall," William said as he straightened up in his chair. "We had a big yield on oats and corn. I think we might be rentin' more land next year."

"We did OK, Mr. Big Shot. Ain't got the nice land you got, though."

"You boys want to play some cards tonight?" Forest asked as he lit up a cigar. "I got a pocketful of pennies and a lucky streak that feels like it's comin' on strong."

He produced a deck of cards and dropped some coins on the table. William went to the bartender and got some change from a silver dollar, enough to last a while, although he didn't think he'd go through all his pennies.

"I'll give you a dime for ten of those," Arthur grinned as William sat back down. "I'm too lazy to get off this here stool."

William counted out ten pennies and pushed them over to Arthur as he slid his dime back to his own side of the table.

"I ain't played poker for a *long* time," William said as he slid down to get comfortable in his chair. "You boys had better be easy on me."

They ordered another round of beers and received their food as the first hand ended, with Forest winning rather quickly.

"All you do is play cards," Arthur scolded him. "Some of us got young'ns and gotta work for a livin'."

"Ain't no need to work when I can make money off dummies like you," Forest bragged loudly.

The men ate their meals and took a hiatus from card playing, joking and laughing about their time at dances, working as hired men together, and catching up on the local gossip.

"We gotta enjoy this here beer while we can, boys," Forest said with a belch. "Those drys are gonna make this stuff illegal yet."

As meals were finished, another round of beers was bought, and now that each had paid for a round, it was Dutch treat. Language started slurring, and voices grew louder. Each man had made at least one trip to the outhouse by now. They dared each other to bet more on their poker hands, until there was no money left on Arthur Davis's part. He had cashed in over two dollars on the games, betting more and more each round.

"Dang it, Forest!" Arthur yelled. "I ain't got any money left after you done cleaned me out!"

"We can end the night with one last round, paid for by Forest," William said, punctuating his pronouncement with a belch. "You'd be payin' with *our* money anyway!"

"I'll buy a round with your money," Forest bragged, crushing his third cigar into the old metal ashtray. "Glad you picked me up tonight, Art. I'm gonna be sleepin' on the way home, not drivin'."

"You'd better be stayin' awake to help me stay awake," Art responded with a yawn. "It's been a long day."

William pulled out his pocket watch. It was almost ten o'clock. It would be a long six miles home. "It's been fun, boys, but I gotta get home. Night ain't gettin' any younger. Now I don't want you tellin' any of this to Maud about us drinkin' and gamblin' tonight, ya hear?"

The men nodded and grinned. They parted ways after agreeing they needed to get together more often. William knew his two buddies would be staying at least another hour or more at the saloon, but it was time for him to go home.

He staggered slightly as he moved down the wooden sidewalk and into the street to his parked Ford. He could see the fog of his breath as he panted. The cars that had been parked in front of his Model T had left hours ago, and he had a straight shot to drive forward.

"Glad I ain't gotta back that car up," he said under his breath. "At least all that beer makes it feel warmer out here."

He set the car's throttle and turned on the ignition. Bending over in front of the car, William cranked the car once, and the metal crank kicked back, striking him on the arm.

"Damn it!" he yelled as he rubbed his right arm. "I forgot to set the spark lever."

The Model T required that the spark lever be set to RETARD before starting or it would kick back on the driver, sometimes so hard it would break an arm. William trudged to the steering column and moved the spark lever off ADVANCE and to RETARD. Returning to the front while rubbing his arm gently, he cranked the car one time, and it roared to life. He climbed in and slowly pulled out. When he reached the edge of Morgan, he finally felt comfortable enough to put the car in road gear to drive faster and get home.

Home never sounded more inviting. The car ride from Morgan was cold, and he stopped once along the way to urinate out one of his many beers. As he pulled into the driveway, he could see candlelight in the living room. He parked the car in the shed and staggered into the house. Duke raced out of the door as soon as William unlatched it. William wasn't the only one who had to urinate that evening.

The house felt especially warm as he entered. He heard the Victrola playing a familiar waltz through its large horn speaker. Someone must have just cranked it because it only played records for a few minutes before it finished. As he rounded the kitchen and faced the living room, he saw the curve of a bare shoulder above the edge of the metal bathtub, which was pulled in front of the roaring fireplace. This time, there was no bedsheet hanging from the hooks he'd placed in the ceiling.

CHAPTER 35

SUNDAY BECKONS

Sᴜɴᴅᴀʏ ᴍᴏʀɴɪɴɢ ᴄᴀᴍᴇ ᴡɪᴛʜ ᴛʜᴇ ᴄʀᴏᴡ ᴏꜰ ᴀ ʀᴏᴏsᴛᴇʀ as the sun lit up the Minnesota sky. William knew that the previous night had been filled with a number of vices that would best be forgotten, and all related parties agreed that secrecy would be the best way to move forward. He dressed and went about his routine to get the morning chores done, starting with milking. In keeping with their prior arrangement, he'd meet Maud and the children at the Petries' for Sunday dinner around noon.

Once the rest of his morning tasks were done, William took a gas can and topped off his Model T for the drive over toward Redwood Falls. Upon entering the house again, he realized his best clothes lay on the living room floor from the night before, and they reeked of tobacco smoke and beer.

"I've got the choice of smellin' like smoke and beer or cow manure," he muttered to himself as he stood in the kitchen in wonder.

"I guess I got one other outfit to put on." William didn't think Maud would mind if he wore a work shirt and pants, even though they were terribly tattered. Better than an incriminating set of clothes infused with the distinctive aroma of a saloon or dirty work clothes that stank of manure.

Mary had retreated upstairs.

"I'm leaving for the Petries'!" William hollered up the steps. "We'll be comin' back before chores this afternoon."

There was no answer in return.

William threw a few pieces of small kindling on the fireplace and grabbed his long coat and hat for the drive to the Petries'. He cranked up the Model T and bid Duke farewell. The seven-mile drive offered a lot of time for thinking about what had transpired the night before.

As William pulled into the Petries' driveway, he saw Frank walking from the barn. Frank glared at him without a wave or a sound. It was almost as though he knew every detail of what had happened hours before. He wheeled into the yard and parked the car in front of the well pump, forcing Frank to acknowledge him.

"Top of the mornin', Mr. Schottenbauer," William said with a smile. "Chores goin' all right?"

"Just finishin' up." Frank pumped water into a large wooden pail and spun around to leave quickly.

William took off for the house, where Gladys came running off the porch to greet him. A nest of black crows fussed and cawed in the oak tree next to the house.

"Daddy, Grandpa and Frank got us candy!" Gladys bragged. "We get to take some home with us. Momma said."

"Can you share with me?" William asked teasingly as he stooped down to pick her up. "I love candy."

"Grandpa said we get candy only if we're good," she snapped back with a serious glare. "Have you been good, Daddy?"

William stared at her eyes as he held her. It would be a difficult lie to bear. The crows stirred in their branch-strewn nest and alternated in their loud cawing, as if to laugh at him.

"I'll leave the candy for you and Lois," William answered with an uneasy voice. "You girls deserve more candy than me."

He set Gladys down and took her hand. Together they entered the Petrie home, which was full of prancing children, the smell of good cooking, and lots of conversation.

"Daddy, I'm a horse rider!" Lois yelled as she rode atop Henry's shoulders. "Grandpa's name is Trigger!"

Maud looked through the kitchen to see her father playing with the girls. She was now visibly pregnant with their fourth child.

"William, we've got a great meal for you—steaks, fried potatoes, buttered sweet corn, and apple cider. Your favorites. We planned it especially for you."

Clara had Gordon in one arm and a large fork in the other, turning the steak in the frying pan. The baby smiled brightly as soon as he saw his father.

"Gordon wants Daddy?" Clara teased.

William took Gordon from Clara. The baby resisted at first, then cooed softly.

"William Kleeman!" Maud said through gritted teeth. "Why are you wearing those rags? It's Sunday dinner."

"Sorry, Maud," William answered, flushing with embarrassment and guilt. "My other clothes are dirty. These are the only clean ones I had."

"Your town clothes were dirty?" Maud replied with a frown. "Did you go to town last night?"

"We'll talk about it later, Maud." William stepped toward the stove again. "Clara Petrie, you are one good cook! Just smell that sweetness!" William winked at his mother-in-law, who stood aside and gave him a disgusted scowl. She'd overheard the conversation and thought he was likely up to no good.

"Henry, please call in Frank so we can eat soon," Clara said to her husband, who was still frolicking with his granddaughters in the living room.

Henry went to the front door, with Gladys and Lois in tow, to call in his hired man. Maud set the table. When the last cup was placed on the table, William walked toward the door as Frank entered the kitchen with Claude Petrie close behind.

Clara brought the food to the table as Maud settled the children in their chairs, and everyone but William found their chairs as well.

"Had too much coffee this mornin'," William said with a smirk. "Headin' to the outhouse."

As he always did, William found an excuse to step out just as the family was about to say grace.

As he entered the outhouse, William looked down and noticed a small hole about the size of a nickel. Next to it, a large, dry snake-skin had been shed as the animal tore it off going down into the hole for hibernation. The skin must have been lying there for weeks or more. William crushed it with his boot. The crows cackled loudly once again as he slammed the door shut behind him.

CHAPTER 36

MARY TAKES ILL

As THE WINTER CONTINUED AND THE CALENDAR TURNED to 1917, Minnesota was unseasonably warm. Unlike typical winters, they didn't see piles of snow and frigid cold. Dr. Adams from Morgan was summoned by telephone to the Kleeman household on Wednesday, February 7, when Maud's water broke. He roared out to the farmhouse in his Cadillac, one of the fastest cars of the time. Knowing that Maud was close to the birth, Clara Petrie had been staying with her daughter to assist with the delivery. William and Maud's fourth child, Rosadell, was born that day, with both mother and baby handling the occasion well.

Over the winter, William and Maud decided they would continue to rent the farm, but they wouldn't expand into renting additional soil. They had enough work and now another child to fuss over. The extra rent payments from the school board were helpful, as was the help Mary Snelling provided with the cooking, cleaning, and child-rearing. That help was needed now more than ever.

March arrived with gentle weather, not the bitter cold and heavy snow that usually pounded the area in late winter.

One Friday morning in the third week of March, Mary politely thanked Maud. "I appreciate your help with my lunch again. I'm going to leave for the schoolhouse a little early today."

Maud helped prepare a lunch for Mary—pieces of leftover chicken and homemade bread. Some applesauce that had been stored down in the root cellar rounded out the meal. Mary almost always drew water from the school pump to drink with her lunch.

As was usual on Fridays, the schoolhouse was somewhat ripe with the mixed aromas of the farm children. The odor seemed particularly overwhelming to Mary that day.

The morning school routine went on as usual. Mary soon started to feel light-headed, and she sat at her desk more than she stood. Her stomach rolled, and she started to sweat profusely.

"I think we'll have an extended lunch today," she announced to the children as she stood, spying the time on the oak school clock that hung on the south wall. "It's Friday, after all—and you've all done so well with your lessons this week that you deserve a longer recess."

The children chattered with excitement at the rare treat, and with a ring of the small brass bell that sat on top of her desk, they darted outside to play.

Mary sat back down quickly and sighed. She opened her wicker lunch basket, revealing the chicken, surrounded by the baked bread and jarred applesauce. She slowly consumed the meal, having a difficult time swallowing and keeping the food down. Out of courtesy to Maud, Mary felt obligated to eat the entire meal. After several minutes, she was forced to grab the metal trash can and vomit, being careful not to spill on the wooden schoolhouse floor.

Her lunch wasn't large or exotic, but she felt sick in a way she'd never felt before. She put her head down and knew that the rest of the school day would be too difficult to bear.

Mary glanced at the clock, which showed twelve forty-five. Recess was more than fifteen minutes longer than normal, and the children streamed back into Sunrise Schoolhouse from their game. The wretched smell of vomit was wafting across the room.

"Are you OK, Miss Snelling?" asked eight-year-old Joseph Blake. "You don't look so good."

"You are correct, Joseph, I'm not feeling well, and I don't wish for any of you to catch it. We are going to end school a bit early today, after spelling."

Mary finished the spelling tests for each grade. Friday's usual routine was to give each grade level their spelling tests and to end the day with assignments that needed to be completed by the following Monday.

"You've earned no homework for the next two days," she announced to a grateful and bright-eyed group of students. "Be ready to work hard on Monday, though. Remember that school will dismiss early on Thursday, and there will be no school on Good Friday. Class is dismissed for this week. Have a lovely weekend."

Not knowing what Monday would bring—how could they?—the children cheered and exited quickly. The March sun had prematurely melted most of the snow and gave way for some outside playtime for a few students who lingered behind before starting home. Most students slogged back to their farms, where they would immediately be put back to work with various chores.

At the Sunrise Schoolhouse, sweeping the floor and erasing the chalkboard were always assigned to students, but her hasty dismissal left the tasks unfulfilled for this week.

The chores can wait until Monday, she decided, focused on getting the basics done and getting to a doctor.

She grabbed the trash can and exited to the hand pump that the children had just used for drinking. She pumped the massive handle to bring up fresh water from the well below to rinse out the smelly pail of vomit. She set the trash pail on the back step to allow it to air out over the weekend. Then she dragged herself to the outhouse to relieve herself, feeling even worse now that diarrhea had set in.

After finishing, Mary went back inside to pull the shades closed. She collected her lunch basket and grade book and then locked the schoolhouse and trudged toward home. The almost half-mile walk seemed longer than usual. Mary vomited again along the way, leaving chunks of chicken and bread on the side of the long farm driveway.

As she staggered up the yard, William spied her from the yard and quickly met her before she entered the house.

"What's the matter, Mary? Are you sick?"

"William, I've thrown up three times in the last hour. I dismissed school early. Can you hitch up the team and take me to Dr. Adams? I feel as if it won't stop."

"Sure thing. Let me tell Maud that we're goin' to Morgan. We'll go right now."

William stuck his head in the open porch door and informed Maud that Mary needed Dr. Adams, and they'd likely be back before sunset. Then he hitched his new team of black horses, Luci and Diablo, to the buggy and helped Mary up into the seat.

The bouncing of the buggy made Mary even more uncomfortable as they made the trek to Morgan. After two miles of trying to contain herself, she asked William to pull the rig over so she could vomit again. After that, she simply had a massive headache and dry mouth.

"Hang in there, Mary," William soothed as they whisked down the dirt road, straight east to Morgan.

"I've never felt sick like this before. Food isn't agreeing with me. I've been throwing up violently, and I'm dizzy and sweaty. I'm never sick, William, never."

William was no doctor. He couldn't think of what it might be. Maud would get sick periodically, but maybe only four times since they got married. The Kleeman household was a hearty bunch. Perhaps the chicken Maud packed in Mary's lunch had gone off?

The buggy rumbled to a halt at Dr. Adams's office. William helped Mary down from the buggy and escorted her into the waiting area. Dr. J. L. Adams was a respected solo physician whose office was located on Main Street in Morgan. As Mary and William entered the front door, he greeted them from his desk.

"Hello, Mr. Kleeman. I hope that new baby is doing well," he said politely. "Your wife rang me on the telephone and said your boarder has taken ill."

"This is Miss Mary Snelling, Doc. She's been throwing up for the last half day," William answered. "Can you help?"

"Well, since Miss Snelling is the patient, Mr. Kleeman, you can wait in the saloon for about a half hour. I'll take care of Miss Snelling."

William nodded to Dr. Adams and told Mary he'd return in a half hour. He glanced at the ornate wall clock with its swinging brass pendulum to check the time as the doctor escorted Mary to the exam room in the rear of the office.

He backed out through the door and headed down the block to the Morgan Saloon, where he knew many of the patrons.

"Well, how do you do?" asked the waitress in a sultry voice through the tobacco smoke. "How's the most handsome man in Redwood County, and what's he drinkin'?"

"The usual," William said with a wink.

He joined a card game and started carrying on with the locals he'd grown up with. In many ways, Morgan felt more like home than Clements. August and Minnie Kleeman lived near Gilfillan Station, which was closer to the more established Morgan than the newly formed hamlet of Clements, which had been platted barely seventeen years before.

As William swilled his Schell's, a large white curtain was abruptly pulled back at the office of Dr. Adams, revealing a solemn-faced physician with news that made Mary grimace. He assured her that professionalism and courtesy would always dictate that medical determinations were kept strictly confidential, especially in small towns like Morgan.

Just then, he was interrupted by the telephone, which jangled with a familiar spurt of rings that usually meant he was being summoned to something urgent. He excused himself to take the call, and Mary took a few deep breaths before moving to the waiting area.

William had finished his two beers and looked at his pocket watch. It had been more than thirty minutes. He thought it'd be best to bring the team to the front door of the doctor's office. He dropped two dimes on the bar and bid farewell to his card-playing friends. After a quick wink to the barmaid, he hopped up on the buggy to get Mary from Dr. Adams.

She was sitting alone in the waiting area of the doctor's office. She looked out the enormous plate-glass window, peering around the large lettering of DR. J. L. ADAMS, MD that was stenciled in gold paint across the pane of glass. She spotted Luci and Diablo pulling William's buggy and hurried out the door.

"Please send me a bill, and I shall make sure you're paid," she called out to Dr. Adams as she exited.

The drive back to the farm seemed like an eternity for Mary. William tried to make small talk, inquiring carefully first about her health and then about the school.

Mary offered few facts about her medical case, other than she was ill and needed to watch what she ate. The buggy bounced down the road and returned to the Kleeman farm in time for William to get the cows milked and the livestock fed. Duke barked a greeting and trotted around the yard to bid them welcome upon their return.

"I'd like to visit my parents in Mankato tomorrow," Mary announced during supper as she pushed her food around her plate instead of eating. "It will only be for about a day, but I want to see them."

Maud thought it was unusual for Mary to go home this weekend when Easter was just the following week. Surely she'd leave to spend the holiday with her family in Mankato then. School was never held on Good Friday, and she could leave by train Thursday afternoon, especially in light of the planned early dismissal.

"William can take you to the depot tomorrow morning. You'll be leaving via Clements, won't you, Mary?"

Mary nodded. She helped gather up the children for reading and play in her usual fashion as Maud cleared the table and tended to dishes. William picked up the newspaper and struggled to read the tiny print by lantern in his rocking chair. He squinted over articles about Germany attacking ships and the weekly obituaries. Duke was allowed inside to sit by the fireplace and keep warm. Maud had fashioned some rags into a nest for Duke to lie on to make the floor more comfortable. William stroked the dog's long black coat as he finished reading the paper. By this time, the baby was asleep, and the other three children were going to bed.

Keeping with his usual routine, William said good night to the older children who had climbed into the trundle bed in the smaller bedroom. Mary retired to her lonely room upstairs. Maud finally sat down, exhausted from churning butter and tending to the children all day.

"What's wrong with Mary?" she whispered to William. "What did the doctor say?"

"He didn't say nothing. Just that she needs to watch what she's eatin' and that she's just ill."

Mary lay motionless on her narrow bed. The outward signs of her sickness had passed. Though she supposed she hadn't eaten enough supper to vomit it out again. Various thoughts raced through her mind as she tossed and turned on the small bed.

The clock ticked louder than usual for Mary Snelling on the night of March 22, 1917. She was sleepless and aware of every small change of the bright moonlight spilling through her window and illuminating her pillow.

What on earth am I going to do? she asked herself frequently through the night.

A barn owl gently hooted in the moonlit tree outside her room. It was her only company for the night.

CHAPTER 37

TILL DEATH DO US PART

WILLIAM'S EARLY BREAKFAST CONSISTED OF a couple of fried eggs from the Kleeman flock, along with bacon. William always liked his bacon sloppy, subjecting the rest of the family and guests to eat it the same way.

"No bacon, please," Mary said, rebuffing Maud's attempts to give her more food. "I need to watch what I eat, and the grease may not agree with me today."

"Good morning, everyone," William cheerfully sang as he entered the house from morning chores. He looked as striking this morning as ever.

Maud fed the two youngest children while William prepared to get Mary off to the train station in Clements that morning. He snatched up her small overnight bag when she set it down momentarily to take a cold drink of cistern water before their trip. He brought the bag down to the waiting buggy and let the women know the rig was ready. Mary set the tin cup down on the cupboard and stepped outside.

"I'll be back right quick, Maud," he teased with a grin. "Might take a little longer if Miss Snelling still feels a tad sick." He winked at Mary.

With his usual boyish chivalry, William assisted her into the buggy, snapped the reins, and whistled for his team of horses to pull down the driveway.

"You behave," he hollered back to Gladys and Lois as they played with a weathered leather kittenball in the cool March breeze.

By the time they reached the end of the half-mile driveway and pulled onto the dirt road, Mary worked up the nerve to discuss heavy matters with William.

"Whoa!" William yelled to the horses, pulling back on the reins with a forceful tug, stopping the buggy cold in its tracks.

She finished sharing her news and responded to his questions.

Eventually, William prompted the horses to get on their way again. The final two miles to the depot seemed to take an eternity. William and Mary both sat silently for most of the trip, with Luci and Diablo trotting at a steady pace to reach the morning train bound for Mankato. In Clements, William stopped a city block short of the depot, looking around to see if anyone saw them together.

"I want to avoid those cars and people," he quickly said. "Your overnight bag is in the back."

William skipped the usual chivalry and pleasantries with Mary when arriving. Mary grabbed her bag and let herself off the buggy, the first time she had to do so in years with any adult man. In a bit of a daze, William was awkward and fumbled over his words.

"You'll miss your train from Mankato tomorrow," William said, not making much sense. "You take care now."

"I'll see you tomorrow, William."

"Don't plan on me getting you tomorrow. The train on Sundays only runs to Morgan. Plan to rent a livery rig. I don't feel well." He struggled to look Mary in the eye. He gave her a quick nod and snapped the reins to pull the team away. Mary watched as William blankly stared ahead. He never turned to face her or wave good-bye.

A good beer was always refreshing, but the uncomfortable conversation he'd just had required a stop at the bar for reasons that extended well past refreshment. He decided to change his original plans to immediately return to the farm. Instead, he'd patronize the Clements tavern to spend some time pondering.

In a trance, he entered the saloon and was greeted with the usual piano music, talking, and card playing. Cigar and cigarette smoke plumed out of the doorway when William entered. Peanut shells lay strewn throughout the dirty floor. Brass spittoons sat next to each table and were lined up along the edge of the bar. The stench of sweaty farmers, spilled beer, and tobacco smoke permeated the air. Sentences in German were overhead from the back table of moustached card players. He recognized a familiar crew of regulars swilling beers across the room: Carl Otto, Joe Rothmeier, Matt Seifert, Nick Walter, and Adam Goblirsh, among others. William didn't acknowledge anyone in the place. Unlike usual, he kept to himself.

The familiar, small slot machine that took nickels—the kind the regulars called a one-armed bandit—stared at William from atop the bar as he entered. Maybe he could strike up some quick money by hitting the jackpot. He fumbled in his pocket and found two nickels. The buffalos that were struck into his coins were worn dull from age.

He put in the first and pulled the handle, only to be disappointed when a mixed group of fruits showed themselves on the machine window. He kissed the second nickel.

"Come on, baby. I need some luck," he whispered.

He pulled the handle swiftly. In less than ten seconds, he was disappointed again. Aghast at his strokes of bad luck, William ordered a beer. The barkeep's name was Robert Schmidt, but among the locals, he was known as Schmitty.

"Schell's, right?"

William gave Schmitty a quick nod.

He sat by himself next to the machine along the long mahogany bar. The stools were high and uncomfortable, especially today. Avoiding his usual social glad-handing, William finished the beer quickly and avoided any conversation, even though he knew many of the men in the tavern. He soon ordered another mug of beer.

"Better enjoy that beer while you can," Schmitty said in a sullen voice as he wiped off freshly washed beer mugs. "Word is, Congressman Volstead out of Granite Falls is going to outlaw every kind of drink known to man, including beer. Might be within a year or two that Congress passes it, and then this place will be shut down for good. So will the Schell's Brewery over in New Ulm and every saloon in these here United States."

"What in the hell is wrong with some people?" Out of all the stupid congressmen across the United States trying to outlaw alcohol, he thought, the most vocal representative had to live forty miles away.

"I'll bet we're fighting the Fatherland by the end of the year too," Schmitty said, on a roll and feeling indignant. "Wilson said he'd keep us out of war, but looks like if we get in, the whole world will be at war with each other."

Just like William, Schmitty and more than three-quarters of the patrons at the Clements saloon had German ancestry. War was already declared in Europe and much of the rest of the world. The German populations in Brown and Redwood Counties weren't big fans of the idea of fighting relatives who remained in Germany.

At age thirty-one, married, and with four children, it was unlikely that William Kleeman would have to go fight the Germans, and he was in no mood to visit about the politics of the day. As William tried to focus on his own problems, Schmitty talked about how Minnesota overall, and Redwood County in particular, had voted for Teddy Roosevelt in 1912—so it wasn't their fault Woodrow Wilson was now in the White House.

"Well, I've got a lot goin' on, Schmitty. Thanks for the beer. I donated two more nickels for you," William teased, pointing to the slot machine nearby. "I guess I'd better have one more. It'll have to be my last."

The beer was cold, and William swilled it as quickly as the first two. He rarely got inebriated from his beers, but then usually he stopped at two. The circumstances of the day called for one additional brew.

The other patrons whispered to each other, curious about why he didn't want to socialize. Usually, William was the first one to crack a joke, share a flirtatious smile with the barmaid, or join in a card game.

It was time to go home. He had run out of luck in more ways than one with his trip to Clements.

Through the tavern's plate-glass window, Reverend Abernathy had noticed William losing his nickels and swilling his beer. He accosted William on the wood sidewalk as he left.

"Mr. Kleeman. You know, we don't believe in gambling or drinking," the reverend said belligerently, feeling the same chill that had swirled around him during his visit to the Kleeman farm last year. "The Lord doesn't either."

"Then I'd recommend you not do it," William snapped as he pushed his way back to where the horses were tethered.

"I'm sure I won't be seeing you tomorrow morning!" the reverend called out prophetically.

William scurried to his buggy and looked around the bustling street. The village was busy—a train had just departed for the east and the bar was almost full of people on a Saturday morning. But he decided the twentieth century was passing him by, and he was still young, only thirty-one. The International dealer had a showy display of shiny new tractors and implements for farmers to buy and was advertising for a spring machinery demonstration that would be held in April, just in time for farmers to begin tilling and planting. William was one of the few men in the area who still didn't own any sort of tractor, as Carl Otto had not so subtly reminded him last season.

He also dwelled briefly on what Schmitty had predicted—alcohol outlawed, the whole world going to war with itself. Who would want to live in that world? Things were changing, and not for the better. The bigger war, and the bigger problem, would be with himself.

William unhooked the horses from the hitching post and climbed on top of his buggy. He ordered his team to pull north, toward home.

As he drove back to the farm, he couldn't stop thinking about his conversation with Mary, which created a deep and sinister darkness that completely overshadowed his soul. Circumstances were pressing against his conscience. He began to consider the unthinkable. It was an illogical, insane choice offered only by Lucifer himself. William hatched the complete scheme as he drove home.

As he pulled into his farm, the nest of black crows cried loudly from the big cottonwood tree.

William pretended nothing was wrong as he went about with his usual chores. He couldn't let on to Maud or the children that anything was out of sorts. He had difficulty eating his noon meal but forced himself to do so in order to shield his plot, which would be carried out that night.

"Did you get Mary dropped off at the train depot?" Maud asked casually as she cleaned off the table.

"She got dropped fine," William replied as he chewed on a piece of fresh bread. "She's probably most of the way to Mankato by now."

As in most rural households in 1917, Saturday was a time of cleaning and preparation in the Kleeman household. Maud and the children were sweeping floors and getting the weekly house chores finished. Maud baked bread from scratch every Saturday afternoon so it could be enjoyed on Sunday.

As they worked inside, William excused himself to go outside to finish his chores. The livestock would be fed and tended to as usual. Because Saturdays culminated in evening baths, it made sense to fork out cow manure from the barn into a stinky pile outside. Later the filth could be loaded into a manure spreader and cast upon the black fields for fertilizer when the dirt was dry enough. Clearing manure from the barn was an especially rancid job, so it was logically done Saturday afternoon so the smell could be washed off of him and cast out in bathwater later that evening—and from his clothing on Monday as Maud did the household laundry.

He played with Duke, the beloved dog he cared for as if it were one of his own children, as he finished up scooping manure. Luci and Diablo would get fed their ration of oats for the day, and the cattle would get their hay.

With six milk cows to tend to, William pulled out his small wooden milk stool and got to work. Milking was when he most regretted that he had no hired man and that his children were too young to do any real farmwork. He sighed and got about the routine of pulling on the teats of each cow until the udder was fully drained of milk. The buckets would have to be brought to the milk parlor, where fresh milk was strained of any straw or large particles and then poured to the top of a cream separator. The shiny aluminum tank captured the fresh milk and then, with the turning of a crank, would gravitate into the machine and divide the cream from the milk. Large steel cream cans and milk containers would hold the finished product until they could be brought to the creamery in Clements to be sold every few days. It was a routine he followed regularly since they'd moved to the farm.

After he finished the afternoon milking in the dairy barn, William retrieved the ax he'd used to chop the large woodpile next to the shed last fall. Since it was a milder than normal winter, the pile stood higher than usual and would last a long time. The enormous grove of trees on their farm site provided a mighty haul of fresh firewood, which was needed both in the fireplace and in the large potbellied stove that provided heat, served as their cookstove, and was used for heating water for clothes washing and bathing. There was a lot of wood left on the farm, even after the Kleemans' years here and the Nelsons before them. Holmer Johnson, the original homesteader on the property, had barely made a dent in the enormous grove, and he'd done a spectacular job of seeding trees in the bare and empty prairie for future generations to enjoy. The ax William was after had been dulled from the cutting required to build the woodpile, and it had suffered from neglect as it sat outside in the elements.

William was muscular and hardworking. However, the unceasing daily drudgery of farm chores was challenging for him. Since the farm had no running water, no electricity, and no modern tractor, he was relegated to doing a lot of work by hand, including chopping the wood. Unfortunately, farming on this particular plot hadn't advanced much from when Holmer Johnson had established the homestead decades ago.

As he stood by the massive woodpile, he saw the first snake of the year slithering along the edge. Indeed, the weather was unusually warm this year. With a look over his shoulder, William moved to the small workshop on the north side of the farm and pulled out his sickle grinder. He sat upon its small, triangular seat and pressed his boots on two flat pedals in an alternating fashion, powering the mechanism that made the massive sharpening stone turn. After getting the machine going fast enough, he held the ax carefully against the stone as it whisked along and ground the blade to the sharpest edge possible.

As sparks flew off the blade of the ax, a shadow suddenly appeared behind William at the entrance of the aged shed.

"Daddy!" Gladys called from the shanty's entry, startling him. "Why are you sharpening an ax when the woodpile is almost full?"

"There's more cutting for me to do, darlin'. You run along and help your ma now."

After finishing, William pushed the sharpener back into the corner of the workshop and quietly moved across the yard to lay the newly sharpened ax on the porch where it could be easily accessed later. He tethered Duke to the porch pole with a rope long enough that he could find protection from the impending storm if needed. The southwestern Minnesota sky was turning a grim gray, and it had started to sprinkle. Nature would help predict what was to come that night.

Supper was ordinary, as it always was on a Saturday evening. However, snitches from the newly baked bread were a wholesome treat everyone enjoyed. William fidgeted with his food but again forced down enough to avoid drawing any suspicion from Maud that something was awry.

"I'm not sure about church tomorrow with all this rain," Maud said as she scurried around the kitchen putting dishes away.

"Well, we have a new baby, there will be a cold rain, and the driveway will be too muddy to get out in the morning. You'll have to do your prayin' at home like some of the other weeks."

"Next Sunday is Easter, and we are *all* going to church *that* Sunday, Mr. Kleeman," Maud warned sternly. "My family are regulars in that congregation, and Easter is one of the most important Sundays of the year. You've given enough excuses about never going to church, but next week you will."

That evening, Maud heated the bathwater over the large black stove. Baths started with the oldest person and ended with the youngest. The shared bathwater would be thrown out in the yard after the baby was done bathing.

Since the snow was almost all melted, March seemed like a gentle paradise compared to past years, when brutal snowstorms and icy weather had pelted southwestern Minnesota more times than not this time of year. The rain that had started dropping gently in the afternoon was steady by the time supper ended. Thunder boomed, and lightning crackled in the blackened sky.

"Aren't you going to bring Duke in from that rain?" Maud asked. "You never leave him out in this type of weather."

"I'll bring him in when I go to sleep," William lied. "I don't want the wet-dog smell in here right after we all get clean from our baths. We'll get the kids to bed early, and then I'll bring him in."

Maud thought the answer was still unusual, since Duke hadn't been put out in rainy or stormy weather before.

"Let's use the chamber pots tonight," William said. "It's too cold and wet to use the outhouse."

The Kleeman house lacked indoor waterworks for bathing, cooking, or toilets, resulting in often cold trips across the backyard for family members to relieve themselves. The children's diapers were all made of cloth and had to be washed by hand frequently. With two children in diapers at the same time, Maud Kleeman would have piles of feces- and urine-stained cloth diapers on her porch, waiting to be washed on Monday. Because Mary laundered on Saturday, though, Maud would do an additional load of diapers to catch up when Mary finished with her water. It would be such an enormous accomplishment when Lois was finally trained to sit on a chamber pot. They looked forward to having only two of the four children in diapers.

Clean and well-mended Sunday clothes were laid out for the children on the oak dressers, even though everyone knew that church would be missed this week. Maud Kleeman would make sure her children dressed well when Sunday morning arrived, regardless of where they'd be praying.

Maud pulled a large galvanized bathtub in front of the roaring fireplace that William had prepared. She poured warm water from a black cast-iron pot and asked Gladys to pull down all the heavy shades on the main-floor windows. There was no need to place the large privacy curtain in front of the tub this week since Mary was in Mankato.

William stripped naked in his bedroom, throwing his manure-stained clothing in a large wicker basket he and Maud used to hold dirty laundry. It contained only one other set of clothing that he'd placed in the basket Wednesday night. William walked to the fireplace and swished a hand through the bathwater to test its temperature. He slid into the awaiting water and took a hasty bath with a homemade stick of soap made from lye and other ingredients the previous autumn. When he finished, he grabbed a large towel Maud had laid out for him, dried quickly, and partially dressed. Maud, ever the prude, tried to keep herself modestly covered in front of the children, so William went to watch them while she bathed. After Maud finished and pulled on her nightclothes, each of the children had their turn, ending with baby Rosadell. Between each member's immersion, Maud dumped in a kettle of piping-hot water fresh off the cookstove to keep the water warm. A week's worth of farm dirt and animal smells was now gone. Unfortunately, the water was quite dirty by the time the youngest member of the family took her turn.

One by one, the children got dressed for bed, and Maud read to them quietly from the Bible in their room, trying to make up in a small way for missing church in the morning. But since they'd share a more extensive Bible reading in the morning, Maud was brief. The candles and lamps burned dim from wicks that had been lit hours earlier. The long day of chores, cleaning, cooking, and baths left her weary, and she retired to bed early.

The storm became louder and more violent as the night wore on. Mary's second-story room was empty. Baby Rosadell slept peacefully in her crib in William and Maud's room. The other bedroom contained Gordon, Lois, and Gladys, lying like cordwood in their trundle bed, girls on the top and Gordon on the lower mattress. The once mighty bath-time fire now burned dim. The house creaked and groaned as the thunder boomed across the sky.

Maud and the children had finally fallen deeply asleep. They were all tired from the long day, so the storm didn't keep them awake.

With little brooding, William carried out his sinister plot. He decided to scrawl out a note he believed would mislead the authorities when they arrived. With his unpracticed handwriting, he scribbled out a simple statement in pencil:

> *Dear folks—*
> *When woke this morning someone in house. Says money*
> *or lives. It is in dresser. Happy. I hang myself.*
> *Good Bye Bye*
>
> > *With love*
> > *W. Kleeman*

On the back of the note, he penciled "He killed them" in barely legible script.

He thought everyone would believe a robber had threatened the family for money or be killed. They would surmise the robber killed Maud and the children and left. They'd believe William was distraught and hung himself because he couldn't properly protect his family from the clutches of the invading robber.

Not bothering to put on socks or shoes, William crept to the porch door and snatched the long, newly sharpened ax he'd left leaning against the side of the porch. He swallowed hard and ignored Duke's whimpering as he begged for entry to the home.

With only a dim lantern, he edged toward his own bedroom, where Maud and baby Rosadell were sleeping. As the thunder crashed and lightning lit the sky, William held the weapon high, aimed the sharp edge for Maud's temple, and struck a hard and fatal blow. Her body jolted and writhed briefly as an enormous amount of blood pumped onto the bed and spilled onto the floor.

Their almost seven-year marriage ended at that moment.

Maud's body was abandoned for younger prey. Knowing the older children might awaken, he moved quickly to their room and struck them in order of age from oldest to youngest with one violent blow to the head for each. He used the blunt side of the ax for his children, believing that perhaps it might be better for them. As the children lay flailing and gasping for life, he returned to the other bedroom to finish the job with the six-week-old in her crib. One savage blow killed the infant instantly.

The deadly deeds were now done. He threw down the blood-stained ax on the floor in his bedroom—where Maud lay lifeless—and fled to the kitchen. He secured a sturdy pole into the unpatched hole in the kitchen ceiling where a stovepipe must have been in earlier years. That hole had always bothered Maud.

A rope he'd left on the porch that afternoon was fashioned into a noose. He slung the rope over the pipe and climbed on a dining chair. He fashioned a neatly tied loop and tightened the rope around his neck. As he jumped from the chair, sixty-six dark angels snapped a precisely coordinated salute from the earth's core at Lucifer's command. With a crack of thunder, William Kleeman's body jerked several times and went limp.

William's soul would return from whence it came.

Rain continued to pour for the rest of the night and into Sunday, but more gently. Wind and water blew down the chimney, and the fire slowly went out and its ashes cooled. The house grew colder by the hour. Massive amounts of rain slopped over the dirt driveway and began to pool in the yard.

The smoky lantern William left on the kitchen table grew dim, and eventually the wick had extinguished itself of life. The Kleeman house was now fully dark.

CHAPTER 38

THE DISCOVERY

On Sunday, as the entire Kleeman family lay lifeless at the farm, Mary Snelling bid her parents farewell and prepared to board the steam train at the Mankato depot.

Her father helped her down from the Packard, while Mary's mother remarked, "Mary, you don't seem to be yourself."

"I haven't been feeling well. I'm not sure why." Mary hoped the half lie would satisfy her mother. "I'll take good care of myself. School will be done a bit early on Thursday, and I'll take the first train to Mankato in the afternoon."

She hugged her parents good-bye. Although she was now in her twenties, she was still quite attached to her parents, like a much younger child. Little did they realize Mary would be returning on a permanent basis in just two days' time.

The rain and storm didn't let up as Sunday wore on. The train bellowed black smoke and chugged its way from Mankato to the depot in Morgan. Mary stared out the window next to her seat. She had no idea what was awaiting her that day, but she knew that soon her life was going to change radically. Just as William advised, Mary planned to hire a livery rig to take her from Morgan to the Kleeman farm. Edward Tolman, the local livery driver, had a stable just a short walk from the railroad depot. Mary trudged through the wind and rain with her bag to reach the livery. Since it was a Sunday, she had to knock on the door of the house next to the stable to find a driver. The old wood door creaked open. A frustrated and bewildered man answered the door after Mary continued pounding louder and louder.

"My name is Mary Snelling. I wish to rent your services to take me six miles west out to the William Kleeman farm. It's the old Holmer Johnson place."

"My name's Tolman. Ed Tolman. But are you out of your mind? This storm has left over a foot of water along the roads coming into town." Tolman looked up to the dark skies. "Plus, it's Sunday."

"I need to reach the Kleeman farm as soon as possible. I have to prepare to teach in the morning at Sunrise Schoolhouse. I don't know anyone in Morgan. I have no other way to get there."

Tolman relented and told her he'd hitch up a team. "We need to leave right now if we're going to make it. A car or truck won't be able to get through the mud, but my high-wheel wagon should do it."

As he hitched the horses to the wagon, Mary fastened a bonnet tightly under her chin. Tolman grabbed Mary's bag and tossed it under the primitive spring seat. He assisted her up the step and handed her a tattered black umbrella borrowed from his wife. The wind and rain pelted them all the way out of town. It was getting darker and more difficult to see every minute. What should have been a quick ride straight west took an enormous amount of time and toll on the riders, in addition to the horses and equipment pulling them.

"Now that we've made it across the road that connects the Indian Reservation with Springfield," Mary said as the wagon creaked, "we're more than halfway there."

They continued another mile and a half, fighting the storm every foot of the way. As the team struggled through the sludge-filled road, the wagon's whiffletree broke.

"Whoa!" Tolman yelled at the team as they struggled and whinnied in response to the broken rig. "Easy, girls!"

"I'm sorry! This wagon can't make it any farther west!" Tolman yelled through the windy sleet. "Why don't you ride back with me? My family will put you up for the night."

"We're past the Zamzow land, which is only about a half mile from the farm," Mary called back. "I can manage to walk that far on my own."

By this time, the water had grown to be well over a foot deep in front of the team.

"Suit yourself, but I think you'd be better off staying with my family tonight."

After Mary insisted, Tolman helped her down from the rain-slick wagon and watched her stagger through the mud into the storm. He pulled the team of horses around and aimed them straight east back to Morgan, never to see Mary Snelling again.

Mary, carrying her soaked bag, plodded through the mud and running water, knowing she was getting close. Tolman had left the umbrella, so she had a little shelter from the pelting rain. It was dusk, so she could still see, but barely. After a couple of minutes sloshing through the mud, she spotted the familiar grove of trees lining the southeast side of the farm. In the distance, between lightning strikes, she saw the outline of Sunrise Schoolhouse to the west of her destination. She struggled through the mud and was relieved to reach the yard and the shelter it promised.

The farm was eerily still, yet the bellowing of unfed cattle rang across the sloppy yard. The distinctive sound of the hungry animals was vaguely familiar; she'd heard them once when William was late getting home to feed them several months ago. This struck Mary as abnormal, since it would have meant that the cattle didn't get their ration of feed that day. She heard Luci and Diablo whinnying loudly from their side of the barn. Apparently they were hungry too.

Upon reaching the house, she was surprised to discover that it was completely dark. No lantern or candles were lit, which was odd for a Sunday evening. Since the home looked empty, she decided to rap on the kitchen window, which faced the yard. Mary tapped on it, hoping someone might come to assist her. The curtains remained fully drawn, keeping her from spying a glimpse of what awaited her inside.

Mary navigated around to the porch door and saw Duke tied up to the support pole. He was muddy and soaked to the bone. He jumped at her and barked, anxious to see her, or anyone.

"What on earth are you doing out here, Duke?" she asked the dog. "This is no weather for a beautiful boy like you." *They never leave Duke out in bad weather like this, especially all tied up*, Mary thought.

Perhaps the family was visiting the Petries or August and Minnie Kleemans' farm today and the weather kept them from returning. Since Maud was the only daughter of Henry and Clara Petrie, it wasn't unusual for them to share frequent visits, especially on Sundays. Mary knew it was a small and tight-knit family on the Petrie side.

Not wanting to startle the Kleemans, she gave the door a quick knock. As usual, it was unlocked. By this time, the sun had totally set, and the farm was in darkness. The wood door creaked as she gently pushed it open, a little apprehensive about the darkness. The house was unusually cold. Maud always had a good fire roaring for the baby and other children to stay warm this time of year.

Soaked and chilled, Mary fumbled for matches, which she felt for in the darkness. She found them with little effort and lit one to produce enough light to locate a lamp or lantern. As the match lit up, she held it up only to reveal the ghastly figure of William hanging from the rope right in front of her. His neck was twisted at an unnatural angle, and his body was limp.

"Oh my Lord!" Mary cried out as the match extinguished itself, masking the corpse in darkness once again. With the momentary glare of light, she had noticed a lantern on the kitchen table. It was the one William had left on the table before jumping from the chair. Quickly, she grabbed another match and felt for the lantern, lighting it with trembling hands.

She again saw William's remains hanging from the rope and thought he might still be alive. Not aware of the other outrageous crimes he'd committed in the adjoining rooms, Mary frantically reached for a butcher knife. She struggled up the same chair William had jumped from and sliced at the rope until his body crashed to the floor.

The massive grandfather clock in the living room struck eight times.

"Oh, William, what have you done!" she screamed at the corpse. "Are you there?" she asked while slapping his still-handsome face.

Mary loosened the noose and pulled it over his head, and then opened up his collar another button. For a moment, she though that she may have heard a breath. She quickly pressed her mouth against his to administer resuscitation, something she learned at the Mankato Normal School in her teacher training. His lips were cool, dark, and familiar.

After a few shared breaths, Mary feverishly pumped water into a pitcher from the kitchen cistern pump. She splashed his face with water and tried to move his arms up and down to gain any circulation. It was all for naught. William Kleeman had successfully committed suicide.

"Lord, give me strength to carry on," she pleaded aloud as she collapsed near William's corpse.

Believing Maud and the children must be at the Petries', Mary rose and went to the primitive wooden telephone and desperately cranked it for almost a minute. She finally was able to reach Ted Crocker, a distant neighbor who farmed the first tract of land west of Morgan.

"My name is Mary Snelling! I'm a teacher boarding at the William Kleeman farm. Mr. Kleeman is dying, and I need a doctor. He may be dead, I don't know! It looks like he hung himself. It's the old Holmer Johnson place six miles west of Morgan. Section 16 of Three Lakes Township!" she called out in desperation.

"Hold on! I'll send someone to help you," Crocker replied quickly. "Stay there, and try to give aid. It's still raining heavily, though, so it may take some time."

Crocker called Dr. Adams at his office in Morgan and Wayne Werring, the local lawyer. They were professionals who were used to harrowing and stressful situations like this one, so they were the perfect duo to dispatch to the Kleeman farm.

"I know it's raining somethin' terrible, but this woman is desperate. She said a man hung himself at the old Holmer Johnson farm. Five miles straight west of my place. I'll call her back and keep her busy on the telephone."

Werring ran to Dr. Adams's house and said they should start by calling someone who lived closer to the Kleeman farm to assist Mary until they could get there.

"Doc, do you know who lives out that way?" Werring asked. "With this rain, we aren't going to get there very fast. A neighbor could be there right quick."

"Use my telephone and call Henry Reding! I know he lives out that way!" Dr. Adams yelled. "I'm going to hitch up the team, and we'll get moving. I was just out to the Kleeman place delivering a baby last month. I know exactly where to go."

Werring reached Henry Reding, the neighbor who farmed several miles east of the Kleemans, and told him the situation. He asked Reding to get to there as soon as possible and assured him that he and Dr. Adams would arrive as soon as they could.

Adams and Werring mounted the doctor's small, sleek black buggy with high wheels. The doctor was known to have some of the fastest horses in Redwood County, due to the nature of delivering children and circumstances like the Kleeman death. In better weather, he could have used his magnificent Cadillac, which could have roared out of town at fifty miles per hour. But on this occasion, they slogged through the mud as best they could. His horses were more suited for racing than pulling difficult loads like the workhorses that area farmers commonly owned. It took them over an hour to navigate the mud and darkness.

Henry Reding was a short, but solid, man. He'd settled in the area just a few years before, purchasing land from W. F. Davidson, a wealthy landowner who purchased most of the land that ran from the Minnesota River south ten miles to the old Sioux Reservation line. After the Sioux Uprising in the 1860s, the treaties that had given the swath of property to the Sioux were nullified. Davidson had snatched up the bulk of it and starting selling it, parcel by parcel, to eager farmers.

Reding saw William Kleeman from time to time, but he was a Catholic, so he tended to have different social circle—and he was busy as the Redwood County Registrar, so they didn't have any type of close friendship. Many neighbors joked about the political power on the corner of the Morgan-Springfield road, with Representative Bendixen serving in the state legislature, the next property west being owned by Redwood County commissioner Chris Frederickson, followed by Henry Reding, the Redwood County registrar.

William Kleeman's newness to the area kept him from forming very many neighborly relations around Three Lakes Township, but his family was familiar with many people in and around Morgan because they'd farmed in the area farther north for many years after his father had traveled there from Janesville, Minnesota.

Upon being alerted to the initial calamity, Reding told his family that he was needed at the Kleeman place for a medical emergency, and he rushed out the door. He didn't give his family any details since he didn't have very many to share. In less than a half hour, Reding arrived at the Kleeman farm, where he found Mary sitting on the floor by the telephone, still speaking to Ted Crocker about William's condition. Crocker had continued conversing with Mary to keep her focused and calm.

"Heavens, girl," Reding said as he entered the ghoulish scene. "Let me help you."

Reding bent over the remains of William Kleeman, who was still sprawled out on the floor from where Mary had left him. By this time, rigor mortis had started to set into the corpse. While his eyes and mouth were open, his body had become stiff and cold.

"Ted, this is Henry Reding," he called into the telephone. "Call the county sheriff and get the law out here!"

The grandfather clock down the hallway chimed loud nine times.

"He's gone, Miss Snelling," Henry replied calmly as he inspected the rope cut from the stem where Mary had filleted it. "We don't know what this is about, so let's not move anything around. We'll stay put right here until Doc Adams and the others can get here."

He found another lantern in the kitchen and lit it. Reding then wondered about the rest of the family. Maud Kleeman rarely went anywhere without William, unless she was at her folks' place by Redwood Falls. He wondered if she and the children went to church with Henry and Clara Petrie over in Redwood Falls and stayed late on account of the rain. William might have had to stay back to do chores. Most knew he wasn't much for churchgoing.

"I found this note by William's body on the kitchen table," Mary said, shoving the cryptic piece of paper toward Reding. "It's definitely his handwriting, but I'm not sure what it means."

Reding took the paper from Mary's trembling hand and squinted as he tried to decipher Kleeman's scrawl. He turned the note over, which Mary hadn't yet done, discovering the words *He killed them* on the back.

"You stay here, Miss Snelling," he said anxiously as he stood up, absorbing what he'd just read. "I'm just going to take a look around."

Henry grabbed the spare lantern. He assisted Mary to a chair and then discovered the horrific scene in the adjoining bedrooms. He peered into the main Kleeman bedroom. Blood had poured out of Maud's body, soaking into the bedding and dripping to the floor.

"Dear God Almighty," Henry muttered to himself as the flickering lantern lit up the bloody images of the murdered family. "Miss Snelling, stay in the kitchen!"

Henry peered into the large bedroom to witness the gore. The ax William used to murder his family lay near the crib, with thick, red blood on both the sharp and blunt ends. He looked across the hall and saw the three other children, all dead, with a terrifying amount of blood on the bedding and on the floor. He looked back in the larger bedroom.

"Even the baby," he whispered, looking at the caved-in head of an otherwise angelic child. "What on earth . . ."

By this time, Henry heard the jingling of the horse harnesses and the sound of the animals braying. Adams and Werring were pulling into the muddy yard. Henry pushed through the kitchen past William's body and told Mary to stay put.

"Men, we've got a huge mess in there!" Reding quickly told the men as he ran to the buggy in the rain. "Someone killed this entire family. I think it might have been Kleeman!"

Reding, Adams, and Werring rushed into the house. Werring comforted Mary while Adams checked William Kleeman's vital signs.

"No pulse, rigor is set in. He's dead. I'm guessing for almost a day now," the doctor proclaimed in a professional tone.

"Doc! In here," Reding said, pointing to the room where Maud and the baby lay. "Any chance anyone is still alive?"

"Holy Lord, I've never seen anything like this," Dr. Adams confessed as he surveyed the carnage. He moved from body to body, starting with Maud and the baby, then moving to the other room to check vitals on Gladys, Lois, and Gordon. All had been dead for almost a day. Adams shook his head at Reding, signaling all were dead. "I'm guessing they were murdered around sundown yesterday. We need the sheriff out here."

"Sheriff Hassenstab lives a ways west, so we'll have to be patient," Werring declared.

Redwood County had a revolving door of sheriffs over the past decade. In fact, the men recalled, Maud Kleeman's father had been a candidate for the office a few years back. The current sheriff, Frank Hassenstab, didn't live in Redwood Falls, but in the small village of Seaforth, which was almost twenty miles from the Kleeman crime scene.

Dr. Adams told everyone to leave all items as undisturbed as possible. "One way or another, this is a crime scene. I'm not the county coroner. Dr. Brey in Wabasso is. The sheriff will have to get him out here tomorrow, and an inquest will have to be held to determine who killed these people."

Reding gulped. As the Redwood County registrar, he'd have to sign each of the death certificates after the county coroner certified the identities and types of death.

By this time, Werring shoved the suicide note at Dr. Adams. Adams looked it over and sighed.

"Kleeman was trying to make it look like someone broke in to this place and demanded money in the dresser or something," Werring surmised. "Does he think we're a bunch of fools?"

Mary demanded to look in the bedrooms. "Mr. Reding has kept me from looking at those rooms," she insisted. "I've lived here since last fall with this family, and I need to see these children one more time."

"All right, go ahead," Dr. Adams said. "But it's a mess, Miss Snelling."

She took a lantern and made her way slowly through the dark hallway. She peered into the room that contained the three children first. They were all snuggled on the trundle bed, each bearing crushed skulls, with blood soaked through the mattress and pooled on the floor.

"Gladys, Lois, and Gordon," she said gently. "You precious little babes."

Mary had loved the Kleeman children. They were so beautiful and full of life. Memories of reading to and playing with them filled her mind as she looked across the barely lit room in a daze. Gordon was as handsome as his father with his light-brown hair and steely blue eyes. Gladys was old enough to start school in the fall, presumably with Miss Snelling as her teacher. But now the roster at Sunrise Schoolhouse would have four fewer pupils who would have adorned its floors for many of the coming years. All snuffed out of existence by their father. Mary crept across to the other bedroom, holding the lantern above her face with a trembling hand. Maud had a massive wound from the sharp side of the ax. The baby was barely recognizable. Blood was everywhere. Mary wondered how William could carry out such atrocious deeds on his own wife and children.

"William, what have you done?" she muttered. "Satan himself helped you figure this out." She saw the bloody ax on the floor where William had dropped it.

"Miss Snelling," Henry interrupted from the hallway. "I think it'd be best if you got some things together and rode with me over to my place for the night. Doc Adams and Mr. Werring can wait for the sheriff."

Mary shuddered, feeling permanently chilled from her rain-soaked clothes and the dire situation. It was difficult to comprehend what had just happened.

"Yes, let me get a few things. I would be obliged to stay with your family tonight, Mr. Reding."

The Kleeman clock bonged ten more times as she finished her sentence.

Mary quickly climbed the creaky steps to her second-floor bedroom and assembled a loose collection of clothing and personal items. She dumped out the wet clothing from her bag and replaced it with dry items.

"I'll pick up anything else I need later," she said to herself. "I need to get out of here."

The rain slowed to a halt, and the air warmed. Mary and Henry Reding made it safely to his home. He quickly briefed his wife on the murders and suicide that occurred down the road and asked that she make Mary as comfortable as possible.

"I just don't know what would have gotten into him," Henry said in astonishment as he threw wood into the fire. "While I didn't know him well, he seemed like such a popular young man."

"Mr. Reding, I'm sure that no one will ever know what happened last night," Mary said with a whimper.

Mary was shown to an extra bed, but her body refused to sleep that night. She'd slept better at her parents' house in Mankato the previous night, but today's circumstances were so horrendous that a sleepless night would plague her again, just like Friday. Now, following the violent deaths of six people, she had to decide her own immediate fate. Obviously she couldn't stay at the Kleeman farm anymore. While the Redings and other neighbors were kind people, she didn't want to face the schoolchildren, the neighbors, or anyone in the area again.

The best decision, she concluded, would be to cancel school Monday and resign her teaching position at Sunrise Schoolhouse immediately. Everyone in Three Lakes Township would understand. They would excuse her from teaching the remaining two months of the school year.

While Mary was lying there, thinking about the situation at hand, her train of thought was interrupted as the old crank telephone rang: two short rings and a long ring, which was the intended ring pattern for Mr. Reding on the party line. He answered.

"Yes, I'll let her know. I can attend too. I'll tell you everything I know." He placed the black mouthpiece back on its hook.

"Miss Snelling," Henry said as he knocked on the door of the spare room. "The sheriff is requesting that we come back to the Kleeman farm in the morning. He wants all the information we can provide. Also, the county coroner will be on hand to conduct an inquest with the county attorney out of Lamberton." Henry paused. "They want to determine soon if Kleeman was the murderer, or if a robber broke in."

CHAPTER 39

THE INQUEST

AFTER A SMALL BREAKFAST, MOST OF WHICH remained uneaten, Henry Reding and Mary left for Morgan, where Mary made arrangements to travel back to Mankato on Tuesday on the noon train. She stopped at the switchboard operator's office to contact her parents and inform them of the tragic events from the past day. They agreed she should resign from her teaching position immediately and abandon the idea of staying in Redwood County to teach.

"Mary," her father pleaded over the telephone, "your mother and I will always be here to help you. Take the train tomorrow. We'll be waiting at the main depot."

Mary finished her brief conversation and plopped the earpiece down on the telephone receptacle. Hettie Beran, the Morgan telephone switchboard operator, asked Mary to step into the reception area. There, Dr. Adams, Henry Reding, and Wayne Werring were all waiting.

"Dr. Brey, the county coroner, has ordered an inquest, and the sheriff needs to hear firsthand from all of us," Dr. Adams stated plainly. "We'll be happy to take care of your transportation and other needs, Miss Snelling."

The force of the tragedy thrust the four unwitting souls together to perform this grisly task. The wagon ride back to the Kleeman farm was filled with conversation, mainly among the three men. They wondered how the bodies would be removed due to the large number and the tragic nature of their deaths. Conversation centered around who would inform their parents of the tragedy and who would tell the Illinois landowners what had happened in the farmhouse that they had rented to the Kleeman family.

Werring wondered aloud what could have provoked William to kill his entire family and himself. Since the economy had been up and down, he surmised that William may have been deeply in debt and decided to end the financial misery with the murders and suicide.

Henry Reding quickly debunked the theory. "William Kleeman is August Kleeman's son," Henry pronounced. "That family has more than enough money to settle any debts he might have had. And Henry Petrie has even more money. They sold the land where Clements was built."

They wondered if William had brooded over something and then just lost his mind.

Werring had seen William at the saloon in Morgan not that long ago. He was having a beer, flirting with the barmaid, and visiting with friends. "He was acting like his usual self when I saw him in Morgan last week."

Mary had thinking of her own to do. She had to decide if she should leave before the funerals or services, as she'd made arrangements to do. After further considering the situation—and imagining how difficult it would be to attend a funeral for the children or Maud or even William—she decided it would be best to end her relationship with Redwood County, Sunrise Schoolhouse, and the few people she'd grown to know. Her six-month stay in the area kept her mainly isolated. She couldn't say she'd made any close friends in that short time. Fleeing to Mankato to live in the safety and certainty of her parents' home seemed the most logical decision. She did want to pay her respects to the children she had lived with and grown to love since September. She decided she could have flowers sent to the surviving family.

"I've seen a lot of crimes and heard a lot of motives," said Werring, the attorney. "But this one may be tough to figure out."

The four arrived at the Kleeman farm to greet Sheriff Frank Hassenstab, who'd driven from his home in Seaforth. He looked shaken up. "Thank you for comin', gentlemen. Ma'am, you must be Miss Snelling?" he asked awkwardly as he looked at Mary.

Mary nodded.

"We still have the bodies in there, so maybe we can just talk out here," Hassenstab continued. "Dr. Brey is here for the inquest with a group of men Mr. Weldon has designated as a grand jury. I haven't handled much like this before, so I'll need your help."

"I'll help in whatever way that I can," Mary responded quietly.

"Mr. Petrie and Mr. Kleeman will be out soon to claim these bodies, so let's get this done," the sheriff urged the group.

W. G. Weldon, the Redwood County clerk of court, had consulted with Albert Enerson, the county attorney, and Judge A. R. A. Laudon in Redwood Falls as to how they should conduct the proceeding.

The men questioned Mary and the others as to how they found the bodies, where the note was, if she saw other muddy shoe prints into the home, and if they saw any sign of other car or wagon tracks leading to or from the farm. When asked if they knew of any motive as to why William Kleeman would murder his family and commit suicide, no one produced a solid answer.

"It is my recommendation, gentlemen, that we find that Mr. William A. Kleeman committed five murders with this ax and then hung himself with this rope to commit suicide, and that any pursuit of other imagined parties be ceased," Dr. Brey stated to the small assembly. "There is no need to bring official charges against anyone or to form a posse to pursue a fictional robber."

"I concur with Dr. Brey," said Enerson.

Sheriff Hassenstab asked each man on the hastily convened grand jury if they had enough evidence to support Dr. Brey's recommendation of what happened. One by one, they nodded and said yes as they were questioned by the sheriff.

"We'll have newspapermen from all over the place calling the sheriff's office," Hassenstab said. "I ain't about to have different stories coming out."

As word of the murders spread, family, neighbors, and curious onlookers started appearing at the driveway leading up to the Kleeman farm Monday afternoon. The circus-like atmosphere led the sheriff to order that no pictures be allowed and that the bodies be shown respect after Brey and Enerson finished their inquest.

Later, the reporters trying to report on one of the worst murder mysteries in the country all asked themselves one simple question: Why did this handsome, successful, and popular young farmer with a beautiful family commit such a heinous act? Many surmised that

William was deeply in debt. All came to the conclusion that he suddenly became insane, which was closest to the truth, without rational motive.

A check of the merchants in Clements showed that William Kleeman had good credit and that he owed, at most, five hundred dollars in total. He did almost no trading in Redwood Falls, and his bills in Morgan were in good stead.

Sheriff Hassenstab had dispatched deputies to the homes of Henry Petrie and August Kleeman to break the news about the horrific act to the surviving family members.

With his entire family wiped out, William Kleeman would have no known direct descendants.

CHAPTER 40

CLAIMING THE BODIES

Henry Petrie pulled into the driveway of the former Holmer Johnson place in his high-wheel triple-box wagon led by his best team of horses. He'd come to take the body of his precious Maud to the Grapp Furniture and Funeral Parlor in Redwood Falls, along with remains of his granddaughters.

Behind him, driving a larger wagon, was Frank Schottenbauer, the loyal hired man who had admired Maud for so many years. Tears streamed down Frank's face as he turned the wagon toward the farm. He took a deep breath before snapping the reins to follow Henry's rig. The wagons pulled hard in ground that was still mushy from the inordinate amount of March rain that had just fallen. Deep ruts had already formed due to all the traffic the place had witnessed in the last two days.

As Henry and Frank arrived, they saw August Kleeman conversing with the sheriff as they leaned on August's wagon. The deputies and other men were gathered outside the entrance to the house. A mixture of automobiles, farm trucks, and wagons with teams were parked alongside the barn.

Henry was reminded of his unsuccessful race for sheriff in 1910. Had he been elected and reelected, he would be both in charge of the investigation and a mourner. Henry remembered that he'd been critical of his opponent for not giving out more specific information to the public on the Tibbetts murder near Delhi back in 1909. At the time, he thought everyone, including the press, should have gotten more details on the murders, including motives. Now, the shoe was on the other foot. He was the one seeking privacy and time to mourn. Henry swallowed hard and whistled at his horses to stop. He pulled back the massive wooden handle next to his left side that set the brake on the wagon wheel and snapped it into place.

Hassenstab dropped his cigar and crushed the simmering butt into the muddy ground as Henry and Frank dismounted their rigs. The men could hear Duke, who was tied up near the barn, barking. He was unaware of what was drawing so many visitors but apparently still felt the need to protect his master and his family.

August and Hassenstab tipped their hats to Henry.

"Henry, I . . . I don't know vhat to say," August Kleeman stammered in his heavy German accent. "I am so sorry about this."

Henry walked solemnly to the men and tried to keep his composure. "Sheriff," Henry stated, ignoring August for the moment.

"Mr. Petrie, you got my sympathies," Hassenstab said sympathetically. "My folks will be happy to help you and your missus in whatever way we can."

"Where are they?" he asked the sheriff. "Where's my family?"

As they started their conversation, Frank had dismounted his wagon and taken his place beside Henry like the dedicated friend he was.

"They're in the house, Henry," Hassenstab replied. "My men can help with the bodies. Whatever you need."

"Henry," August injected again, with his lips quivering. "I'm not sure we should go in there yet."

"I must, August. They're my babies, and I need to take care of them."

Knowing the ghoulish scene the mourning fathers would encounter, Hassenstab decided to personally escort them into the home and not relegate the unpleasant task to one of his junior deputies. The lawman turned to Henry and Frank with his right hand extended, temporarily halting them at the foot of the porch steps. "I'm warning you that this is an awful sight. Dr. Brey is finishin' up his exams, but we can go in. Don't bother takin' your shoes off; it's a muddy mess. The schoolteacher testified that the house had no mud or water in it when she arrived Sunday, which tells us that no one else was in the home before her."

Sheriff Hassenstab led the way, followed by Henry, Frank, and a bewildered August Kleeman.

The house was empty of life, other than the county coroner making notes at the kitchen table. He sighed, slid the chair back, and stood as he saw the men enter. He was clearly disgusted by the horrific nature of the crimes, but he tried to stay as professional as possible. He sympathized with the Kleeman and Petrie families. In all his years of doctoring, he'd never seen anything so sinister or detestable.

Brey had started a series of preliminary death certificates that would eventually need to be filed with the county registrar. The six death cards were laid out across the table neatly. Since the inquest had concluded, he'd filled in some basic information, but he thought it'd be best to have the fathers' assistance for dates and other required personal details. The task would also provide a needed initial distraction from the grisly scene they would soon encounter.

"This here is Henry Petrie, daddy of the woman," the sheriff told Brey. "And that there is August Kleeman, the man's daddy."

"I'm Dr. Frank Brey, county coroner. I'm sorry for your losses."

"This is my hired man, Frank Schottenbauer," Henry said, rounding out the introductions. "He's my right-hand man, and he's here to help me out with all this."

William's body had been pushed to the edge of the dining room floor, and a pure white cadaver sheet had been placed over it. Unlike the sheets atop the other bodies, the linen on William was exceptionally clean—not one drop of blood or dirt on it. His remains lay there, silent but unmistakably present, as the men conducted their business.

Frank glanced over at the body with a sneer. Trying to ignore the corpse's presence, the group listened to Dr. Brey's prognosis.

"Men," Dr. Brey explained, "the situation is grim. I think it'd be best to have you give me the information required for these certificates before you go in the bedrooms."

"That's fine," Henry replied, his left hand visibly shaking. "Just let me know what you need."

August nodded in agreement, remaining conspicuously silent. He was working hard to disregard the presence of his dead son lying on the floor behind them, only a few feet away.

Dr. Brey seated himself again and pulled over the first certificate. "Let's see," he said in a businesslike voice, "I need information on Rosadell Eilene Kleeman."

Henry burst into tears. The thought of his six-week-old grand-daughter being slain was too much to bear. Hearing Rosadell's name triggered a wave of grief he wasn't expecting.

Frank Schottenbauer, who rarely touched another human being, put his arm on Henry's shoulder.

"Mr. Petrie, the baby is in heaven with Maud and the other kids," Frank said in a deep, quivering voice. "Take your time, sir."

August started to sob, and Hassenstab looked down at the ghostly sheet that covered Kleeman's body. As the top lawman in the county, he tried to never show emotion in such circumstances, but this was far from a usual situation. He fumbled for a handkerchief in his pocket and blew his nose.

Brey, who'd had the misfortune to witness more death and sadness than everyone in the group combined, kept his composure and continued.

"I just need birth dates for the most part," he said calmly. "Everything else, I can do on my own."

"February 7," Henry managed through his sobs. "The baby was born last month on the seventh."

The men collectively exhaled. The announcement of the baby's birthday broke the initial tension and helped transition to the next question.

"You're the woman's father, so it would be correct to state that the maiden name of the child's mother is Maud Petrie?" the doctor inquired.

"Yes, sir."

"And the father is William Kleeman?" Brey asked, turning to August.

Frank visibly winced.

August nodded solemnly. "Yes, sir."

Brey scribbled on the document.

August, who was standing closest to the table, craned his head slightly to spy what the doctor was writing on the papers. He squinted to see Rosadell's completed death certificate. The coroner slid it to the far end of the table, making it easier for August to read.

His eye trained toward the middle side of the page, on the right side, under the heading CAUSE OF DEATH printed in bold, capital letters.

"Comminuted fracture of skull from blows of axe struck by father (murder)" was scrawled there.

August gasped. The technical medical terminology brought a stark realization of the horrific crime his son had just committed.

"Mr. Kleeman?" the physician loudly asked for a third time, breaking him from his trance. "I need your son's birth date."

"I cannot stay in dis place right now," August blurted out. "I just cannot."

August turned, tears streaming down his unshaven cheeks, and left the room quickly.

"We'll put this one aside for now," Dr. Brey said as he pushed the death card to the side.

August never returned inside the home.

William's death certificate would have an empty space for his birth date when it was officially filed. Dr. Brey guessed William's age to be about thirty-two to thirty-three years old and scrawled a number that could be either number on the card and moved on. William was actually thirty-one.

The coroner didn't want to bother Henry Petrie with details of his daughter's murderer, so he put NOT KNOWN next to the box asking for William's mother's maiden name and birthplace.

For the cause of death, Brey scribbled, "Strangulation from hanging by neck, suicidal."

Dr. Brey knew that August was born in Germany, so he put that information down under BIRTHPLACE OF FATHER and then set the card on top of Rosadell's.

The tense moments after August's flight were broken by Henry. "Continue, Dr. Brey. What's your next card?" Henry asked calmly, wiping a tear from his cheek.

Kleeman's departure may have made things a bit easier for Henry Petrie, Brey thought. "We'll fill out your daughter's next, Mr. Petrie. Her date of birth?"

Henry thought for a moment. "August 12, 1888," he said, and he couldn't stop a whimper. "One of the best days in my life."

Just then, the apparently emotionless Frank Schottenbauer started to sob. For years he'd yearned after and loved Maud like a beautiful, untouchable flower. Henry put his arm around Frank. He'd known about Frank's secret crush on his only daughter.

"I'm sorry, folks," Frank said as he wiped his nose with a grimy kerchief. "It's just that Miss Petrie sure didn't deserve this."

Frank had always struggled to call Maud by her married name. Under the current circumstances, he gave himself permission to go back to calling her by her maiden designation, as he had from his first days working for Henry Petrie.

He'd believed, without reservation and from the very beginning, that she'd deserved better than William Kleeman, who'd never earned the right to land Maud Petrie. His immature behavior, his shameless guile, and his lack of respect for the elder Petries all pointed to an undeserving scoundrel. Frank had sensed William's weakness the first time he laid eyes on him.

Piercing the emotional scene, Dr. Brey cleared his throat and continued. "I need the parents' names—including your wife's maiden name—and places of birth."

"Clara Johnston, born in Canada," Henry replied, sniffing up phlegm. "I was born in Wisconsin."

Henry remembered the old days when he and Clara traveled west to settle in Redwood County. They were overjoyed when they discovered Clara was pregnant with Maud, their firstborn. Try as they might, they never had more daughters—so they heaped mounds of attention on the beautiful prairie girl who was the light of their life for so many years. Henry and Clara had lost two young sons to disease, so burying another child—this beloved daughter who had reached adulthood and bore them four grandchildren—was insufferable.

Now, it was Frank's turn to sneak a look at the documents. His limited reading skills made reading Maud's death certificate difficult, but he was determined. Frank scowled as he deciphered the cause of death: "Compound comminuted fracture of skull from blows of axe struck by husband, murdered."

The coward! Frank thought as he looked at William's lifeless body. *What an absolute coward.*

Dr. Brey finished with the certificates in the order he found the bodies in the next room. He started with Gordon, the Kleemans' only son, who had been admired as one of the most handsome boys in the township.

"Gordon Wallace Kleeman was born March 15, 1915," Henry replied as the doctor inquired. "We just celebrated his birthday less than two weeks ago."

Since Brey had the other necessary information from Rosadell's certificate, he refrained from repeating questions.

"We'll do that younger girl next," Dr. Brey stated unemotionally. "She looks about three years old or so."

"Lois Rosamond Kleeman, born November 15, 1913," Henry stated with a grimace. "She was beautiful, just like her mother."

As Henry starting sobbing again, Sheriff Hassenstab cleared his throat as he tried to keep his emotions in check. The pure innocence of the lives that were snuffed out in such a cruel and demonic manner shook even the most stoic of men.

"I'm sorry," Dr. Brey continued. "We have one child left."

"Gladys Alice Kleeman," Henry said, sniffing. "She was our first grandchild. Born June 12, 1911. It's a day I'll never forget."

Henry and Frank both recalled that Clara had been staying at the house with Maud because her pregnancy went a full nine months and birthing was almost always difficult for a first-time mother. Maud and William had lived next door on the rented place Frank had vacated upon their marriage. Henry and Clara had been ecstatic at Gladys's birth, knowing their lineage would continue.

"Well, that'll do it, men," Dr. Brey concluded. "Once again, I'm so sorry about your losses, Mr. Petrie."

The coroner gathered up the pile of death certificates, grabbed his black bag, and moved toward the door.

"Frank, you can handle it from here," he said confidently to the sheriff. "I've got a woman ready to have a baby north of Wabasso. I have to get over there quick."

The men turned toward the south wall and stared at the white sheet that covered William Kleeman.

"I think my deputies can load him up on August's wagon," the sheriff declared. "Don't look like August wants to come back in here."

"Don't have your men come in quite yet," Henry said. "I want a few minutes first."

Sheriff Hassenstab shuffled into the hallway to lead Henry to the other bodies.

The house was very familiar to Henry. He'd spent time here ever since they had toured the place eighteen months ago with the Nelson family. Now that spacious and comfortable home was transformed into a morgue.

"Here's the bigger bedroom," the sheriff said softly, as if not to awaken the corpses. "We have them covered."

It was room in which Maud had delivered baby Rosadell only six weeks earlier. The room that had so recently seen the arrival of a new life was now a somber mortuary. Henry and Frank entered the room slowly and looked around at the ghastly sight. They noticed blood splattered on the walls near the head of the bed and some puddles of it that had dripped to the floor.

Frank looked at the dusty black drape that hung over the window. The curtain made the room darker than it needed to be, he thought. Tiny droplets of blood could be seen dried along the midsection.

In his initial tour of the home, Henry remembered the cross the Nelsons had attached on the wall near the foot of the bed. Dust and frequent woodsmoke had created a hazy outline around where Christian symbol had been. William never allowed it to be replaced. Like the family before them, the Kleemans' marriage certificate was framed and nailed above the bed. Frank squinted to read it. September 10, 1910. It was an infamous day as far as Frank was concerned. Second only to March 24, 1917. He'd rather look at a bloody corpse than view the license William Kleeman had used to violate Maud Petrie. He quickly cast his gaze back to the bed.

Henry lifted the sheet gradually, with a trembling hand, and was shaken to his soul at the sight. His only daughter lay lifeless in a pool of blood, most of which had sopped into the mattress. The fresh sheet the coroner supplied had splotches of red on the top, with a brilliant shade of white over the rest.

"Dear God," he whispered. "My beautiful Maud."

Henry and Frank scanned the body intently. Maud Petrie's left temple was caved in from the sharp side of William's ax. At least a third of her face had a deep hue of dried blood covering it. Her blue eyes were open, staring straight up at the dusty ceiling. Her shoulder-length, light-brown hair was matted with blood on the left side, but clean and neat on the right side. Her skin had turned pasty white. She was still wearing the off-white nightgown Clara had made for her several Christmases back. Her lips were dark and dry, her mouth agape just slightly.

Frank put his arm on Henry's shoulder and squeezed as Hassenstab studied the red puddle of blood that had soaked through the bed and spilled to the faded hardwood floor.

"Mr. Petrie, she was a beautiful woman and a good mother," the loyal farmhand stated with a quivering voice. "Now she is with our Lord."

Henry pulled the sheet back over his daughter's face. They turned to face the small crib. A small blanket was placed over the tiny baby. Henry nodded at the sheriff as he stepped toward the bassinet.

Hassenstab slowly pulled the blanket back, revealing the shattered cranium of an otherwise angelic infant. The baby's face was unrecognizable. She was wearing a plain nightgown that was spattered with blood. She looked more like a life-size doll that had broken than a lifeless human being.

"She's an angel in heaven, Mr. Petrie," Frank said serenely. "Just like her ma."

Henry continued to sob and quake as the sheriff covered the baby's corpse again.

"Are you finished in here?" the lawman asked quietly. "We can go next door, if you'd like."

Henry nodded, and the three exited the main bedroom and moved toward the smaller, second room where the children slept in their permanent slumber. The door opened slowly with a loud creak as the sheriff gently pushed his way in. Henry mopped his brow with a monogrammed handkerchief and took a deep breath as Frank followed closely.

The children lay on a trundle bed separated by gender, with Gordon, the toddler, on the lower mattress and the two older girls sharing the top bunk. One large white sheet with red stains soaked into its left side covered the two girls. A smaller ghostly linen with a more moderate splotch of blood covered the boy, who was lying crossways.

Henry jerked his neck quickly to signal the sheriff to lift the sheet off his only grandson.

Hassenstab slowly revealed Gordon Kleeman, his head smashed in on the right temple.

Henry visibly shuddered. The good-looking boy had a fractured skull, and blood covered the majority of his face. His body was turned toward them, as if he were ready to spring up and run to the door. The energetic toddler was rendered lifeless like his parents and siblings.

"Hard to see him not runnin' around," Henry sniffed as he knelt to the lower section of the trundle bed. "This is the most still I've seen him in over two years."

"He was a fine boy," Frank added softly. "So full of energy."

The sheriff pulled the shroud up and back over the boy's face and released it, allowing it to float down to surround his head and body.

"Let's see my precious girls," Henry stated between sobs as he stood erect.

Hassenstab tugged the sheet to uncover the girls' faces.

"Dear Gladys and Lois, my sweet girls," Henry said in anguish. "Grandpa's little sweeties."

Henry had spoiled the two girls more than he did Maud, which was a feat in itself. He was so proud to have his lineage continue and never failed to produce a candy treat for them on their frequent visits to the farm. Rarely a week went by in which he and Clara hadn't seen the girls since they were born. On occasion, they would watch the girls for a week or more, returning the children on Sunday. Clara delighted in baking delicious cakes and cookies for the girls, and they were starting to learn cooking themselves. Henry teased them with rides on his shoulders, old Bible stories, and ribbons for their hair.

Both girls had their heads bashed in from the blunt side of the ax. They were snuggled together, as if to hold on to each other in protective solidarity from their murderous father. Blood covered their faces, but Henry could still envision Gladys's strong resemblance to his wife and Lois's likeness to his daughter.

"Beautiful girls, Mr. Petrie," Frank offered. "They were just like your own."

Frank saw the girls frequently as he worked at their grandparents' farm, entertaining them with rides on the horses and giving them peppermint sticks he purchased at the general store in Rowena. He would never sire children of his own, so Maud's brood was the closest he'd ever come to child-rearing. William Kleeman had snuffed those encounters from ever happening again.

"I think we're done," Henry said, exhaling loudly from the experience of observing the morbid display. "It's time to find August."

The men made their way back to the entrance of the house.

"Not interested in seeing him," Henry said with a scowl as they passed William's covered remains.

Frank walked by quickly, staring ahead only, not wanting to dignify the corpse with further acknowledgment.

Henry was moving into the anger phase of his grief but was aware that August Kleeman wasn't to blame for the rampage carried out by his demonic son.

The men exited the house as neighbors and deputies rustled in the farmyard. There was no laughing or loud talking, just murmuring, smoking, and hushed gossip. August Kleeman stood alone by the barn, gazing south to the plowed black field. He had come early that day to meet with the authorities and do the necessary livestock chores. Someone had to take care of the dog, chickens, horses, and cattle that still remained on the Kleeman farm, and the responsibility fell to the aging father.

"Sheriff, let me talk to August alone," Henry ordered. "We'll just be a few minutes."

"Take your time, Mr. Petrie. We'll be here when you're ready."

"Frank," Henry commanded. "Bring the big wagon around to the front door."

Frank started walked to the awaiting horses and gave them a friendly pat as they patiently waited to carry out their morbid chore.

"August!" Henry called, interrupting the thoughts of the murderer's father. "We should figure this out." Henry wanted to avoid blame and arguing about William's gruesome acts. He didn't want to pull August into more unbearable guilt than he was already suffering. As the two men stood together by the barn, the warm sun lit the sky brightly and warmed them from the chilly breeze that vexed them in the morning.

"What's done is done," Henry said flatly. "I think we need to get the bodies to Grapp's in Redwood and let him prepare for the funerals. We'll figure out what to do about those later."

Grapp Furniture and Funeral Parlor was the mortuary service in Redwood Falls. Like most undertakers in the area, they also sold furniture, including caskets, which loosely fit the definition.

A dazed August looked at him, shaking nervously. "Vhat do ve do, Henry? I'll do vhat you ask." He refrained from looking Henry in the eye. The shame brought on by his oldest son's evil was almost unbearable.

"Frank has the biggest wagon. He's bringing it up to the door. He can help the lawmen get the Maud and the girls into our rigs. I'm proposin' that you go in the house to get Gordon and your son." Henry wouldn't use William's name.

August refused to step foot in the deadly home. His emotions got the best of him. "I vill not go in dat house again!" August snapped. "Your deal is a fair von; I vill ask the lawmen to put William and Gordon in my vagon, and ve'll take dem to da undertaker."

Neither man wanted to participate directly in the dreadful task of removing their children and grandchildren's corpses from the farmhouse.

"The livestock needs to be fed," August reminded him. "Have them put da boys in my vagon, and I will finish da chores. You see me before you leave."

It was a convenient excuse to avoid reentry to the gruesome morgue, and he couldn't blame August for seizing upon it. Henry nodded and trudged through the mud to the awaiting lawmen. He whispered to Sheriff Hassenstab that his deputies should help load the bodies into the wagons and in what arrangement. Not knowing how long it would take for August to tend to the animals, he asked that Maud and his granddaughters be put into his wagons first. They could finish by placing William and Gordon into the Kleeman rig.

Henry had decided he didn't want to be a temporary pallbearer for his slain family. He was overwhelmed enough. Frank and the deputies wanted to be useful, so the grotesque task of removing the dead bodies fell to them.

Frank went in first. The deputies found large wooden boards to act as stretchers, and one by one, they were carried into the house. Maud Petrie's was the first body removed, with Frank on the front end of the corpse, gently carrying it toward his wagon with the assistance of a neighbor and Redwood County deputy. Maud would finally be escorted to Redwood Falls by Frank Schottenbauer, even if only in death.

Another deputy followed with Rosadell, wrapped tightly in a blanket and placed in a large wooden toolbox that acted as a makeshift casket. Maud was carefully placed in the awaiting wagon as the horses switched their tails. The small, interim coffin containing the infant was gently placed at Maud's feet.

Two more neighbors and a deputy assisted with the remaining daughters, Gladys and Lois, who were carefully hoisted aboard Henry's wagon. Additional white sheets were found and placed across each body to give clean linen to the murdered family. Light brown rope was then discreetly tightened around the bodies to keep them from moving.

Frank appeared before Henry as the deputies finished strapping down the bodies.

"We'll leave for Grapp's right now," Henry said, snapping his pocket watch closed. "Frank, can you lead?"

"Yes, sir," Frank answered dutifully. "Let me fetch some water for the horses to get a drink before we leave."

Frank moved across the yard to grab a metal pail that lay by the toolshed. He moved quickly to the large red cistern pump and pulled up and down on the handle until cool water appeared.

Henry decided he needed to say farewell to August and headed for the barn. He found the elder Kleeman shoveling yellow oats into a bunk for the horses.

"August," Henry called across the clamor of the cattle, "Frank and I are going to be leaving. I'll call you tomorrow regarding funerals and such."

August leaned the shovel against the dusty wooden fence.

"Thank you, Henry. I vill await your call. Again, I am so sorry about all dis."

Henry nodded—what was there to say?—and spun around. He wondered if August had thought about how the animals and grain should be divided, the machinery and household items dispensed with, and what to do about the house. Ambrose Hollenbeck owned the makeshift morgue that they were standing on. No one had told him about the crime yet. Time was short, and there were countless other tasks to consider.

Henry Petrie had originally negotiated the leasing of this farm from the Hollenbecks when the Nelson family left. He felt it was his duty to inform them of the gruesome deeds, which undoubtedly would relegate the building site to be uninhabited in future years.

Henry popped his head back into the spider web–adorned barn door. "August, I'll write the Hollenbecks tomorrow about what happened."

"Dhat's fine."

The bodies of his daughter and granddaughters were now secured in the wagons. Henry decided to look in the house one last time as Frank respectfully checked each body to make sure each was secure.

Henry entered the kitchen, remembering the laughter and antics that his grandchildren shared in the home. There was a sense of still and peace.

As he turned left, he saw William's body lying where it had been before, now covered with a dusty black curtain.

CHAPTER 41

MOVING THE BODIES TO TOWN

Frank and Henry left down the soft, muddy driveway for Grapp's in Redwood Falls. Only minutes after they left, Fred Kleeman, William's younger brother and now August's oldest living son, arrived with a small buckboard from the Morgan road. While six years William's junior, Fred bore a striking resemblance to his murderous older brother, which was unsettling to the neighbors when they first laid eyes on him. He was dressed in a simple long-sleeved shirt, with a light jacket and gray trousers. He lived on a farm east of his parents, and he'd been informed by his mother of the terrible deeds committed by his older sibling.

Sheriff Hassenstab greeted the younger Kleeman as he pulled into the yard and stopped his team.

"I'm Fred Kleeman," he said, slightly embarrassed to be reciting his last name to the assembled crowd. "Is my daddy here?"

"He's in the barn," the lawman answered in a monotone voice. "Just finishin' up some chores that needed doin'."

Fred slipped through the muddy yard to see the shadow of a man dumping a pail of water into the trough for the horses inside the barn.

"Daddy?" Fred called across the dirty fence, recognizing his father, whom he hadn't seen since Gordon's birthday party almost two weeks prior. "Ma sent me over."

"I knew you vould come to help me, Fred."

Both men had large lumps in their throats and tears streaming down their cheeks. August dropped the bucket and moved toward his son, embracing him for the first time in almost two decades.

"I cannot tink why William vould do this," August sniffed. "He killed Maud and all da children, den hung himself."

"We might not ever know why," Fred answered as he sobbed. "I want to help you and Ma get through this. I left Rosa and George back with Momma."

"Ve vill *never* get through this," August answered with a scowl. "I vill *never* get over dis my whole life."

"What can I do to help?"

"William's and Gordon's bodies are in da house," August answered, wiping his nose with his handkerchief. "The Petries came and got the girls and took them to Redwood. I need you to help the lawmen load them. It is our job to take them to da undertaker."

Fred considered the gruesome task. "My buckboard is small, but I could take Gordon in mine," Fred answered. "I can help get them to Grapp's."

"I think Ma and the kids need to see William and Gordon *before* we go to Redwood."

Fred stepped back and looked up. "Are you sure that's a good idea? Maybe it's better if they see them after the embalming."

"Ve are in charge of the bodies now, Fred," August replied defensively. "Our place is only a mile out of the vay to the undertaker."

August and Minnie Kleeman still rented their farm several miles north in Paxton Township, between Redwood Falls and Gilfillan Station. The Kleemans had six children, with William being the oldest. Next was Fred, and then August and Minnie's oldest daughters, Edith and Lillian, who were both married. Edith lived far away, in Chamberlain, Saskatchewan, and likely didn't know about the tragedy. Lillian, who was much like her mother, lived near Redwood Falls but had recently undergone a surgery to her throat and was being shielded from knowledge of the murders to protect her health, or so Minnie Kleeman rationalized.

William's two youngest siblings, Rosa and George, were still living at home as teenagers.

"I'll do what you say, but I hope Ma and the kids can handle this."

"I vill handle dhat, Fred. Ask the lawmen to put the bodies in the vagons, and I vill be down in a few minutes."

August turned and trudged back to the water pail and continued feeding and watering the livestock.

Fred slid his way down the slight hill to the awaiting Frank Hassenstab, who was extinguishing another cigar in the sticky mire.

"Sheriff, my father is going to finish the chores, and then we'll be taking my brother and nephew to Grapp's. Could I have some help moving their bodies?"

"Sure can. Where should we move them to?"

"We'd like my nephew wrapped and placed on the back of my buckboard," Fred instructed, pointing. "My brother should go in my dad's rig. I'd like to look in the house first."

Hassenstab directed two deputies and two neighbors to help Fred with loading when he was ready. Fred looked around the familiar kitchen. His place was only a few miles away, so he was able to visit his brother and family when time allowed. As a farmhand himself, he had to work around the schedule of chores and field work, in addition to helping his parents on their farm.

"Your brother is lyin' over there," Hassenstab said. "My men can load him up if you want."

Fred looked at the dirty black curtain that Frank Schottenbauer had taken down from the bedroom window and, unbeknownst to anyone, placed over William's body. The original dazzling white linen had been removed by Frank and was made to be the final covering for Maud's body before her remains were strapped to the wagon.

The sheriff was initially taken aback by the black shroud replacing the pure white cloth initially laid on William's remains by Dr. Brey. However, it seemed a fitting substitution, so he kept quiet.

Fred paled and slowly moved toward his brother's body. He pulled the black curtain down to William's chest. Fred studied his brother's face. His blue eyes were open and staring to the dusty ceiling. His near-perfect skin now had a hint of five o'clock shadow, and his mouth was slightly agape. A light bruise from the rope burn was visible on his neckline. It was like viewing an older reflection of himself.

"What on earth got into you?" Fred scolded under his breath to the corpse. "How could you do this to our folks?"

A single tear rolled down his left cheek and fell onto William's chin. He pushed the cover back over his brother's face and stood.

"Where's my nephew?" he asked the sheriff as deputies brought a long, thick plank into the kitchen to move William's body. "I want to see him before he's moved."

Hassenstab walked Fred into the children's bedroom and pointed to the lower shelf of the trundle bed. The empty top mattress was covered in blood. A window was left partially open window in an attempt to keep the odor at bay. Fred had just seen the toddler at his recent birthday party. The bereaved uncle knelt near the blood-soaked mattress.

"This is going to be tough, son," the sheriff warned as he slowly pulled back the sheet. "I ain't ever gonna forget what I seen in this place." He revealed Gordon's handsome face. Dried blood was caked on the side of his skull.

"Dear Lord, Gordon! What did he do to you?"

The lawman took a deep breath and pulled the sheet back over the child's face quickly.

"We ain't got a clue why your brother done this. The womenfolk looked just as bad."

Fred held his face in his hands as he crouched down next to his nephew's corpse. "I don't know anything, Sheriff. I wish I did," Fred answered, wiping tears from both eyes as he stood up.

"We interviewed your pa this morning. We'd also like to get your statement before you leave, if that's all right."

The sheriff stepped to the side and saw that the deputies had removed William's body to August Kleeman's wagon, which left the kitchen empty. A deputy entered and nodded to Fred.

"We can take the boy out to the buckboard, Sheriff. We're done with the other body."

"No, Sheriff," Fred pleaded suddenly. "I want to take Gordon out to my rig. *Just me.*"

"Go ahead," Hassenstab ordered the deputy. "Fetch Mr. Kleeman from the barn, and tell him that his son's body is in his wagon. And tell Tonak to come in."

The deputy turned and left the house.

"That's a fair request, son. I'd want to do the same."

"You need to interview me, and I understand why. Let's get it over with."

He took a seat at the kitchen table, where Dr. Brey had filled out the death certificates earlier. Another deputy arrived with pale writing paper and a stubby pencil and took a seat next to Fred.

"This here is Anton Tonak," the sheriff said. "He does a lot of our questionin' and writin' for the office."

The young man was trim, courteous, and professional. "I'm sorry for the loss of your family," he stated, holding out his hand.

"Thank you, Mr. Tonak," Fred answered, shaking the deputy's hand. "I appreciate you doing this right away."

The sheriff led off the questioning, informing him that a hasty inquest had already been conducted by Dr. Brey and that it was determined William Kleeman murdered Maud and their four children and then committed suicide by hanging.

"Do you know of any reason why your brother would kill his family?"

Tonak scribbled in his tablet.

"No, sir," Fred answered with a clear voice. "None whatsoever."

"Do you know why he'd kill himself?" he continued. "Was he a drinker and got drunk? Was he up to his eyeballs in debt? Was he and his missus fightin' all the time?"

"I have no idea, sir. He only had a Schell's beer here or there. Maybe two or three at most, and that was almost always in town. I don't believe my brother owed a lot of money to anyone, and my folks would have helped if he was in trouble. I know his in-laws had money too. They was always spoilin' Maud and the kids. As far as I know, Maud and him got along well. I never saw them fightin' much."

"Let Anton catch up," the sheriff directed as the deputy scurried to write as quickly as he could.

Fred took a long breath.

"Is there anyone that might have caused something like this to happen?" the sheriff asked. "Like someone who didn't have a likin' for your brother?"

"My brother was popular—had no big enemies that I know of. That's why this don't make any sense. I think the Petries' hired man didn't care for him much, but nothin' to cause this ruckus."

"Your answers are about the same as your pa's were this mornin'," Hassenstab said, somewhat disappointed. "We ain't got no motive, and we ain't got nothin' to prove out why he done this."

"I saw him at Gordon's birthday party the week before last. He was laughin' and jokin' with everybody. Just the same ol' Willie Kleeman he always was. Maud, the kids, Miss Snelling, Maud's folks—we was all havin' a good time."

"If we have more questions, we'll get ahold of you. Might be after the funerals and such," the sheriff said as he scratched his head. "Anton can help you with loadin' the boy if you need."

Gordon Kleeman's lifeless body was the only one that remained in the house. Fred had just been roughhousing with the boy at his birthday party. He felt it was his duty to carry him to his buckboard alone.

Fred reentered the smaller bedroom with Anton Tonak close behind. He kept the sheet over Gordon's little body and asked the deputy to help lift and wrap an additional two sheets around him, so as to keep the cleanest sheet visible on the outside. Fred could feel that the vibrant and energetic body he'd held two weeks earlier now had become stiff.

He lifted the child into his arms with a loving embrace, cradling him like he did when he was a baby.

"Need any help, Mr. Kleeman?" Tonak asked politely. "I can hold the door if you'd like."

Fred nodded and slowly carried the boy through the front door. The dozen neighbors, lawmen, and others who were previously chattering quickly ended all conversation. With a stolid look on his face, Fred held his nephew close under the white linen and made a solitary procession in silence to his buckboard and gently laid the toddler in the back.

August Kleeman walked toward his son. "Dhat boy was my only grandson and the next generation of Kleemans," August whispered quietly as he sobbed. "Thees is da vorst ting that could happen in my life."

"Daddy," Fred sniffed quietly. "You still have me and the other kids."

They lovingly wrapped the last of the sheets left by Dr. Brey around the motionless boy. August carefully strapped the toddler's body in with rope.

Father and son embraced and whispered to each other as the crowd moved toward the barn and house. Only the sheriff and his loyal deputy, Anton Tonak, remained close by.

"I vill be stopping by my place a few minutes, and then we take them to Grapp's," August said to the sheriff. "I thank you and your men."

"This'll take some time to figure out," Hassenstab responded as he saluted the elder Kleeman. "If there's anything that you know about what caused all of this, please let me know. You and your family have my sympathy."

The Kleeman men mounted their respective wagons and gently slapped the reins to carry their deceased to the home Kleeman farm, and then to Redwood Falls for embalming.

CHAPTER 42

THE BOYS COME HOME

AT THE AUGUST KLEEMAN FARM, THE STOUT MINNIE was surrounded by her youngest children, George and Rosa, who still lived in their parents' home. Some neighbors had stopped to bring food but hesitated to stay.

The youngest Kleeman children stayed close to their mother, who was seated at the kitchen table.

George saw the wagons entering the front yard slowly. "Daddy and Fred are back!"

"Finally," Rosa muttered. "Daddy's been gone a good part of the day."

Minnie rose slowly from her chair, visibly shaking from the horrific events of the past two days. Rosa and George walked out to greet Fred. The men parked their wagons at the edge of the front lawn and pulled the teams to a halt. The horses, tired from their trip, looked around to see if water might be brought to relieve their thirst.

Fred jumped from his buckboard and hugged his younger siblings in a three-way circle as August carefully dismounted his large wagon. The crusty Germans rarely showed emotion or love, at least outwardly. The Kleemans rarely cried or shed tears on even the happiest or saddest occasions. They almost never embraced, and the younger generations kept up the tradition of their stoic ancestry. In silence, Minnie Kleeman joined her children in their awkward, but required, embrace. August trudged to his family, looking dazed.

"Daddy, we're so glad you're back," Rosa said as she broke away from the hug. "How can we help?"

Minnie stood quietly, just as she had most of the morning.

"Ma, Fred and I have brought William and Gordon here," August stammered. "They are in da vagons."

Minnie Kleeman turned pale and leaned heavily on Fred, almost staggering.

"August, you brought them *here*?" she uttered, making up a majority of her words for the past several hours. "What about takin' them to Grapp's?"

"I tink you need to see them," August replied. "Both of them." It was a morbid plan, but he believed William's mother needed to see their son, but more importantly, see Gordon and the evil committed upon him.

"August," Minnie continued. "It might be best that just you and I go to the wagons, and we'll see if George and Rosa can handle it."

"That's fair. I vill go with you." He slowly put his arm around his wife's waist, and they turned to walk toward August's wagon. Fred followed behind, realizing that his mother might faint at the sight of her son or grandson. The black curtain was still covering William's body, which had shaken around on the bumpy road traveling home. August loosened the rope that was closest to William's head.

"Are you all right, my dear?"

Minnie nodded slightly, wondering what lay under the sheet with a morbid curiosity. August gradually pulled the musty curtain to reveal their son's face.

Minnie cringed in horror. His familiar and handsome face was pale, and his eyes were wide open, showing his ultra-blue irises and long eyelashes. By this time, his lips were darkened, and his mouth was open wide.

"My Willie, what have you done?" she sobbed loudly. "How could you do this?"

She turned away from the corpse and folded her arms tightly, standing against Fred. August pulled the drape back over his son's face.

"You needed to see him, Minnie," August said quietly as he leaned toward his wife. "But I tink it's more important dhat you see Gordon."

He took Minnie by the arm, gently prodding her to Fred's smaller wagon. The pure white sheet, covered several times over, did not reveal what might lie beneath. August unfastened the single rope and started pulling the layers of sheets down until the boy's bloody face was showing, including the massive crack on one side of the skull.

Minnie had turned away, unable to bear the unveiling of her only grandson's corpse. She turned gradually and caught a glimpse of the boy's face, the majority of it covered in dried blood, with the huge gash on the temple.

"Lord forgive us!" she shrieked. "My Willie, what did you do?"

It was too much to bear. Fred pulled his mother away and moved toward his siblings, who witnessed their mother's emotional outburst and decided not to come closer. They'd seen enough from where they stood.

"Take them to Grapp's, August!" she said through uncontrollable sobs. "What on earth will people think of us?"

"We vill get them to Grapp's right now," August replied, shaken and stumbling over his words. "You needed to see, Minnie."

"I know, August. I know I did," she said, moving toward Rosa and George with the support of Fred's arm.

Fred released his mother to the care of his younger siblings. He and August climbed back into their wagons and slowly circled the yard, finishing their solemn, two-wagon procession to Redwood Falls.

The startling sight of her dead son and murdered grandson shook Minnie Kleeman from her silence. She now obsessed about what the townspeople and neighbors would think of her family and her child-rearing and how judgment might be passed on her and August. She sat in the kitchen, brooding over the legacy of her son, the murderer of her daughter-in-law and grandchildren.

"I cannot go to these funerals." Minnie shook as she spoke to her younger children. "This is humiliating."

"Mother, you *must* go," Rosa begged. "Daddy and the rest of us, we need to have you there."

"Not another word! I am *not* going!"

Rosa and George stood by and wondered what they could do to convince their mother that attending the funerals of the grandchildren, Maud, and William might help bring closure, but they dared not question the grieving mother and grandmother.

As they pondered the immediate question, the wooden telephone rang out one short ring and four long rings.

"That's our ring. I'll answer it, Mother." She picked up the receiver. "Hello, August Kleeman residence," she said in a quivering voice.

George put his hand on his mother's shoulder.

A person at the other end wondered when the bodies might be arriving and when an obituary would be available to publish.

"Yes, they're on their way to you now, Mrs. Grapp. Probably less than an hour. Yes, we'll put something together. Thank you."

George looked at his sister expectantly.

"Mother, that was Grapp's. They wanted to know when Daddy and Fred would arrive and if we'd get them an obituary soon."

There was barely any time for actual mourning. Now, the painful chores of tending to details like services, obituaries, grave purchases, embalming, and all the other dreadful tasks that accompany death would have to be addressed.

"William wasn't a churchgoer," Minnie said with a blank stare. "That might have been part of his problem."

"Mother, who will have the services?" George asked. "Would Pastor Darrel do it?"

"Your father is going to have to talk to the minister. I cannot face him after all this."

"Maybe we should work on the obituary together," George said, trying to find an activity that his mother would be willing to engage in. "Rosa and I could help write it."

Rosa, sensing the same predicament that her brother did, reached into the drawer and pulled out a small writing tablet and a thick pencil with a dull tip.

"We need to keep in mind that this will be read by everyone in Redwood County and then some," Minnie stated forthrightly, snapping out of her shock.

"How do we handle this . . . you know . . . with how Maud and the kids died?" Rosa asked. "What do we say?"

"We will say, 'Mr. Kleeman was a loving and devoted husband to his wife and children and to his parents as a son,'" Minnie announced as she cleared her voice. "Do you have that written down?"

"But, Momma," Rosa said as she wrote the statement on the paper, "he killed them."

"I will not have my son remembered like that in the obituary *we* are writing, young lady," Minnie said in a short tantrum. "Those newspapers are gonna write all sorts of things that may or may not be true."

"I understand," Rosa said meekly as she finished the first statement.

"This just happened Sunday," Minnie continued. "Do we honestly know that some robber didn't come in and kill Maud and the children, then William found the mess and hung himself or that maybe they killed him?"

Rosa placed the pencil gently on the table and wiped a tear from her eye. Rosa and George could tell their mother was trying to rationalize the abominable things that William had done. Yes, the information was tentative, but it did seem fairly obvious that their brother likely killed the family with an ax and then committed suicide.

"Mother, I understand your point," George added, looking blankly into the air. "We can run this by Daddy and see what he says too."

"Your daddy can look all he wants, but we're doin' this obituary right now, and I'm havin' the final say," she said angrily, pounding her fist on the table. "Now pick up that pencil and start writin'!"

Minnie cleared her throat again. "It should also say, 'His mother was unable to attend due to the accident she had early last fall,' and so forth," Minnie continued confidently. "Word'll get out I wasn't at the funeral, and they need to know why."

Rosa and George looked at each other in disbelief.

"Momma, tell us you ain't decided not to attend William's funeral and the babies' too?" Rosa asked. "Can't we wait for Daddy to come home and discuss all this?"

Minnie ignored her daughter's plea.

"I already talked with Frank this morning," Minnie declared, referencing her son-in-law. "Your sister ain't comin' to the funerals either on account of that throat surgery she had."

Rosa and George looked astonished. Their mother and older sister were going to seclude themselves, while making their father and them face the difficult task of attending the funerals. Boycotting the funerals seemed so unfair, not just to their father but also to them.

"Write this down," Minnie commanded. "It should say, 'Mrs. Frank Huweiler was unable to attend the funeral, having not recovered from a throat operation,' or some such thing.

"We should also say, 'Mrs. Orin Wolverton, another sister, living in Chamberlain, Saskatchewan, was not able to get here in time,' or somethin' close to that."

George's emotions were shifting from mourning his brother and his family to anger. "Momma, I don't mean to be sassin', but this reads more like why no one is goin' to William's funeral than an obituary!" the teenager said with flaring eyes.

"I don't want to hear any more about it, and you'll not cross me on this subject, young man!"

George sat down at the table and cried through barely audible sobs. He had wept more in the last two days than he had his entire life combined.

Rosa decided it would be pointless to argue with her mother without the aid of her father or Fred.

"I got this all written out, Momma," she said, pointing to the paper. "What else should we add before Daddy looks at it?"

"We'll see what your daddy has to say about the funerals," Minnie conceded. "Let's do some cleaning to get our minds off things. Neighbors may keep stopping by, and I don't want them to think we're a family of savages."

CHAPTER 43

PREPARING FOR THE FUNERAL

FRED AND AUGUST ARRIVED IN THE FRONT of the Grapp Furniture and Funeral Parlor in Redwood Falls and parked their wagons parallel along the street, in tandem with each other.

"Daddy, I'll stay and watch the wagons; you go inside to find Mr. Grapp," Fred said as he looked over the horses. "Find out where we should go."

August walked into the furniture store, where he found Cora Grapp behind the counter, writing out bills for the month. Cora owned the store and funeral home with her husband, Otto. As was common in southwest Minnesota, the funeral home doubled with the furniture store in Redwood Falls. She looked up from her books with a pleasant smile.

"Goot afternoon. I am August Kleeman," August said with a tip of his hat. "I am looking for Otto Grapp."

Cora, who had just visited with the Petrie family an hour earlier, was startled. She had dealt with many difficult situations with families and death. In fact, often she was the first person to work with a grieving family. The Grapps had dealt with the bodies from the murders and suicide by Delhi back in 1909, so it wasn't the first death by violent crime they'd experienced. However, it had shaken her to see firsthand the brutality of the crime August's son had committed.

"Mr. Kleeman, I'm Cora Grapp, Otto's wife," she said, masking her dismay. "My husband is in the back."

As Cora stood up to retrieve her husband, August held up his right hand.

"My son is out front with the bodies of my other son and grandson," August said quietly, looking in either direction. "Could you tell me where ve should go?"

"Yes, of course. Please pull your rig around to the right and follow the building until you see a large wooden door. Wait there, and I'll have my husband open it for you."

August nodded and returned quickly to the wagons. He knew Fred would be embarrassed to be standing on the street with two dead bodies in the back of their rigs.

"Ve are supposed to pull da vagons around the side of this building," August instructed. "I vill lead."

They climbed up to the wagon seats and slapped the reins, slowly pulling their rigs to the back as instructed.

Otto Grapp was waiting near a large wooden door. "You must be Mr. Kleeman. Please pull in here."

He pointed to a parking place outside the back door of his funeral parlor and then turned to open the big door. Fred peeked inside, where he could see the sheets with his nieces underneath in various sizes lined up in the back. A larger body was under a white sheet on the end, next to the baby's body. Undoubtedly, it was Maud's corpse.

"I have stretchers and boards to help with the bodies as needed," Grapp said with a monotone voice. "My son is coming to help us."

"I can handle the boy on my own," Fred answered, moving toward the back of his buckboard. "Just show me where to put him."

"Yes, certainly." Otto gestured to a sturdy wooden table.

August knew the Petries had been there earlier and wondered what was discussed. Fred carefully lifted Gordon out of the wagon and gradually made his way to the table, gently placing him on top.

Just then, a young man about twenty years old appeared. "I'm Floyd Grapp," he announced with a polite smile. "Let me know how I can help you."

"There's a large table over here," Otto called from the far side of the room, opposite where the rest of the family were lying.

The unusually large number of concurrent deaths filled Grapp's back room to near capacity. In addition to the Kleemans, two other bodies were under sheets in the front of the room, and the body of a middle-aged man lay in a pine coffin, its cover open to expose a well-dressed chap with a moustache. It was obvious that the visitation would take place soon.

"We have a full house," Floyd said as he pulled the large pine table forward. "You folks from Redwood?"

"We live over by Gilfillan," Fred answered as they turned and exited toward his father's wagon. Looking Floyd straight in the eye, he continued, "My brother in the back of the wagon is the one who died. He's William Kleeman from Clements."

The boy froze in his tracks. Word of the mass murder had spread through the area. Floyd wasn't around when the Petries came earlier, and he hadn't realized that the Kleeman men were standing in front of him. He blushed fiercely.

August and Fred knew what the young man must have been thinking, but they continued to focus on the business at hand.

"Can you help pull him onto that gurney?" Fred asked as he unlatched the back of his father's wagon. "I think we can manage to get him on there."

Floyd pushed the squeaky-wheeled gurney to the back of the wagon.

Fred grabbed William's legs and pulled hard. With the black covering still on top of the remains, Fred, Otto, and Floyd were able to arrange the body in a perfect position. Floyd flipped two straps around the body and buckled it securely onto the cart.

The Grapps wheeled William's remains into their back room, followed by Fred and August. Floyd immediately shut the door. They unloaded William's corpse on top of the table. The pure white sheets that lay across the other bodies in the morgue stood out in sharp contrast to the black cloth covering William.

"I'm not sure if you're ready to discuss funerals and burial, Mr. Kleeman," Otto stated with a hushed voice. "Mr. Petrie has some ideas he'd like to share with you."

"My vife vill trust me. Ve vill stay to make some decisions."

"The plan would be to embalm your son, Mr. Kleeman," he stated professionally. "I assume you will be the responsible person for his funeral and burial?"

"Yes, I am. Ve can decide vhat we can right now."

Otto Grapp went through a routine list of items, some of which August and Fred could immediately answer, and others they couldn't. They picked out a coffin, selected a grave in the Redwood Falls Cemetery, decided that he would be embalmed, and agreed that there wouldn't be a visitation. When it came to arrangements for a church, they were perplexed.

"I may ask our pastor over at da Methodist church," August stammered. "I am not sure how he vill take this."

"Give us just a few hours," Fred interjected. "We can get this figured out."

"It didn't sound like the funerals would be together when talking to Mr. Petrie," Otto added carefully. "He said he'd speak with you about that detail."

August groaned. He didn't expect the Petrie family to want anything to do with William's burial. It was obvious by the initial location of William's body on the opposite end of the room from Maud and the children that the Grapps were instructed to keep his body far away from that of the innocents.

"I'd recommend that his funeral and burial be on Wednesday," Grapp added. "It would appear that the Petrie family and their church would prefer Thursday. Because this death was Saturday or Sunday, waiting any longer wouldn't be prudent. In addition, all churches in town have Good Friday services."

Grapp didn't want to openly reference that the corpse would begin to decompose, especially with his primitive instruments used for embalming. However, if the Petries preferred Thursday for Maud's funeral, August and Fred felt that was more than fair. Besides, Maud's funeral would be packed, while August wasn't sure his own wife would attend their son's funeral.

"Get him ready to bury for Wednesday," August instructed. "You can get gravedigger?"

"We can charge you for a gravedigging crew, or you could do it with your family, Mr. Kleeman," Otto responded plainly. "It is your choice."

"Daddy, I know you're cheap, but this ain't no time for us to be gravediggin'," Fred whispered to August. "We got to take care of Momma and the kids."

August stroked his chin. He was extremely conservative with his money. He knew that his surviving sons, Fred and George, could dig the grave quick enough, especially since the ground was soft. However, he agreed there were enough complications to deal with already, and sending the boys into Redwood Falls to dig an eight-foot grave wouldn't be the best use of their time and energies.

"Ve vould like you to get the gravediggers," August said quietly as he looked down at his shoes. "I vill pay you."

"We'll arrange that then. The other matter is pallbearers for the casket. We could find up to six men if you have difficulty arranging enough people, but they would get paid a nominal fee."

The reaction was instant in this case.

"I vill not pay men to attend my son's funeral!" August called out abruptly, staring at the undertaker in anger. "Ve will find men for pallbearers."

Fred leaned over and spoke quietly in his father's ear. "I can call Forest Van Sant, Art Davis, and the Streeter boys," he suggested. "George and I can round out the bunch if we can't get two others."

"My son here vill be in charge of pallbearers and call you on telephone about who vill do it."

"The newspapers have asked that a preliminary obituary be prepared," Otto said, now a bit irritated. "I had my wife call to your home and ask that your wife start on one."

"Dhat's fine. They need somethin' to do."

"At this point in time, I have what I need to proceed, Mr. Kleeman," Otto replied as he closed his notation book. "Mr. Petrie said he would discuss the arrangements for the children with you. He is taking responsibility for his daughter."

Fred and August thanked the Grapps for their help and said they would telephone with the other information as it was needed.

"Ve need to get home, Fred," August said to his son. "There is much to do."

They mounted their wagons and returned home to a fussy Minnie Kleeman and two bewildered teenagers.

"Minnie, ve have enough embarrassment! Do you have to give public excuse for not attending your own son's burial?" August begged as he read over the initial obituary prepared for their murderous and suicidal son. "And to say he 'was a loving and devoted husband to his wife and children'—Minnie, da readers will see dis as a joke! William just killed them all!"

"Who has proved that our son killed anyone?" Minnie sassed back. "How do they know anything?"

"I was there for dhat inquest Dr. Brey had," August pleaded. "Those men all said William killed Maud and the kids!"

Fred held up both hands, trying to quiet his parents.

"We womenfolk may not have any vote in the elections, August Kleeman," Minnie warned, referencing the recent political fight over women's suffrage, "but I got the final vote on this matter."

It wouldn't be the last heated debate over the murders between Minnie and August Kleeman. The terrible acts committed by their son would haunt their family name, reputation, and mental health for years to come.

George and Rosa hid in their rooms upstairs, listening to their parents argue over the self-serving obituary Minnie Kleeman demanded. Fred tried to referee the shouting match, but he knew that his stubborn mother wouldn't relent.

The funerals and burials were a vexing issue. Maud had been a faithful communicant and regular attendee at the Church of the Holy Communion in Redwood Falls. The Kleemans had attended the Lutheran church back in Janesville, but they'd joined the local Methodist church as casual members after they couldn't find a close Lutheran church to their liking in Redwood County.

CHAPTER 44

NEGOTIATING BURIALS

AFTER CONCEDING THAT THE OBITUARY for William would outline his love for his wife and children while giving excuses as to why
Minnie and the older Kleeman sisters couldn't attend the funerals,
the details of other arrangements still had to be negotiated.

August brooded over how to continue on with the worst week
of his life. "We have to talk to the Petries and figure out how to do
the funerals, Minnie. Otto Grapp said they have some suggestions."

August rang the switchboard operator in Redwood Falls, cranking steadily until his summons was answered.

"Redwood Falls switchboard," the operator said mundanely.
"How may I direct your call?"

"Operator, connect me to the Henry Petrie place," August requested.

"That's one of the most requested switches all day," she muttered.
"What a sad affair."

The operator rang the Petrie farm, and Henry answered.

"Henry, dis is August Kleeman. Otto Grapp said we need to meet and talk about funerals."

"We do need to talk," Henry replied in a hushed tone.

Claude Petrie, Maud's teenaged brother who had now lost three siblings to death, got up from the table and climbed the stairs to his lonely room.

"August, it might be better for me to come to your place. It would be well for my wife not to be involved right now," he said in a barely audible voice. "I'll be there in less than an hour."

Henry quickly signed off when his wife stood over him.

"You were talking to them, weren't you?" she demanded. "The parents of that good-for-nothin' who murdered our daughter and our grandchildren. You were talkin' with them!"

"Clara, we must have funerals for the children and Maud. They have to be involved. The Kleemans are good people. It's the son that Lucifer seduced, not the parents!"

"I will not have my only daughter buried next to her murderer," Clara said flatly. "You work out what you will, but my beautiful Maud will not rest next to him. If you allow that to happen, I will dig him up myself, and so help me—"

"That won't happen, Clara. I give you my word."

He gently kissed Clara on the forehead as she whimpered in the midst of a fresh burst of tears. Her neighbors had been keeping her company, and they were in the living room eavesdropping on the conversation.

Frank Schottenbauer dutifully stood watch at the front door, welcoming neighbors, relatives, and friends who came to visit and drop off food.

"You know I had misgivings about that charmer," Clara said quietly to her husband. "It was too quick. They up and got married at our house, then churned out a baby in nine months."

"I know, Clara," Henry soothed, ignoring her obvious regrets about their dead son-in-law. "I love you."

"This is worse than when we had to bury our boys, Henry," she gasped out through her silent sobs. "I cannot fathom what's happened."

Henry escorted Clara to the arms of Frank Schottenbauer and gave him strict orders. "Take care of her and the boy, Frank," Henry said to his hired man as he put on his hat. "I have to go see August Kleeman."

"Two orders, Henry," Clara said sternly as he opened the door. "She will be buried separate from her murderer, and we will sing 'How Great Thou Art' at the funerals."

Henry nodded and left Clara to the care of Frank, who held her tightly. He went directly to the car shed. The chickens scratched in the dirt, and the cattle called from the barn, not aware anything was the matter. He started the Buick and chugged his way toward August Kleeman's farm. He had seven miles to drive and ponder.

As Henry was speeding toward the Kleemans' house near Gilfillan Station, August and Minnie determined that they would ask the minister at their church to conduct a funeral for William.

August turned the crank on his telephone.

"Redwood Falls operator," the voice answered.

"I need Reverend Darrel at the Methodist church," August said into the black mouthpiece.

"Please wait, and I'll ring him," the operator announced.

"Blessings. This is Reverend Darrel," the voice said calmly. "May I help you?"

"Reverend," August called into the telephone, "this is August Kleeman."

There was a long pause. "Y–yes, Mr. Kleeman, hello," the clearly nervous pastor responded. "I heard the news."

That would become a familiar and awkward response that the Kleemans would hear for years: avoidance of the topic of their oldest son's deadly deeds. People would change the subject or cut off communication entirely. The reverend's nervousness was understandable.

"I am calling to ask if you might do a brief funeral for our son William?" August asked, his hand shaking. "We are looking at Wednesday afternoon, according to Mr. Grapp."

"After reading the *Gazette*, it looked like your son is getting buried out of the Lutheran church," he sidestepped. "I don't want to intrude."

"Dhat vas a mistake on their part," August replied, clearing his throat. "William vas baptized Lutheran, but as you know, ve've sorta been Methodist since comin' to these parts."

"Well . . . Mr. Kleeman," Reverend Darrel responded, "it is one of our duties to bury the dead. I can talk with Mr. Grapp about details."

"Thank you, Reverend," August replied. "I know dhat this is tough."

"God bless you, Mr. Kleeman. It is you who needs God's strength. Please give my best to Mrs. Kleeman."

The call ended, and August reflected on the bravery it took for the pastor to take on William's funeral when the circumstances were so horrible. "Vhat can a minister say about an ax murderer that commits suicide?" August muttered. "Usually, funerals are filled vith stories about going to heaven."

Even the most loving and generous father would have a hard time believing that outcome for William, given his crimes.

———

Henry Petrie turned into the driveway of August and Minnie Kleeman's rented farm in Paxton Township. Several white chickens flapped across the yard, avoiding the car as it approached the house.

After arriving, Henry dismounted his vehicle and felt the warm sun hit his face. He noticed Fred dumping water into the horse troughs near the west side of their barn. He must be helping his parents with chores.

Minnie hid in the house with the younger children while August quickly walked outside to greet Henry. The men ignored the general pleasantries and got down to the business at hand.

"Henry. I am so sorry. I don't know vhat to say about all of dis. Vhat do ve do about the funerals and graves?"

"August, I'm going to make a proposal because my wife is beside herself with grief right now," Henry pleaded. "Hear me out."

"I am listening."

"Grapp's getting the bodies embalmed. He's keeping William in a separate room from Maud and the babies. August, there's no easy way to say this," Henry said solemnly. "I propose that William be buried out of your church. Gladys and Lois can be buried next to him. You pay Grapp for his trouble and buy their stones. I'll have Maud, Gordon, and baby Rosadell buried through our church. We'll pay Grapp's fees and get the stones for those three. The burials must be separate. I think William could be buried Wednesday and Maud

351

and the children buried on Thursday. Grapp said that waiting any longer wouldn't be wise." He'd barely taken a breath when offering his Hobson's choice to August Kleeman. Now after a gulp of air, Henry asked, "What do you say?"

August kicked the dirt and stared at his worn cowhide boots. He processed the offer through his mind, wondering if there was really any contrary position he could propose. Under the circumstances, it was generous for Henry to offer that any children be buried next to William. He contemplated the offer briefly, then reached out a rugged hand to clutch Henry's waiting palm, shaking it.

"I vill gladly meet your proposal, Henry," August said. "The vomen are probably both going to have issues, so we must tell them that this is the agreement and stay vith it. I just talked to the Methodist minister, and he vill do a service for William. I am sure he vill be able to do something for Gladys and Lois too."

Henry nodded with relief. "We'll plan on Thursday for the funerals for Maud, Rosadell, and Gordon. We got a houseful of people to manage, so I really need to go. August, I'm sure you'll understand why Clara and I cannot come on Wednesday."

"I understand. I vish that I could take the place for all this and have those kids be alive," August said with tears rolling down his cheeks.

Henry stopped in his tracks.

"August, I don't blame you or Minnie for what happened. I've already buried two children. It's the worst kind of pain," Henry said with tears welling up in his eyes. "I have many angels waiting for me in heaven—and so do you." He turned to get into his car. "Tell Minnie that I give her my best."

"The same to Clara."

While their children had only been married for a scarce six and a half years, they had respected each other as parents. Now they shared a new bond, the loss of children under terrible circumstances and for unknown motives.

Henry stooped over to crank his Buick, and it sputtered to life. He stepped onto the running board, climbed into the driver's seat, and backed up the car so he could point it down the driveway. After accelerating briefly, Henry tipped his beaver-pelt hat to August, who waved in return. The Buick rumbled down the wet driveway to return him back to his beloved Clara and his remaining child.

While the wives weren't overly satisfied with the terms, Henry kept his word to Clara that William Kleeman, the murderer of her daughter and grandchildren, wouldn't be buried next to her precious daughter, Maud.

CHAPTER 45

FUNERALS

BESS WILSON, EDITOR OF THE *REDWOOD FALLS GAZETTE*, decided that her paper might sell better if she visited the Grapps and reported on what she saw. On Tuesday morning, she went to the furniture store and sheepishly asked for Otto Grapp.

"Miss Wilson?" Grapp asked, a bit bewildered. "What brings you here? I paid for my ads last month, didn't I?"

"Oh yes, Mr. Grapp. I'm actually here to see if I might be able to view the Kleeman bunch."

"Well, I haven't gotten them embalmed yet. Perhaps later today or tomorrow."

"Well, I think the people of Redwood County have a right to know more about this terrible crime. May I just take a quick look and be on my way?"

Against his better judgment, Grapp cracked open the door to

the back area of the store. He knew that if Wilson wanted to print things in a bad light, it could hurt his undertaking and furniture business.

"You've got five minutes," Grapp said firmly. "No pictures."

He pointed to two rooms where the Kleeman family lay separated. Maud and the four children were in one room, with William isolated in the other. Grapp hadn't yet tried to do any repair on the damaged skulls, other than an attempt to clean the blood from their faces.

Wilson almost gagged as she pulled out her notebook. She noted that Maud had been hit on the right side of head and her skull crushed. She scribbled that the children had been hit on the temple with the blunt side of the ax. She hadn't witnessed anything so gruesome in all her years reporting in Redwood County. *There is no more to see here*, she thought, grateful to walk away from the carnage.

She spun around and backed into the room that contained William's body. His light-brown hair and fair skin were as perfect as ever. His looks were striking, even in death. She saw no sign of violence as she viewed the murderer, only the murdered. Wilson jotted down that William Kleeman was thirty-three (though he'd actually just turned thirty-one a month earlier) and headed back to the door where Grapp waited for her.

"It's a bit shocking how good lookin' that boy is," Wilson said with an astonished frown.

"Ironic, isn't it? The devil looks like an angel, and the angels look like hell. Good day, Ms. Wilson."

The funerals for William, Gladys, and Lois were held Wednesday at the Methodist church in Redwood Falls. Reverend Darrel, the local minister who knew the Kleemans, was forced to preach for a murderer who rarely attended his church and two of his victims who were still innocent children. It was an awkward and sparsely attended affair. A small group of relatives came by train from Janesville and were joined by a handful of neighbors, including Carl Otto and his fellow school board members. Omer and Grace Streeter sat in the second row, behind their two sons, who had agreed to be pallbearers. As promised, Minnie Kleeman didn't attend the funeral for her son and grandchildren, nor the later service for her daughter-in-law. She continued to attribute her absence to an accident she'd had more than six months earlier.

The pallbearers, who made up almost a third of the small group of mourners, consisted of John Streeter, the young man William had loved like a brother; Lester Streeter, John's older brother and William's workmate for over three years; Arthur Davis and Forest Van Sant, William's best friends since he was a teenager; and his brothers Fred and George.

The loudest cries and deepest sobs at William's funeral were from John Streeter, who hadn't uttered a word since his mother had informed him of the murders and suicide two days earlier. Even when William had been busy with his family and farming, he'd kept his promise to take John fishing, hunting, or driving at least every month since he had married almost seven years earlier.

After the funeral service at the Methodist church, William's body was taken to the Redwood Falls Cemetery on the northeast side of town. A noisy nest of black crows called out from the cemetery entrance as the mourners arrived. William was buried quietly; few were in attendance to see his casket dropped into the earth. Gladys and Lois would be buried next to him the following day. The family headstone only stated KLEEMAN upon it. His grave was placed on the east edge of the burial grounds, as if exiled from the other families.

Lester and John Streeter noticed a familiar oversized garter snake darting across the cemetery as they got into their parents' car. It seemed too early for them to be out of hibernation. Actually, John realized he hadn't seen one of the creatures since he'd fallen off the ladder while painting his father's shed with William several years earlier.

A small, gray footstone would be placed eventually at William's grave, stating simply WILLIAM with the years 1886–1917 below his name. The brownish-red headstone to the west of his grave would have to suffice for a last name if someone sought out his existence in the future.

Gladys A., 1911–1917, and Lois R., 1913–1917, the oldest of the Kleeman children, shared a modest footstone next to their father that, like his, stated no last name. August Kleeman, ever the miserly German, decided that one small footstone could suffice for the girls and be shared equally. They were buried on Thursday, after their mother and other siblings' services. In that way, William's burial was kept separate, and the grieving Petrie family didn't have to attend the graveside service for the murderer of their daughter and grandchildren. Still, Thursday's mourners couldn't help but notice the fresh dirt immediately next to the girls' graves.

Funerals for Maud, Gordon, and Rosadell were held at the Church of the Holy Communion Episcopal Church in Redwood Falls on Thursday. Throngs of relatives, friends, neighbors, and the curious made their way to the small church to pay their respects. The noticeably small pine boxes for the children kept mourners mindful of the young lives snuffed out by their father. Reverend Joss read the service, and, as Henry had promised to Clara, the congregation thundered "How Great Thou Art" when the funerals concluded. The crowd accompanied the bodies to a different cemetery, in keeping with Clara Petrie's determination that her daughter would be buried separately from her murderer and husband.

CHAPTER 46

THE AFTERMATH

THE *REDWOOD GAZETTE* MISTAKENLY MENTIONED on the front page that William Kleeman was "of the Lutheran faith" in its first, hastily printed sensational article about the murders.

Reverend Aloysius Abernathy of Clements threw down his copy of the *Gazette* in disgust the day after the murders. He burst into the office of the paper's editor, Bess Wilson, and demanded to know why the worst murderer in the modern history of Minnesota—who had never stepped foot in his church, she might like to know—was listed as "of the Lutheran faith" on the front page.

"You will print a correction!" Abernathy bellowed. "Or I'll have every Lutheran minister in this county order a boycott of your newspaper next Sunday!"

"Hold on, Reverend," Wilson pleaded. "William Kleeman was baptized Lutheran. That was confirmed!"

"He's not Lutheran now, and to advertise on your front page that the most murderous fiend in the state of Minnesota is a Lutheran is sacrilege to our faith! Baptism or not, Mr. Kleeman was *not* Lutheran. Print that in your correction."

Wilson pulled out a tablet and scrawled out a statement that she would print in the next edition of the *Redwood Gazette*, to be listed right after William Kleeman's obituary. "Reverend, I'm going to print this next to the Kleeman obituary, so any curious readers will immediately see this statement," Wilson stated as she pushed the tablet toward him.

> The Gazette is requested by the pastor of the local Lutheran church to state that Wm. Kleeman was not affiliated with the Lutheran church, misinformation having led us to state, in our issue of last week, that he was a member of that denomination. Mr. Kleeman, however, was baptized in the Lutheran church, although he was not a communicant of the local church.

Abernathy quickly squinted at the statement through his thick spectacles. "Fair enough. Never make a mistake like that again," he warned as he stormed out and slammed the heavy wooden door behind him.

John Streeter retained his boyish looks and innocent charm into adulthood. His stutter had grown worse over time. However, when he was with William Kleeman for their monthly adventures, he opened up in periodic conversation. He lived alone in the old ramshackle house that William had occupied years earlier. Two weeks after William's funeral, John took his own life inside the wooden shed he'd painted back in 1910. He performed his suicide in same manner William did, and his body was discovered by his father when John didn't show up for supper. A simple note next to his body read: "I lost my only friend. Forgive me, Momma. J. Streeter." He had just turned twenty-four years old.

Lester Streeter married the portly Julia Christensen, whom he initially met at the Kleeman-Petrie wedding. While Lester had served as a pallbearer for William's funeral, Julia refused to attend out of loyalty to her lifelong friend Maud. When Julia was over forty years old, she conceived with a set of twin boys. They were named John, after their deceased uncle, and Omer, after Lester's father, who had passed away from a heart attack just a year before the babies' birth. Lester took over his father's farm and cared for his ailing mother in addition to his children.

Mary Snelling had agonized over how to handle her exit from Sunrise Schoolhouse, finally concluding that she should leave immediately. Before she left, she needed to submit her resignation to Adella Pratt, the superintendent of schools for Redwood County. Mary had phoned Mrs. Pratt from the Reding home on Monday afternoon when she returned from the inquest.

"Mrs. Pratt, you may have heard of the horrific circumstances that require me to ask your permission for a midyear resignation from my position at Sunrise Schoolhouse. I hope you understand."

"Miss Snelling, I've been informed by the sheriff about the murders at your boarding place. It's an awful situation. Please send your resignation in writing. I'll visit with Mr. Otto and the other members of the school board to find someone who can substitute the rest of the year. Do you plan to teach in the area again?"

Mary thought for a moment. "I don't believe I'll ever come here again. I plan to obliterate all thoughts of my experience here from my mind. You'll receive my letter of resignation this week."

Mary left for Mankato the next morning. No funerals. No chance of anyone discovering the secret that only she knew. She made arrangements at the local flower shop that an arrangement be sent to each funeral under her name. The last time Mary was seen in Redwood County, she was boarding the noon train in Morgan on Tuesday, March 26, 1917, bound for Mankato.

But Clara Petrie made sure Mary was personally mentioned in the notation of thanks printed in the *Redwood Falls Gazette* that acknowledged her daughter's mourners. It read:

> Mr. and Mrs. Henry Petrie wish to thank their friends for the many kindnesses show them at the time of the death of their daughter, Mrs. Maud Petrie Kleeman, and her children. To all those who attended the burial service and to those who sent flowers, they especially wish to express their gratitude. The flowers sent by Miss Mary Snelling were greatly appreciated, as they were symbolic of the tendencies and kindness she had shown Mrs. Kleeman and the children while they were living.

In the late spring of 1917, before the land was sold to a local farmer, neighbors near the site secured permission from the Hollenbecks to burn the house to the ground. The rest of the buildings were left empty. No one has lived on the site since March 24, 1917, but several of the outbuildings stood for more than a century, a testament to their sturdy construction by Holmer Johnson. The mighty grove of trees that kept the Kleemans protected from the cold northwest winds and provided ample firewood for them to stay warm still stands today. The long driveway connecting the farm to the road also stood the test of time, although it's grassed over and somewhat shabby.

Sunrise Schoolhouse, which opened its doors to students in 1904, was used by area children until the late 1960s, and then it was taken down after the school closed. The tall cast-iron pump that provided cold drinking water to decades of thirsty schoolchildren stood sentry for another thirty years after the school was dismantled. Eventually, the pump and its aging cistern were also dug out and removed, leaving no sign that scores of rural farm children had once trudged there to earn their elementary education.

August and Minnie Kleeman survived their son William by more than thirty years. They died within a year of each other—August on December 19, 1948, and Minnie only four months later on April 29, 1949. They were survived by five other children.

Henry and Clara Petrie stayed in Redwood County, and they also both died within a short time frame. Clara passed away on November 18, 1938, and Henry died less than eight months later on July 8, 1939. Many area residents attributed their deaths to broken hearts from which they never recovered.

Mary Snelling moved to Huntley, Minnesota, to room with her sister, Esther. She died on October 12, 1918, only a year and a half after the murders and suicide. She is buried next to her parents in a simple grave at the Glenwood Cemetery in Mankato, next to a simple marker that reads: MARY J. SNELLING 1895–1918. She was twenty-three years old.

The ax used in the murders was taken to Redwood Falls and kept in the evidence room at the sheriff's department for many decades before it was eventually donated to the Redwood County Museum, where it remains to this day.

ABOUT THE AUTHOR

MARTY SEIFERT WAS RAISED ON A SMALL FAMILY FARM near
Clements, Minnesota. After graduating from Southwest Minnesota
State University he became a high school teacher and a university
admissions counselor. He served seven terms in the Minnesota House
of Representatives, three years as House Minority Leader, and was a
candidate for governor in 2010 and 2014. As executive director of
the Avera Marshall Foundation, he played a key role raising millions
of dollars to build and operate a new cancer treatment facility. Since

2015, he's worked in government relations with Flaherty & Hood, P.A. Seifert is active in his Catholic church and a volunteer counselor with the American Legion Boys State Program. He holds memberships in the Lyon County Historical Society, Sons of the American Legion, SMSU Alumni Association, and Shades of the Past Car Club. He dabbles in real estate, politics, and travel. Seifert lives in Marshall, Minnesota with his wife, Traci, and children, Brittany and Braxton.